Optimizing Salesforce Industries Solutions on the Vlocity OmniStudio Platform

Implementing OmniStudio best practices for achieving maximum performance

Dmitri Khanine

Optimizing Salesforce Industries Solutions on the Vlocity OmniStudio Platform

Copyright © 2024 Packt Publishing

Portfolio Manager: Aaron Tanna
Publishing Product Manager: Kushal Dave
Book Project Manager: Deeksha Thakkar
Senior Editor: Aditi Chatterjee
Technical Editor: Vidhisha Patidar
Copy Editor: Safis Editing
Proofreader: Aditi Chatterjee
Indexer: Manju Arasan
Production Designer: Shankar Kalbhor
DevRel Marketing Coordinators: Deepak Kumar and Mayank Singh

First published: March 2024
Production reference: 1280324

Published by
Packt Publishing Ltd.
Grosvenor House
11 St Paul's Square
Birmingham
B3 1RB, UK

ISBN 978-1-83546-847-0

www.packtpub.com

Contributors

About the author

Dmitri Khanine is a certified Vlocity and OmniStudio developer, trainer, and consultant based in Canada. He has spent the last 7 years of his over 25-year-long IT career focusing exclusively on Salesforce Industries.

Dmitri combines training with hands-on development, creating industry apps with OmniStudio. This keeps his skills sharp and ensures he never runs out of fresh tips, tricks, and trade secrets.

The recipe for Dmitri's training success is simple. He gives students a complete view of the OmniStudio platform, followed by best practices and anti-patterns, and then takes it a step further by showing an actual percent improvement that each best practice is expected to bring.

"There's no point in repeating what can be easily found in online documentation in under 5 minutes," says Dmitri, *"It's the tips and tricks that people are interested in."*

Dmitri is available for a limited number of training, speaking, and consulting engagements and can be contacted at `dk@ecmsolutions.ca`.

About the reviewers

Sam Lienpanich is a recognized expert in Salesforce OmniStudio, specializing in Communications Cloud, CPQ, and Billing. With a robust background that intersects technology, innovation, and strategic implementation, Sam has dedicated his career to mastering and advancing the capabilities of Salesforce Industries and OmniStudio. His technical acumen and solution-oriented approach have set industry standards, particularly in his roles that span from a pivotal tenure at Oracle, Vlocity, and Salesforce. As the Salesforce Industries Global Lead at Sabio Group, a Premier Salesforce Partner, Sam leads the strategic development and execution of Salesforce Industries solutions, with a particular emphasis on telecommunications companies. He is highly regarded for his leadership in OmniStudio development, where his innovative methods establish benchmarks for scalable, efficient, and transformative solutions. Sam is dedicated to upholding and promoting best practices in OmniStudio development, ensuring that his team consistently delivers superior quality and groundbreaking results in their projects.

I would like to express my appreciation to the author for crafting such an insightful and informative book. Heartfelt thanks to my family for their love and support during this review process. I am also grateful to Sabio Group for providing me with the opportunity to review this book, underscoring their commitment to continuous learning and professional growth.

Rathin Mojumdar has over 24 years of experience as a seasoned Professional Services Leader and CRM professional. Throughout his career, he has successfully led CRM, data, and AI projects across diverse business environments, facilitating companies in achieving enhanced business agility and optimal customer satisfaction, and delivering niche business value propositions with a remarkable return on investment. His focus extends to assisting clients in their digital transformation journey, offering top-notch CRM/Industry Cloud solutions seamlessly integrated with ERP, mobile, social, and various other cloud applications. This integration results in a comprehensive omnichannel experience across both digital and traditional channels. His expertise encompasses a range of specialties, including CRM solutions, digital transformation, cloud architecture, solution design/IT strategy and framework development, managing complex implementations, building and overseeing cross-functional teams, system integration, and the formulation of enablement and transformation roadmaps.

Table of Contents

Part 1: The Platform Overview

1

Understanding the Vlocity OmniStudio Platform 3

2

A Sample Application 21

Part 2: Getting to Know the Tools

3

4

5

Part 3: Best Practices for Improving Performance

6

Options for Async Execution   127

7

Understanding Caching   145

8

Non-Selective Queries and Data Skew   159

9

Improving the Performance of the Service Layer   171

10

Improving the Performance of the Presentation Layer   195

Preface

OmniStudio is the engine behind customized, industry-specific offerings that run on the new part of the Salesforce platform called Salesforce Industries. It was originally built by Vlocity (who pioneered the concept of the Industry Cloud) and was acquired by Salesforce in 2020.

While each industry has its common business processes, the OmniStudio platform along with the Industries data model offers the tools and components that support all types of industries, saving new and existing customers months and even years of development. Industries have really never been more important, says Salesforce Co-CEO Bret Taylor, highlighting that these offerings provide customers with quicker time to value.

In 2022, Salesforce called Industries one of its three strategic growth pillars, along with Customer 360 and the company's geographic expansion. The platform then continued to grow rapidly, and it is currently supporting 15 industries—up from 6 just 3 years ago at the time of the acquisition of Vlocity.

However, as out-of-the-box solutions are customized and new apps are developed, clients often face performance and scalability issues. Just like with any new technology where the best practices and design patterns are still being refined, Salesforce Industries solutions built with OmniStudio may underperform or crumble under load.

This book provides a foolproof system built on a set of proven best practices, tools, and specific metrics of improved performance and scalability. It will benefit administrators, developers, hands-on application architects, and business professionals involved with Salesforce Industries solutions.

Beginning with the 1,000-foot view, zooming in on the performance and scalability issues of its key components, the book will provide critical insights, helping you deliver better-performing and more reliable OmniStudio apps.

While some of these performance-related best practices are available, they are often scattered across different sources. The coherent system presented in this book, as well as the never-published performance assessments and anti-patterns, will help you achieve better results faster.

Who this book is for

This book offers technical guidance to IT professionals, administrators, developers, and hands-on application architects who are involved in Salesforce Industries projects. Whether looking to enhance existing Vlocity OmniStudio systems or embark on a new implementation journey, this book is your roadmap to better performance and scalability.

While a basic understanding of the OmniStudio platform is sufficient to benefit from some of the chapters, administrator and developer-level experience would help you get the maximum benefit from this book.

What this book covers

Chapter 1, *Understanding the Vlocity OmniStudio Platform*, starts with the 1,000-foot view of Vlocity OmniStudio, which will drive home the overall vision behind the platform and how the components are designed to work together. This knowledge will make it easier to diagnose problems and improve the performance of your OmniStudio apps.

Chapter 2, *A Sample Application*, offers a quick hands-on refresher, where you will be able to touch a lot of the OmniStudio moving parts so that you are better prepared for the chapters ahead.

Chapter 3, *Evaluating the Performance of an OmniStudio Implementation*, provides a hands-on overview of the key tools and techniques for measuring the performance of OmniStudio components. These tools will come in handy before, during, and after the improvements are implemented.

Chapter 4, *An Introduction to Load Testing*, continues where the previous chapter left off by looking at load testing and exploring the tools, tips, and best practices available for simulating real-life load on the system. This will help you measure the capacity, performance, and scalability of your OmniStudio apps and get ready to handle the expected customer demands.

Chapter 5, *Tracking Code Changes and Deployment*, presents the tools and techniques that will make it easy to see, track, and reverse code and configuration changes in your system. These tools will allow you to adjust to better performance with complete peace of mind.

Chapter 6, *Options for Async Execution*, discusses the best place to start by focusing on the area where a simple configuration change could produce massive performance improvement with just a few clicks. This chapter provides several options and step-by-step guidance for applying them.

Chapter 7, *Understanding Caching*, reviews the second tool that can produce large performance gains quickly. In this chapter, we will explore the caching architecture of OmniStudio and the underlying Salesforce platform and how it can be applied to speed things up.

Chapter 8, *Non-Selective Queries and Data Skew*, reviews a frequent reason for sub-standard performance in DataRaptors and Integration Procedures. While the first instinct usually is to blame OmniStudio, the issue may often originate in the underlying queries we're running. In this chapter, you will find an example query on an indexed field that may run slower than one on a non-indexed field. We will then explore the reasons and look at the tools we can use to improve performance and prepare our apps for increasing data volumes.

Chapter 9, *Improving the Performance of the Service Layer*, offers a few quick, sure-fire ways to spot and improve sub-standard performance in the OmniStudio Service layer: Integration Procedures and DataRaptors.

Chapter 10, Improving the Performance of the Presentation Layer, explores the ways to spot and improve sub-standard performance in the OmniStudio Presentation layer: OmniScripts and FlexCards. This chapter also looks at the impact that some of the recommended Presentation layer best practices may have on our applications.

Chapter 11, DataRaptor Formula Performance Considerations, reviews the out-of-the-box and custom Apex-based formula performance considerations and different options available to improve the performance of formulas in our DataRaptors and Integration Procedures.

Chapter 12, OmniStudio Performance Anti-Patterns, introduces the concept of OmniStudio anti-patterns and reviews three common anti-patterns, the negative performance and scalability effects they may have on your apps, and ways to avoid them.

To get the most out of this book

To get the most out of this book, you should have some developer-level understanding of the Salesforce platform. Basic knowledge of Salesforce Objects, SOQL Queries, and some understanding of Apex and governor limits is assumed as these are foundational for developing and improving the performance of applications built on the Salesforce platform.

Some developer-level familiarity with OmniStudio is required to get the most out of *Part 3* of the book. Furthermore, a basic understanding of HTML and Chrome Developer Tools would be beneficial to get the most out of *Chapter 10, Improving the Performance of the Presentation Layer.*

There are many short code snippets in this book provided solely for demonstration purposes, and you do not need to execute them directly to understand them. That said, it is recommended to practice the topics discussed in the book in a sandbox with a recent version of OmniStudio installed.

The following is the software covered in the book:

- Salesforce platform/Sales Cloud
- Salesforce Industries/OmniStudio

You will find a list of the supported browsers and devices at `https://help.salesforce.com/s/articleView?id=sf.getstart_browsers_sfx.htm&type=5`

> **Note**
> As OmniStudio is still very new, Salesforce is actively updating documentation as we speak and some of the links we have placed in this book may no longer work when you will be reading it. If this happens, please use the search feature in Salesforce documentation.

Disclaimer on images

Some images in this title are presented for contextual purposes, and the readability of the graphic is not crucial to the discussion. Please refer to our free graphic bundle to download the images. You can download the images from `https://static.packt-cdn.com/downloads/9781835468470_ColorImages.pdf`

Conventions used

There are a number of text conventions used throughout this book.

`Code in text`: Indicates code words in text, database table names, folder names, filenames, file extensions, pathnames, dummy URLs, user input, and Twitter handles. Here is an example: "To call an Integration Procedure from Apex, use the `runIntegrationService` method of the `IntegrationProcedureService` class."

A block of code is set as follows:

```
Map <String, Object> ipOutput =
  (Map <String, Object>) omnistudio.IntegrationProcedureService
    .runIntegrationService(
      'sample_IPCalculate',
      new Map <String, Object>(),
      new Map <String, Object>()
    );
```

Any command-line input or output is written as follows:

```
"error": "You have uncommitted work pending. Commit or rollback before
calling out"
```

Bold: Indicates a new term, an important word, or words that you see onscreen. For instance, words in menus or dialog boxes appear in **bold**. Here is an example: "We can just throw our objects on the **Extract** tab of a DataRaptor and connect them using **Filter** expressions."

Tips or important notes
Appear like this.

Get in touch

Feedback from our readers is always welcome.

General feedback: If you have questions about any aspect of this book, email us at customercare@packtpub.com and mention the book title in the subject of your message.

Errata: Although we have taken every care to ensure the accuracy of our content, mistakes do happen. If you have found a mistake in this book, we would be grateful if you would report this to us. Please visit www.packtpub.com/support/errata and fill in the form.

Piracy: If you come across any illegal copies of our works in any form on the internet, we would be grateful if you would provide us with the location address or website name. Please contact us at copyright@packt.com with a link to the material.

If you are interested in becoming an author: If there is a topic that you have expertise in and you are interested in either writing or contributing to a book, please visit authors.packtpub.com.

Share Your Thoughts

Once you've read *Optimizing Salesforce Industries Solutions on the Vlocity OmniStudio Platform*, we'd love to hear your thoughts! Scan the QR code below to go straight to the Amazon review page for this book and share your feedback.

https://packt.link/r/1835468470

Your review is important to us and the tech community and will help us make sure we're delivering excellent quality content.

Download a free PDF copy of this book

Thanks for purchasing this book!

Do you like to read on the go but are unable to carry your print books everywhere?

Is your eBook purchase not compatible with the device of your choice?

Don't worry, now with every Packt book you get a DRM-free PDF version of that book at no cost.

Read anywhere, any place, on any device. Search, copy, and paste code from your favorite technical books directly into your application.

The perks don't stop there, you can get exclusive access to discounts, newsletters, and great free content in your inbox daily

Follow these simple steps to get the benefits:

1. Scan the QR code or visit the link below

https://packt.link/free-ebook/9781835468470

2. Submit your proof of purchase
3. That's it! We'll send your free PDF and other benefits to your email directly

Part 1: The Platform Overview

The first part of this book will provide a high-level overview of Vlocity OmniStudio. It will help drive home the overall vision behind the platform and how the components are designed to work together. This knowledge will make it easier to diagnose problems and improve the performance of your applications.

If you are new to OmniStudio, you will also find a quick hands-on refresher, where you will be able to touch on a lot of OmniStudio's moving parts, getting ready for the technical chapters ahead.

This part has the following chapters:

- *Chapter 1, Understanding the Vlocity OmniStudio Platform*
- *Chapter 2, A Sample Application*

Understanding the Vlocity OmniStudio Platform

Let's start with the 1,000-foot view of Vlocity OmniStudio—the new part of the Salesforce platform that runs all of the Industries Solutions. While you may be familiar with tools such as OmniScripts and DataRaptors, this chapter may still help as it will drive home the overall vision and how the components of the platform are designed to work together, building the foundation for understanding the chapters ahead.

Knowing the building blocks and moving parts of the platform will make it easier to diagnose problems and improve the performance of our OmniStudio apps. This knowledge will help us narrow down the issues to a specific layer, building block, and component and then follow the best practices and techniques designed to be effective in that part of the system.

We will build on this foundation throughout the book while studying layer- and component-specific best practices for improving performance and scalability.

In this chapter, we will cover the following topics:

- The OmniStudio platform—the engine that runs Salesforce Industries solutions
- The Process Library—the open repository of the reference solution templates
- The three layers of the OmniStudio Digital Interaction Platform and how they fit together
- How the existing Salesforce low-code tools, such as Flows, fit with new OmniStudio tools

Let's start with the big question of what OmniStudio really is.

Technical requirements

To follow along with this chapter, you will need access to an OmniStudio installation. If you don't have one handy, you can always request your free trial development environment from the Salesforce Developers site, which is (at the time of this writing) available at `https://developer.salesforce.com/free-trials`. Once on the site, head over to **Industry-Based Trials** and get yourself a trial org for the industry of your choice. Please refer to our free graphic bundle to download the images used in this chapter and throughout this book. You can download the images from `https://static.packt-cdn.com/downloads/9781835468470_ColorImages.pdf`

What is OmniStudio?

OmniStudio is the engine behind the customized, industry-specific offerings that run on the new part of the Salesforce platform called **Salesforce Industries**. It was originally built by Vlocity, an independent company that was acquired by Salesforce in 2020. Founded in 2014, Vlocity pioneered the concept of *Industry Cloud* on the Salesforce CRM platform, quickly gaining momentum and making it to the Forbes Cloud 100 list for three consecutive years in 2017, 2018, and 2019.

As of the time of this writing, Salesforce Industries caters to 15 industries. Just three years ago, before the acquisition of Vlocity, it served only six. Then, nine new industries were recently added, sharing the OmniStudio toolset, reusing existing and adding new industry-specific components:

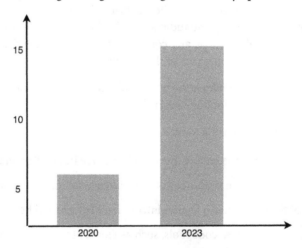

Figure 1.1 – The acquisition of new industries over three years by the Salesforce Industries platform

While each industry has its common business processes, the OmniStudio platform along with the Industries Data Model offers the tools and components that can support all types of industries, saving new and existing Salesforce Industries customers months and years of development.

Based on independent studies, the use of OmniStudio tools alone may result in a boost of over two times the productivity as compared to custom development.

To learn more about productivity boosts, you may want to read this article by Konstantin Sitkin, published on SalesforceBen: Salesforce Industries vs. Custom Salesforce Development: Benefits of OmniStudio (`https://www.salesforceben.com/salesforce-industries-vs-custom-salesforce-development/`)

Let's now look at the platform components that enable this kind of productivity boost.

Digital Interaction Platform

The core OmniStudio components such as OmniScripts, FlexCards, DataRaptors, and Integration Procedures, along with other tools such as **Configure, Price, Quote (CPQ)** and Vlocity Industry Services, all form the **Digital Interaction Platform**.

Each of the specific industry solutions gets most of the Digital Interaction Platform tools built in. They come with the industry's most common business processes already implemented and ready to be customized and deployed. For instance, the *Public Sector Cloud* comes pre-built with *Permits and Inspections* and the *Energy & Utilities Cloud* comes with *Utility Self Service* and *Clean Energy Program* reference implementations.

The following diagram shows the building blocks and core components of the Digital Interaction Platform:

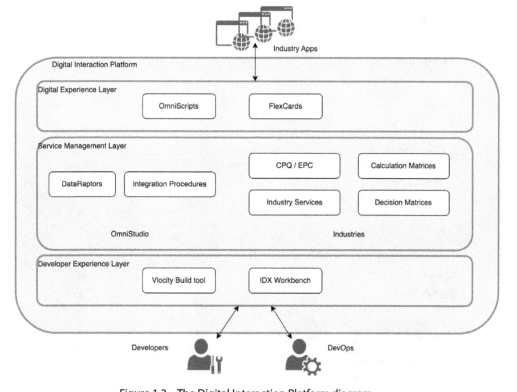

Figure 1.2 – The Digital Interaction Platform diagram

Salesforce Industries also shares its **Process Library** — an open GitHub repository, where clients can download samples and complete reference implementations.

The Salesforce Industries Process Library

The Salesforce Industries Process Library contains ready-to-use, high-level business process reference implementations. These can be easily downloaded, configured, and customized to fit business needs.

Let's take a quick look at the steps involved in downloading a business process from the Salesforce Industries Process Library.

Begin by going to the Process Library that is currently available at

`https://github.com/Salesforce-Industries-Process-Library.`

Then proceed to your industry's repository:

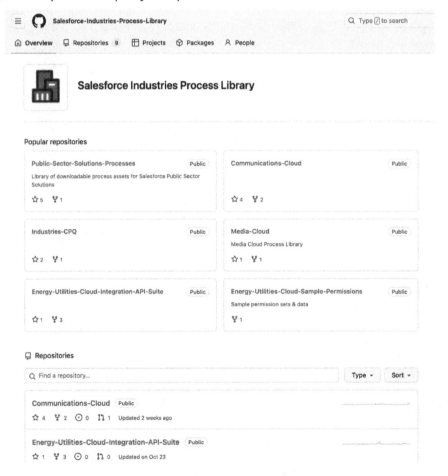

Figure 1.3 – An overview of the Salesforce Industries Process Library

Each of the business processes available comes with a PDF describing the solution that usually includes the flowchart, details of the reference implementation, and the steps required to get it up and running in your org.

The following is the flowchart that comes with *Apply for Business Authorization* reference implementation that is available for Public Sector Cloud customers:

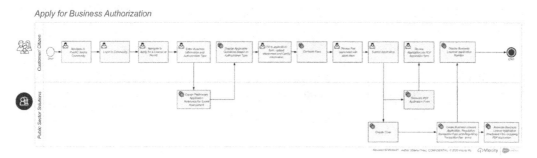

Figure 1.4 – A flowchart with the reference implementation of
the Apply for Business Authorization process

The following figure shows a list of the OmniStudio components that are included with this specific downloadable process:

Process Package Includes

Zip file includes the following:

Omniscript (1)
1. Business License Application
2. Salon Licence Application

ExpressionSet (1)
1. Fee_Calculation

Data Raptors (13)
1. Salon License Form
2. TransformCalculatedFeeOutput
3. DRBusinessAccountProfileInfo
4. DRGetBusinessLicenseApplicationWasReturned
5. UpdatePremAppRefCustom
6. DRCreatePreliminaryApplicationReference
7. DRGetBusinessActivityAuthorizationTypeId
8. DRGetApplicationId
9. DRUpdateIsSubittedPAR
10. DRGetContactForUser
11. DRUpdateBLA
12. DRCreateSalonLicenseApplication
13. DRGetRegulatoryFee

PDF (1)
1. BLA_Fillable_PDF_v3_pdf (Document)

Figure 1.5 – An overview of the Process Library's process package
content for Apply for Business Authorization

> **Note**
>
> The Salesforce Industries Process Library used to be called the **Vlocity Process Library** (**VPL**) and the downloadable processes and reference implementations are sometimes called the VPLs.

Install the OmniStudio DataPack of the Process by going to the OmniScripts page and clicking the **Import** button, then follow the steps in *Configuration Requirements* in the reference process's PDF.

(We have a step-by-step demo of downloading, installing, configuring, and running a VPL on this book's companion site. Head over to `https://maximumvlocity.com/` to see it.)

And now that we've seen how easy it is to add reference implementations to the OmniStudio Digital Interaction Platform, let's look under the hood to see the components that make it all possible.

Digital Experience Layer

The **Digital Experience Layer** (**DEL**) contains two OmniStudio components: OmniScripts and FlexCards. The following diagram shows the building blocks and core components of the DEL:

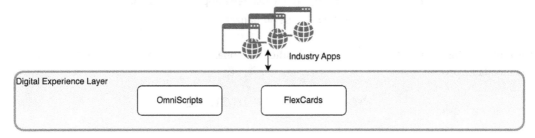

Figure 1.6 – Diagram of the Digital Experience Layer

These point-and-click tools make it easy to quickly build rich user interactions, guide users through complex business processes, and display contextual information and context-specific actions.

OmniScripts

OmniScripts are low-code, visual, point-and-click tools that allow developers to quickly create *guided interactions*, where customers are taken through a sequence of screens as required to complete a business process. OmniScripts come with a rich library of **user interface** (**UI**) components and support different and easily customizable looks and feels, step charts, document generation, and other features that are not currently found in Salesforce Flows.

All steps and UI elements are also mapped to JSON, which makes them developer-friendly, and it is easy to load, save, and manipulate the data using other OmniStudio tools. The following screenshot shows a simple OmniScript in the **Preview** mode with its corresponding **Data JSON** view:

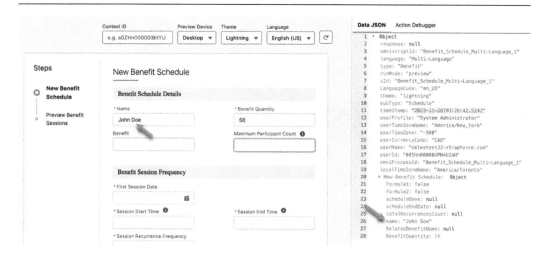

Figure 1.7 – An overview of a sample OmniScript Data JSON

Why would Salesforce support OmniScripts when Flows have been around longer?

While OmniScripts currently offer more control over the user experience through the *Step Chart*, input validation, JSON mapping, themes, and other features such as PDF generation, Flows have been around longer. Why would Salesforce support OmniScripts over Flows?

Can it be because the OmniScript features will be rolled into Flows? Yes, according to what David Schmaier, Chief Product Officer at Salesforce, said at True to the Core '23. He said:

These (the Flows and OmniScripts) will become the same, but they're not going to become one immediately.

FlexCards

OmniStudio **FlexCards** allow developers to quickly build interactive tiles or *Infolet Cards* containing relevant information and context-specific actions. These tiles can then be assembled into consoles or simply added to Salesforce object pages, external sites, dedicated console screens, OmniScripts, and more. FlexCards, once out of the FlexCard Designer tool, are rendered as **Lightning Web Components (LWCs)**, so they are easy to integrate pretty much everywhere an LWC can be placed.

The following example illustrates how a simple arrangement built from just four FlexCards can show a lot of relevant information about an insurance policyholder along with relevant, context-sensitive actions:

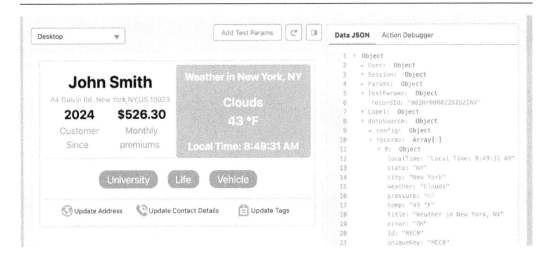

Figure 1.8 – An overview of a sample FlexCard layout

Here's an example of using FlexCards as LWCs on an org's Account page:

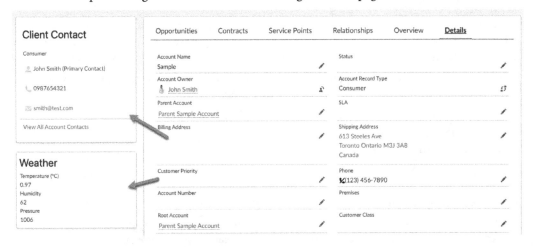

Figure 1.9 – An overview of FlexCards on the Account page

And this is how the previous Weather FlexCard looks in the *FlexCard Designer* tool:

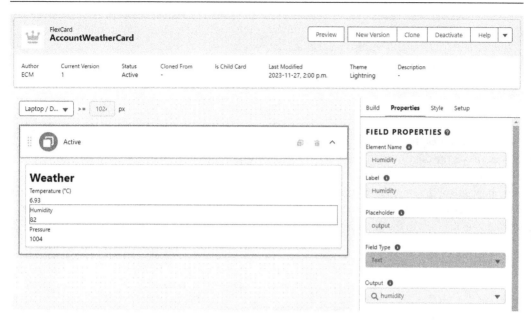

Figure 1.10 – An overview of a FlexCard Designer

And that is it for the DEL. Now let's look at the Service Management Layer.

Service Management Layer

The **Service Management Layer** (**SML**) contains the OmniStudio SML as well as the Industries SML components. The following diagram shows the building blocks and core components of the SML:

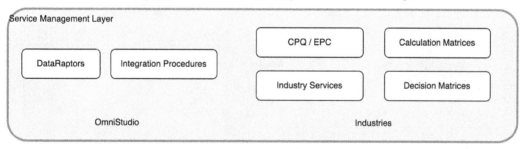

Figure 1.11 – Diagram of the Service Management Layer

The OmniStudio SML is built from two powerful data tools: DataRaptors and Integration Procedures. The Industries SML contains industry-specific components such as the Enterprise Product Catalog (aka Salesforce Industries CPQ), Calculation Matrices, Calculation Procedures, and the Salesforce Industries Service Catalog.

DataRaptors

OmniStudio **DataRaptors** provide an intuitive point-and-click **extract, transform, and load** (ETL) tool that allows the developer to easily manipulate and move the data between various sources and destinations. The following DataRaptor maps values from an input JSON blob to an Account Object, where the value of the `AccountNumber` node will be saved. The JSON blob can be supplied from different sources — for example, from the **Account** step of an OmniScript. The `AccountNumber` JSON node is mapped to the **AccountNumber** field of the Salesforce Account object:

Figure 1.12 – An overview of a sample DataRaptor

There's a wealth of options that can be configured for mapping, default values, formulae, and more to facilitate powerful data manipulation and transformation with just a few clicks.

Integration Procedures

OmniStudio **Integration Procedures** provide intuitive point-and-click server-side orchestration tools where you can build more complex logic by stringing together DataRaptors, web service callouts, document generation, and more.

The following screenshot shows the *Design View* of an Integration Procedure that retrieves a complex set of information related to the client application:

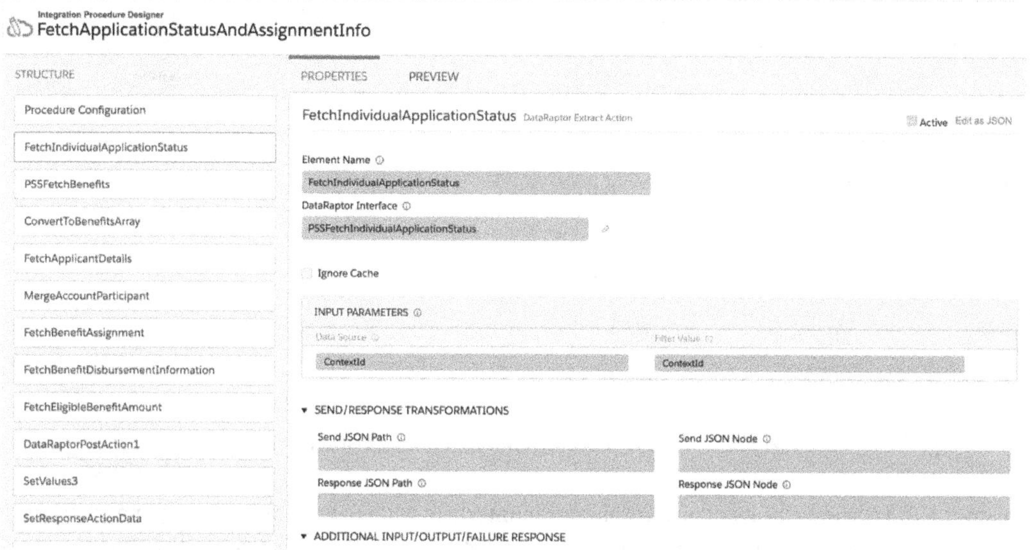

Figure 1.13 – An overview of a sample Integration Procedure

In addition to hosting functional blocks, Integration Procedures can implement their own logic, conditions, and loops. They can also use DataRaptors to implement data, JSON operations, and more, providing an intuitive point-and-click tool for serious server-side processing and data manipulation.

Salesforce Industries CPQ

Salesforce Industries CPQ is one of the core components in the *Communications, Media, Energy & Utilities*, and other industry clouds. It allows for extremely complex business rules to be applied for generating quotes, creating and fulfilling orders, managing promotions, and more. It also comes with a set of performance-enhancing services and is extensively customizable. Industries CPQ supports both B2B and B2C processes.

The following screenshot shows the **Edit PriceList** interface that is a part of the Salesforce Industries *Enterprise Product Catalog*:

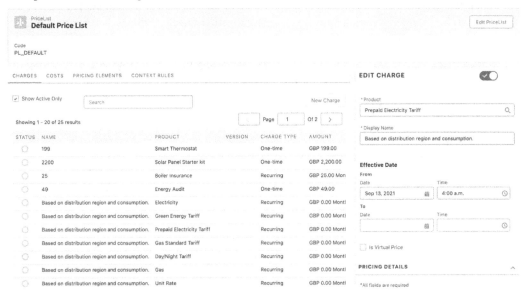

Figure 1.14 – An overview of the Edit PriceList screen

Industries CPQ comes with its own administration interface where an administrator can access key configuration settings and run maintenance, EPC, upgrades, and other CPQ service jobs. The console is shown in *Figure 1.15*:

Figure 1.15 – An overview of the Industries CPQ Administration screen

> **Note**
>
> At the time of this writing, the screen is still called **Vlocity CMT Administration**, which stands for *Communications + Media + Technology* and serves the *Telecommunications, Energy & Utilities, Media*, and other industries.

Core features of the Industries CPQ include the following:

- **Enterprise Product Catalog (EPC)**: It implements the Shared Catalog that allows you to define various product attributes, product hierarchies, bundles, and selling periods using the *Vlocity Product Console*.

- **Pricing Model**: A component–oriented system that allows grouping products and pricing them differently while keeping the original product pricing intact, applying discounts without altering the original product price, creating employee discounts, service-level agreements, and more.

- **Shopping Cart**: It provides a customizable, fully featured user experience for creating and changing orders and dynamically configuring products using the rules and attributes defined in the Industries CPQ.

- **Promotions and Discounts**: It supports pricing adjustments and overrides, contextual discounts, time plans, promotions and redeemable codes, and child product pricing.

- **Guided Selling**: It facilitates the creation of a custom selling experience using OmniStudio Digital Commerce LWCs and features such as Browse, Configure, Cart, Checkout, Qualify Customers for certain products, and the ability to make catalog and functional modifications.

- **Advanced Pricing**: It supports attribute-based and loyalty pricing, repricing orders and assets, event hooks, and usage-based pricing.

- **Context Rules Framework**: It allows you to change standard product and pricing behaviors in the Cart according to business objectives.

- **Advanced Rules Framework**: It supports the design of complex natural language criteria for product compatibility using the Vlocity Rule Builder to make sure that the right products are available to eligible customers at the right price and configuration.

- **Order Management**: It maps *technical* or internal products used in fulfillment to *commercial* products that customers see in the catalog. The mapping is performed in the tool called *Vlocity Product Console*.

Calculation Matrices

OmniStudio **Calculation Matrices** is a versatile tool that allows tabular data to be easily included in processing. Data can be pasted or imported from Excel and CSV and the lookup logic can include exact values, ranges, and more. The following screenshot shows a sample calculation matrix providing electricity rates based on the area and the time of day:

Figure 1.16 – An overview of a sample Calculation Matrix

Calculation Matrices support both individual value and range lookup, making it easy to locate data in business scenarios.

Calculation Procedures and Decision Matrices

Similar to Integration Procedures, OmniStudio **Calculation Procedures**, **Expression Sets**, and **Business Rules Engine** provide point-and-click tools to orchestrate multiple Calculation Matrices and facilitate complex processing.

> **Note**
>
> Calculation Procedures are now being replaced by Expression Sets that offer similar functionality in a more visual and efficient UI.

The following screenshot shows the *Expression Set* that uses our *electricity rates pricing matrix* as a step in a chain of pricing calculation:

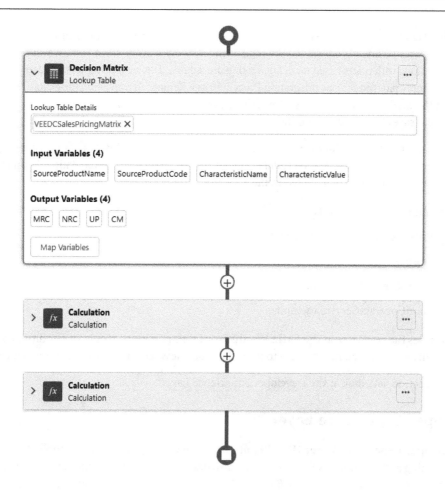

Figure 1.17 – An overview of a sample OmniStudio Expression Set

The new UI makes it easy to see the processing flow and includes a Decision Matrix and several calculation steps.

Salesforce Industries Service Catalog

Salesforce Industries Services are Apex classes, methods, and triggers that are distributed with the OmniStudio Vlocity Managed Package. They contain ready-to-use business logic for OmniStudio components such as OmniScripts and Integration Procedures, as well as Flows, APIs, and other Apex classes.

Industries Services are cloud-specific and are usually well-documented. For instance, the *InsProductService:getRatedProducts* service returns the insurance products currently available to the policyholder along with prices based on defined rating procedures. This service implements complex logic and can be simply plugged into an Integration Procedure as a Remote Action using the *getRatedProducts* method of the *InsProductService* class. Similarly, the *InsQuoteService:calculateTaxesAndFees* service calculates and saves taxes and fees on the target quote.

It's always a good idea to consider using out-of-the-box Vlocity services instead of implementing the logic from scratch. Look for the *Service Catalog* in your industry-specific documentation. For instance, here are a few services that are included in the Vlocity Health Services Catalog:

- ActionListService methods

- HealthFeeScheduleDataService methods

- InsCensusService methods

- InsCensusServiceStd methods

- InsClaimCoverageService methods

That concludes the overview of the SML. We are now familiar with the tools and components we have at our disposal and can match them to implement business scenarios with maximum efficiency.

In the next section, let's look at the Developer Experience Layer.

Developer Experience Layer

The **Developer Experience Layer** (**DEL**) contains the developer and DevOps tools that enable version tracking and Continuous Integration for the Salesforce Industries components. The two core Developer Experience tools are *Vlocity Build Tool* and *IDX Workbench*. In *Chapter 5, Tracking Code Changes and Deployment*, you will find more information on features and how to use these and other OmniStudio DEL tools.

The following diagram shows the building blocks and core components of the DEL:

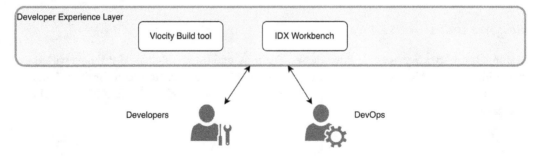

Figure 1.18 – Diagram of the Developer Experience Layer

And that is it for our high-level overview. We have now seen the Process Library as well as the three-tiered OmniStudio Digital Interaction Platform architecture, the tools that make up each of these layers, and how they all fit together. We also got to know about Salesforce's vision for how its new OmniStudio tools are designed to live alongside its existing low-code tools.

Having learned all this, we should now be able to better plan and design future proof OmniStudio apps. This brings us to the end of the chapter.

Summary

In this chapter, we learned about Salesforce's new OmniStudio Digital Interaction Platform, the engine behind Salesforce Industries. We saw how the ready-to-go industry solutions could be downloaded from the Process Library and internalized the three-tiered architecture of the OmniStudio platform. We have seen how all these components fit together.

Furthermore, we learned how existing Salesforce low-code components such as Flows play along with the new OmniStudio tools so that we can build more future-proof applications.

Our knowledge of the building blocks and moving parts of the Industries Platform will make it easier to diagnose problems and improve the performance of our OmniStudio apps. We can now narrow down issues to a specific layer, building block, and component and then follow the best practices and techniques that other developers found effective for improving performance in that part of the system. And we will study these best practices throughout this book.

In the next chapter, we will get started on our quest for maximum OmniStudio application performance by learning about the tools and techniques we will need to measure the performance of an OmniStudio implementation.

A Sample Application

This chapter offers a quick hands-on refresher where you will be able to touch a lot of OmniStudio's moving parts so that you are better prepared for the chapters ahead. If you are currently working on a project or are comfortable with OmniStudio and don't need a refresher, then skip this chapter. I hope you look forward to seeing the performance-enhancing tips, tools, best practices, and the ugly anti-patterns we're heading toward in the following chapters.

If you are new to OmniStudio, you will also be able to find tutorials and good guidance at Trailhead. For instance, the *Build Guided Experiences with OmniStudio* trail) offers a deeper review of the OmniStudio Digital Experience and the Service Management Layer tools. That trail, however, will take close to six hours to complete, so this chapter may be a faster way to get things moving. In this chapter, you will build an example app. More specifically, you will tackle the following: (`https://trailhead.salesforce.com/content/learn/trails/build-guided-experiences-with-omnistudio`) offers a deeper review of the OmniStudio Digital Experience and the Service Management Layer tools. That trail, however, will take close to six hours to complete, so this chapter may be a faster way to get things moving. In this chapter, you will build an example app. More specifically, you will tackle the following:

- Creating, updating, and running an example OmniScript
- Creating a DataRaptor and using it in the OmniScript
- Creating a FlexCard and using it in the OmniScript

In the following section, we will get some hands-on experience with OmniStudio by putting together a simple fully functional OmniScript.

Technical requirements

To follow along with this chapter, you will need access to an OmniStudio installation. If you don't have one handy, you can always request your free trial development environment from the Salesforce Developers site, which is (at the time of this writing) available at `https://developer.salesforce.com/free-trials`. Once on the site, head over to **Industry-Based Trials** and get yourself a trial org for the industry of your choice.

Hands-on lab – creating an OmniScript

Let's explore the OmniStudio by putting together a simple OmniScript. In this section, we will be creating a simple vendor registration app where vendors who are interested in participating in the currently open projects would apply. The app will contain three screens:

1. Vendor company information

2. Contact person

3. Current project openings

Now, because this is a very simple app and its sole purpose is to provide a refresher on the critical OmniStudio components, we will not be spending any time creating custom objects, loading example data, or doing other unrelated prep work. As soon as you can access an OmniStudio environment, you are good to proceed with creating the example app immediately (see the *Technical requirements* section earlier in this chapter for more information on how to obtain an OmniStudio trial org).

Let's go ahead and create an OmniScript with three steps. The first step is to create an account, which we will use to store our vendor company information. The second step will then create a contact, saving the information of the contact person at the vendor company. And finally, the last step will show the list of current project openings. Again, to keep things simple, we will simulate this by showing opportunities available in the system.

Creating an OmniScript

Begin by heading to the **OmniScripts** page and clicking the **New** button:

Figure 2.1 – An overview of creating a new OmniScript

The **New OmniScript** dialog box comes up. OmniStudio components have two-part names: **Type** and **SubType**. This helps in keeping them organized. The OmniScript name, therefore, contains the **Type** and **SubType** values:

Figure 2.2 – An overview of the new OmniScript dialog box

With the creation of a new OmniScript, step one is complete. Let's call our first step Account because we're using the Account object to store this information, and we will use two of the standard fields readily available in the system to simulate our vendor company information: **Name** and **Account Number**. This way we will not have to create any fields.

Go ahead and change the name of the first step of our OmniScript to Account (see *Figure 2.3*):

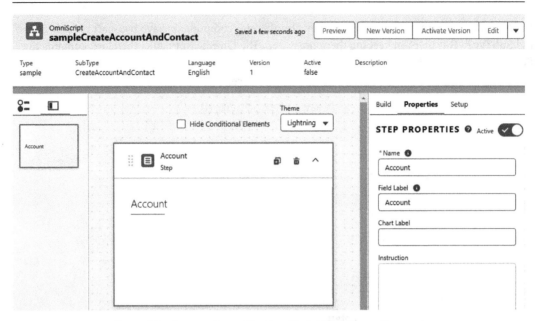

Figure 2.3 – An overview of the OmniScript Step Properties pane

Now switch to the **Build** tab and add a text input by dragging the **Text** element over to the step's canvas:

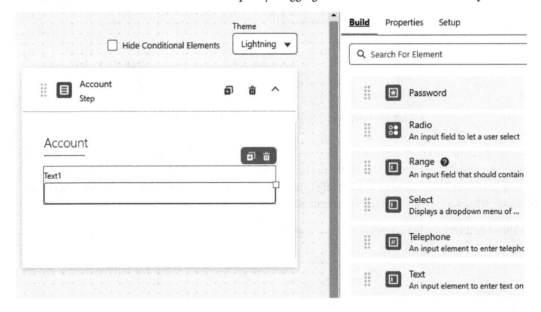

Figure 2.4 – An overview of adding a text element

Let's now adjust the name and label of our new text field:

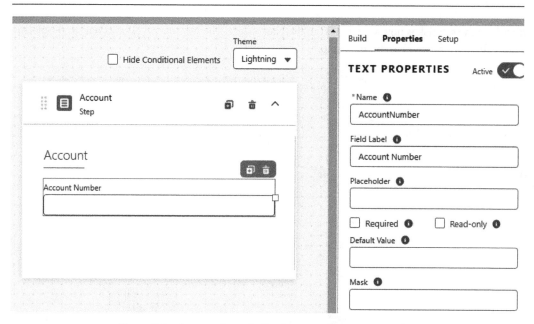

Figure 2.5 – An overview of adjusting text element properties

Let's now add another text element and set its properties as shown below. Then, also check the **Required** box (see *Figure 2.6*):

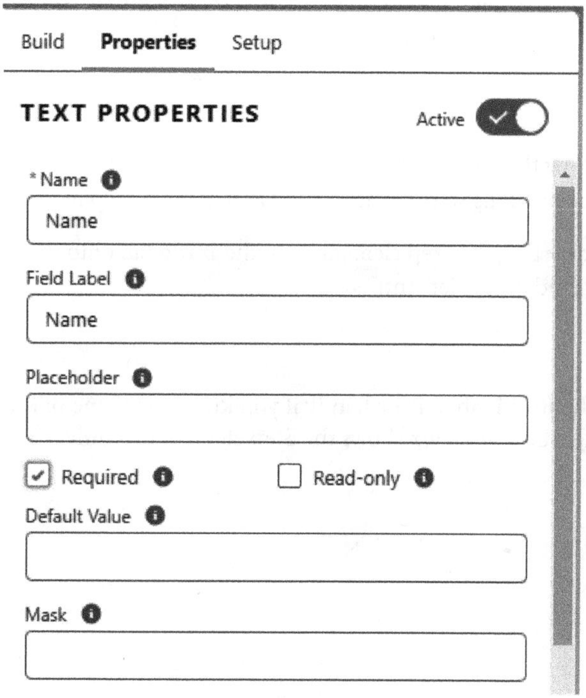

Figure 2.6 – An overview of marking the element as required

Notice how the asterisk is now shown next to the **Name** field. The user now will be asked to complete it before they can proceed to the next step:

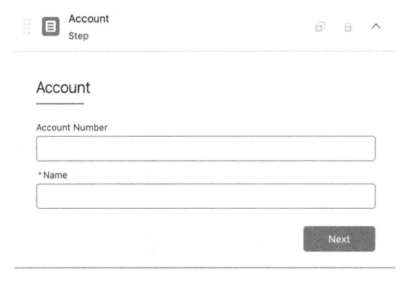

Figure 2.7 – An overview of the required field in the OmniScript UI

We now have our first screen completed! Let's add the second step now that will capture the name of our contact person.

Adding steps

Our second step will allow the user to create a Contact that will be linked to the Account that we created or updated in the previous step. Go ahead and add another step to OmniScript.

Create another step by dragging the **Step** element from the **Build** tab onto the canvas, just below the **Account** step—our last (and only) element.

> **Note**
> The **Search** box in the **Build** tab may be handy if you know the name of the element you are trying to add. Typing `ste` in the box shows the **Step** element instantly:

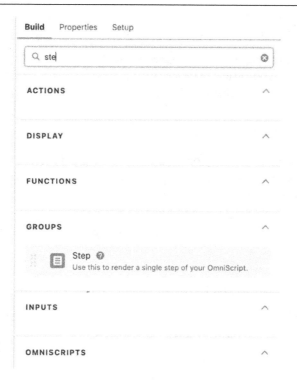

Figure 2.8 – An overview of using the search feature of the Build tab

Once the step is added, give it a name, and add the **First Name** and **Last Name** fields (see *Figure 2.9*).

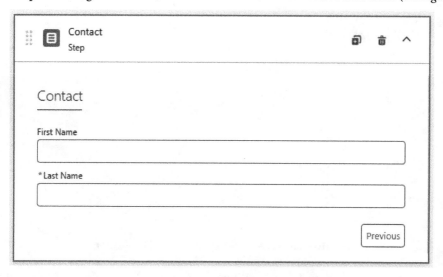

Figure 2.9 – An overview of a sample Contact edit screen

Hope it was easier to add the step the second time around!

We now have our **Account** fields storing our example vendor information and our **Contact** fields storing the contact person. These data points are now captured, and we are ready to save them to the database. Let's accomplish this by creating a DataRaptor.

Creating a DataRaptor

Let's begin by opening a new tab to keep our OmniScript handy in the previous browser tab. Begin by heading to the **OmniStudio DataRaptors** page and hitting the **New** button on the top right. Give it a name and select **Load** in the **Interface Type** field:

Figure 2.10 – An overview of creating a Load DataRaptor

The DataRaptor is now created. Click on the **Add Object** button and select **Account**. This will allow our DataRaptor to create or update accounts:

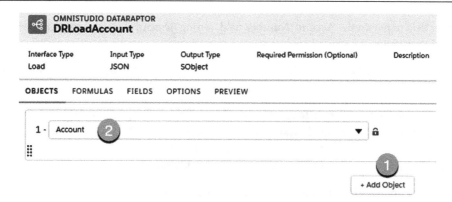

Figure 2.11 – An overview of editing the Objects tab in a DataRaptor

Let's now tell our DataRaptor what *Account* fields we want to persist. Go to the **Fields** tab (see *Figure 2.12*):

1. Begin by clicking the small plus sign on the top-right corner of the list of fields. This will create a new field.

2. Type `Account:Name` into the **Input JSON Path** field. This is the name of the OmniScript step and the name of the Text field we added in the previous section.

3. Finally, select **Name** from the **Domain Object Field** dropdown, so that the value will be put into Account's name.

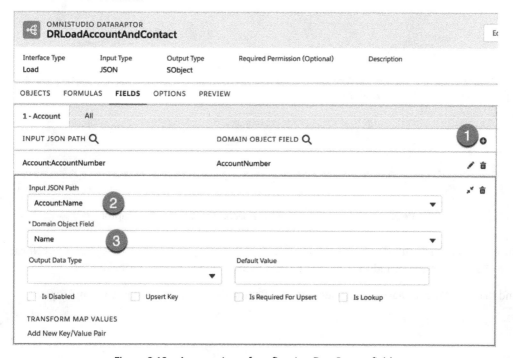

Figure 2.12 – An overview of configuring DataRaptor fields

Add another field to persist the **AccountNumber** field, setting `Account:AccountNumber` as our **Input JSON Path** value.

Now let's go ahead and add another Object to our DataRaptor so that the name of our contact person can also be saved. The DataRaptor will automatically create a new Contact record to store it.

Begin by going back to the **Objects** tab in our DataRaptor and clicking on the **Add Object** button, just as you did before, then select **Contact**. We now need to tell the DataRaptor to link our newly created Contact to the Account that was just created. This will be done by setting the value of the `AccountId` field on the Contact to the value of the `Id` field of our new Account.

Begin by clicking on the **Add Link** button and then configure the **Domain Object Field** and **Linked Object** fields (see *Figure 2.13*):

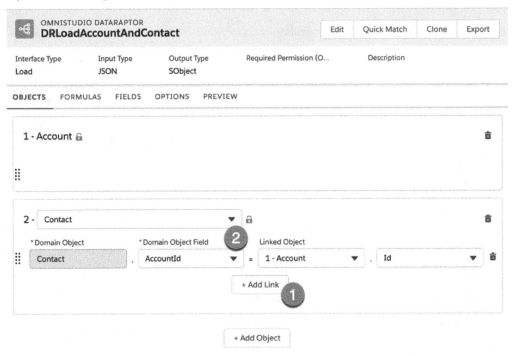

Figure 2.13 – An overview of adding a second object to a DataRaptor

Once completed, return to the **Fields** tab, and configure the mapping of the `Contact:FirstName` to the `FirstName` field and the `Contact:LastName` to the `LastName` field.

And that is it. We now have created our first DataRaptor. Go ahead and add it to OmniScript.

In our OmniScript Designer, switch to the **Build** tab and then find the **DataRaptor Post Action** element:

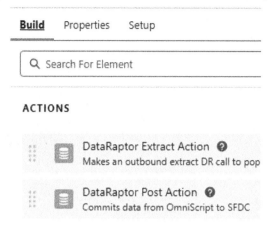

Figure 2.14 – An overview of finding the DataRaptor Post Action element

Drag it to our OmniScript's canvas below the bottom edge of our **Contact** step, so that the new element is added as our **DataRaptor Post Action** (see *Figure 2.15*):

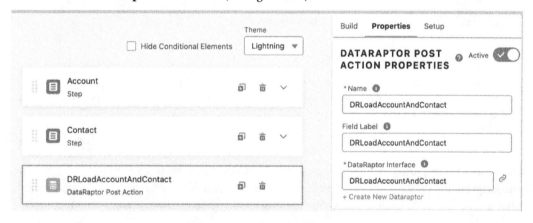

Figure 2.15 – An overview of adding a DataRaptor Post Action

Give it a name and select our DataRaptor in the **DataRaptor Interface** field. Once the DataRaptor **Post Action** step is added, the data we enter should be saved to the database, so let's now give it a try.

OmniScript preview

Click on the **Preview** button on the top right. You should now see the **OmniScript Preview** screen where you can test your OmniScript (see *Figure 2.16*):

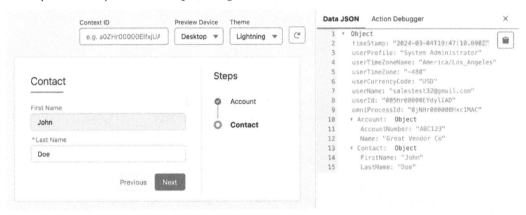

Figure 2.16 – An overview of an OmniScript preview

On the right-hand side, there's a **Data JSON** window where you can see a node added for each of your steps containing the data points collected as you progress through the screens.

> **Real-time data mapping**
>
> If you were watching the Data JSON pane closely, you would notice that it is being constantly updated. Every time you move your cursor out of a field, the value gets transferred to that field's JSON node, which I find to be neat! It's kind of like what's happening inside an LWC, yet the OmniScript is more fun to watch.

Well, we have accomplished quite a bit with just a few clicks! And now, let's add one last step to our OmniScript so that the list of opportunities is displayed to our vendors after they have completed an application. And while doing that, let's get familiar with another OmniStudio UI component: FlexCards.

Adding a FlexCard

Before adding a FlexCard, let's add one more DataRaptor so that we have some data for it to display. Let's go ahead and create a DataRaptor, but this time, let's create an **Extract** one.

Give our DataRaptor a name and select **Extract** from the **Interface Type** dropdown:

Create: OmniStudio DataRaptor

* DataRaptor Interface Name

DRExtractOpportunities

* Interface Type

Extract ▼

* Input Type

JSON ▼

* Output Type

JSON ▼

Required Permission (Optional)

Description

Cancel   Save

Figure 2.17 – An overview of creating an Extract type DataRaptor

Once the DataRaptor is created, select the Object we're going to extract. In our case, this will be **Opportunity**. You can also select the **Filter** criteria that you want to apply during the extraction. The following screenshot shows an example filter criterion where opportunities with the **Stage Name** of 'Qualification' are selected:

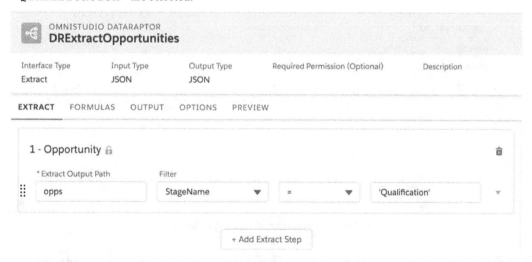

Figure 2.18 – An overview of configuring the Extract DataRaptor

Now we need to specify the Opportunity Object fields for DataRaptor to extract. Just as before, click on the round plus-sign icon and add the fields shown in the following screenshot:

Figure 2.19 – An overview of adding fields to Extract DataRaptor

Our DataRaptor is now ready to go, and we are ready to create the FlexCard! Go to the OmniStudio **FlexCards** app and click on the **New** button at the top. Let's give our FlexCard some **Name** and **Title** values:

New FlexCard

Figure 2.20 – An overview of creating a FlexCard

We will now need to select a data source for our FlexCard. Let's go ahead and select **DataRaptor** so that we can use the one we just created:

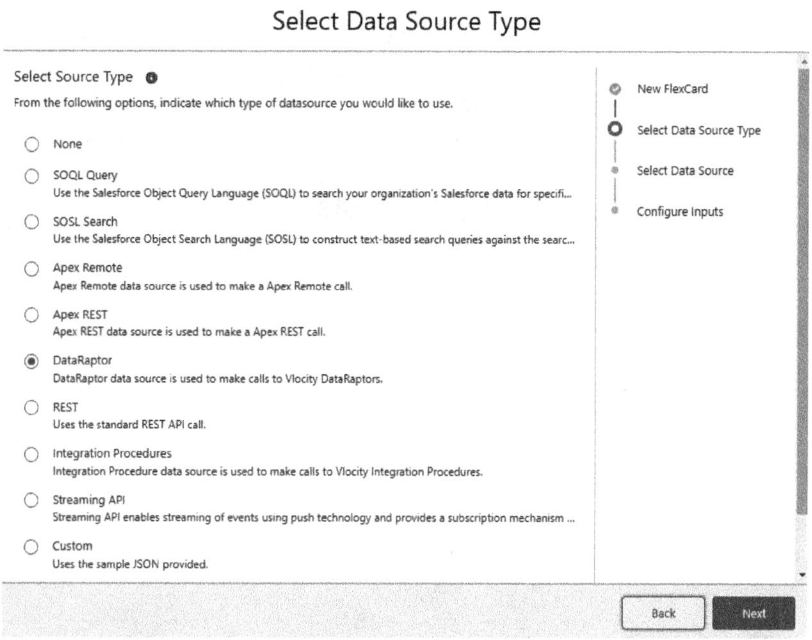

Select Data Source Type

Figure 2.21 – An overview of selecting a FlexCard data source

When you click **Next**, the **Select DataRaptor** dialog box opens. Specify the DataRaptor we created in the previous step.

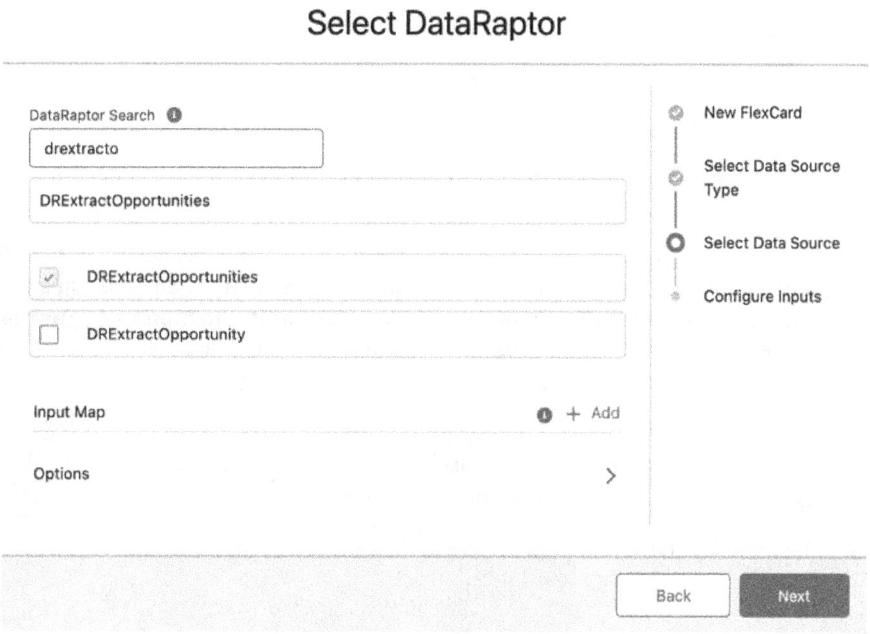

Select DataRaptor

Figure 2.22 – An overview of configuring FlexCard DataRaptor

After clicking **Next** in the dialog box, you will be taken to the final screen of the FlexCard creation wizard where you can test your data source. Since we are not using any parameters, our job here is done and we can test our data source by clicking the **Fetch** button (See *Figure 2.23*). The result of the query will populate the small table below, so you can view the data source in action:

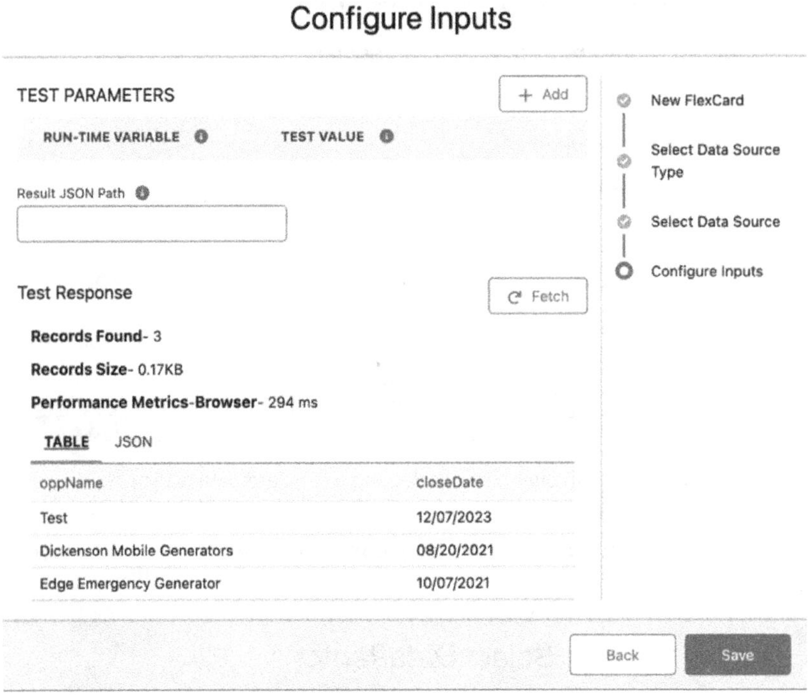

Configure Inputs

TEST PARAMETERS		+ Add
RUN-TIME VARIABLE ⓘ	TEST VALUE ⓘ	

Result JSON Path ⓘ

○ New FlexCard
○ Select Data Source Type
○ Select Data Source
○ Configure Inputs

Test Response   ↻ Fetch

Records Found- 3

Records Size- 0.17KB

Performance Metrics-Browser- 294 ms

TABLE   JSON

oppName	closeDate
Test	12/07/2023
Dickenson Mobile Generators	08/20/2021
Edge Emergency Generator	10/07/2021

Back   Save

Figure 2.23 – An overview of testing the FlexCard data source

> **Note**
>
> If you are seeing the `error: No bundle is specified` inside the table instead of the list of sample opportunities, this may indicate an OmniStudio installation issue and you may be able to resolve it by going to **Setup** > **Omni Interaction** > **Omni Interaction Configuration**, then click the **New Omni Interaction Configuration** button and add an entry with the **Name** and **Label** of `RollbackDRChanges` and the **Value** of `true`.

Your FlexCard is now created and ready to edit. Just like in the OmniScript Designer, you will see the canvas on the left and the list of available controls on the right.

Go ahead and drag the **Datatable** component over to the canvas (see *Figure 2.24*):

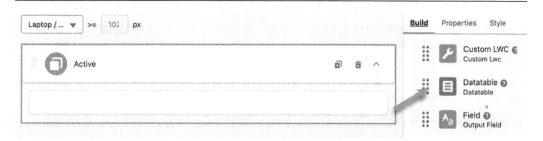

Figure 2.24 – An overview of adding a datatable to a FlexCard

In the **Properties** tab on the right, you can now customize your **Datatable** component. Click on the pencil icon to edit the columns and set the column order:

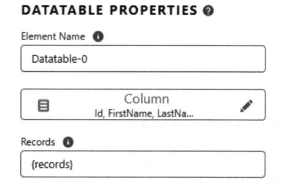

Figure 2.25 – An overview of updating the Datatable properties

This brings up a grid where you can configure our **Datatable**. The rows represent the fields available in the data source we set for the FlexCard. The columns represent the properties of those fields:

Add DataTable Columns

↻ Reset To Default								+ Add Column

TABLE JSON

*Field Name ⓘ	Field Label ⓘ	Is Sortable ⓘ	Is Searchable ⓘ	Type ⓘ	Is Editable ⓘ	Is User Selectable ⓘ	Is Visible ⓘ	
oppName ▼	Name	True ▼	False ▼	T... ▼	is Edit... ▼	is User Select... ▼	is Visible ▼	🗑
closeDate ▼	Date	True ▼	False ▼	T... ▼	is Edit... ▼	is User Select... ▼	is Visible ▼	🗑
oppDes... ▼	Description	True ▼	True ▼	S.. ▼	is Edit... ▼	is User Select... ▼	is Visible ▼	🗑

Save

Figure 2.26 – An overview of configuring the datatable fields

Since we are using a table to display our records, we only want one instance of our FlexCard to display all result rows. To configure that, switch to the **Setup** tab on the right and clear the **Repeat Records** checkbox inside the **Repeat Option** section.

> **Repeat Records**
>
> If we were to leave the **Repeat Records** box checked (as it is checked by default), OmniStudio would display a new copy of our card for each record, rendering a new table for each record returned by the data source.

To turn **Repeat Records** off, uncheck the box as shown in *Figure 2.27*:

Figure 2.27 – An overview of Repeat Records setting in the FlexCard Setup tab

Lastly, since we will be using our FlexCard in an OmniScript, we need to enable the **OmniScript Support** option by checking the relevant checkbox in the **Setup** pane:

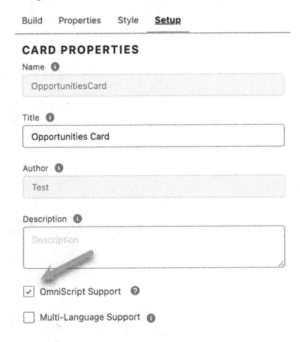

Figure 2.28 – An overview of enabling OmniScript Support in a FlexCard

And finally, we need to activate our FlexCard, so that we can use it in OmniScript. Click the **Activate** button on the top right.

> **Note**
>
> Once the FlexCard is activated, OmniStudio will create an LWC that can be used anywhere in the system as it will be available in the Lightning App Builder. The LWC creation options are configured in the **Runtime** section(s) of the **OmniStudio Settings** page in the Salesforce setup.

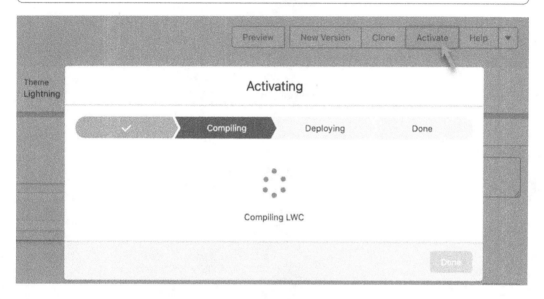

Figure 2.29 – An overview of activating a FlexCard

We're now ready to add our new FlexCard to our OmniScript.

Adding a FlexCard to an OmniScript

Let's begin by adding a step to our OmniScript that will display the list of opportunities. Just as before, locate the **Step** component on the **Build** tab.

Once the **Step** is added, update its **Name** and **Field Label** values:

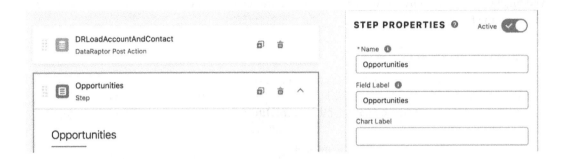

Figure 2.30 – An overview of configuring the step for the FlexCard

Finally, drag the **Custom Lightning Web Component** from the **Build** tab onto the canvas. You can now add your FlexCard LWC.

> **Note**
>
> To find the LWC created from your FlexCard, add `cf` in front of the FlexCard name, so the card named `OpportunitiesCard` will generate the `cfOpportunitiesCard` LWC.

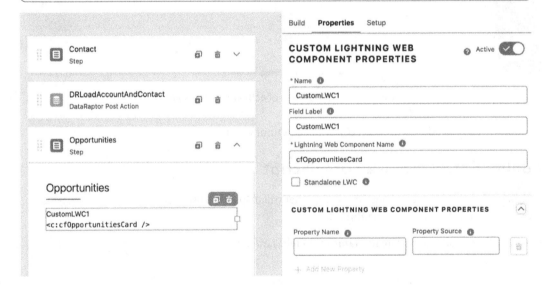

Figure 2.31 – An overview of configuring Custom Lightning Web Component Properties in OmniScript

Now we should be good to preview the OmniScript. The last step left is to activate it.

Note

Normally, you would not have to activate your OmniScript to be able to preview it, but since we're using an LWC, the OmniScript itself needs to be compiled into an LWC as well before you will be able to see the other LWC working inside it. So go ahead and hit the **Activate Version** button in the top right of the screen (see *Figure 2.32*):

Figure 2.32 – An overview of Activating an OmniScript

At this point, we're done with our OmniScript, so we can test it from end to end. When you hit the **Preview** button, you are prompted with the **Account** screen where you can enter some example vendor company information:

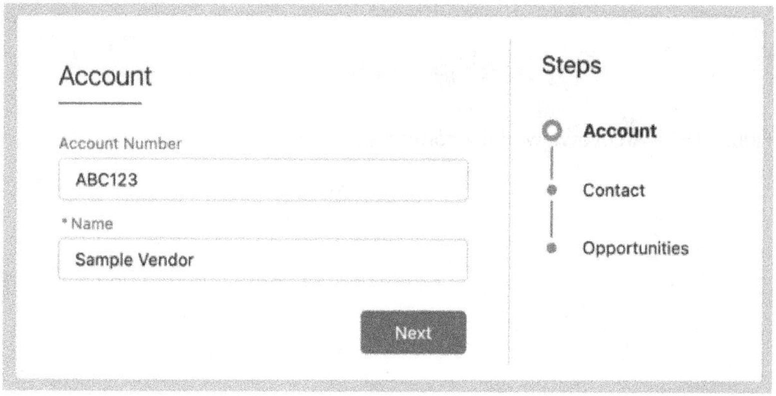

Figure 2.33 – An overview of the completed OmniScript's Account step

Once you click **Next,** you are taken to the **Contact** screen where you can add a Contact to the Account created in the previous step:

Figure 2.34 – An overview of the completed OmniScript's Contact step completed

And finally, on the last screen, you will see a list of all available **Opportunities:**

Figure 2.35 – An overview of the completed OmniScript's Opportunities list

> **Note**
>
> If you do not see the list of opportunities on the last screen (see *Figure 2.36*), hit the **Refresh** button in the top right. If your FlexCard and your OmniScript are both active, the **Refresh** button should flush the internal cache and get your FlexCard LWC to appear.

Figure 2.36 – An overview of how to refresh the OmniScript preview

Well, we've seen a lot of tools in this chapter. We have created an OmniScript, added DataRaptors, added steps and actions to our OmniScript, and previewed our work. We then went ahead to create a FlexCard and finally added it to our OmniScript.

This example app was designed to give you hands-on experience with the most go-to OmniStudio tools. I hope it also got you in the mood for the tech-heavy parts of the chapters ahead.

Summary

In this chapter, we rolled up our sleeves and built a simple OmniStudio app using some go-to components: OmniScripts, DataRaptors, and FlexCards. As a result, we've now seen a large chunk of the OmniStudio platform in action. We've seen most of the go-to OmniStudio tools that make up virtually every app.

If this was your first look at OmniStudio, you should now have a good understanding of what's involved in building the Salesforce Industries apps and how they differ from the other tools (e.g., Flows) available in the core Salesforce platform.

In the next chapter, we will get started on our quest for maximum OmniStudio application performance by learning about the tools and techniques we need to measure the performance of an OmniStudio implementation.

Part 2: Getting to Know the Tools

The second part of this book will introduce the go-to tools that will help you evaluate the performance of your application and its components. You will also find the tools and techniques that will make it easy to see, track, and reverse code and configuration changes in your system.

By the end of this part, you will be able to simulate the real-life load scenarios, measure performance, and adjust to better performance with complete peace of mind.

This part has the following chapters:

- *Chapter 3, Evaluating the Performance of an OmniStudio Implementation*
- *Chapter 4, An Introduction to Load Testing*
- *Chapter 5, Tracking Code Changes and Deployment*

Evaluating the Performance of an OmniStudio Implementation

You can only improve something that you can measure, so before improving the performance and scalability of an OmniStudio implementation, we need to measure its current performance first. In this chapter, we will look at the go-to tools and techniques that come in handy for measuring the performance of OmniStudio components—before, during, and after improvements are implemented.

Here's what you will learn in this chapter:

- How to use the built-in tools to quickly assess the performance of major OmniStudio components
- How to use the OmniStudio Tracking Service for collecting more detailed stats, even when the app runs unattended
- Finding out about other helpful Salesforce and Vlocity tools for collecting stats and debugging OmniStudio apps

First things first—OmniStudio is always providing handy and easy-to-use stats on everything we do, so let's get familiar with these and make sure we're using them.

Technical requirements

To follow along with this chapter, you will need access to an OmniStudio installation. If you don't have one handy, you can always request your free trial development environment from the Salesforce Developers site, which is (at the time of this writing) available at `https://developer.salesforce.com/free-trials`. Once on the site, head over to **Industry-Based Trials** and get yourself a trial org for the industry of your choice.

Measuring execution times in OmniStudio

How would you like to find out that your Integration Procedure is taking 30 seconds to run—simply by previewing it? You don't need the project manager to remind you about the business-level expectations while having to dig through dozens of declarative and code-level components. The OmniStudio platform is already providing you with this info, giving you valuable instant feedback on how long the component you are looking at is taking to execute.

Information is literally at our fingertips, everywhere throughout the platform, yet I'm always surprised to see even experienced developers ignoring these and opting for more complex choices right out of the bat.

Execution times in DataRaptors

Every time you preview a **DataRaptor**, OmniStudio calculates its execution time and shows it at the top, right above the results—see *Figure 3.1*:

Figure 3.1 – An overview of execution times in the DataRaptor Preview mode

The **Preview** window shows the following useful performance information:

- **Browser** shows the total time the full request has taken—from clicking the **Execute** button until a response is rendered by the **Preview** UI

- **Server** shows the total time the Salesforce Apex code took to execute

- Finally, the **Apex CPU** metric shows the total time that DataRaptor-specific code took to execute

Please note that the **Apex CPU** metric cannot exceed 10,000ms or milliseconds, or you will exceed the governor limit and your app will throw an exception.

Execution times in Integration Procedures

As with DataRaptors, each time you run a preview on an Integration Procedure, the OmniStudio platform calculates execution times and shows them at the top, right above the results, as shown in *Figure 3.2*:

Figure 3.2 – An overview of execution times in the Integration Procedure Preview mode

The stats are displayed in a similar manner as done for DataRaptors:

- **Browser** shows the total time that the full request has taken—from clicking the **Execute** button until a response is rendered by the **Preview** UI

- **Server** shows the total time the Salesforce Apex code took to execute

- Finally, the **Apex CPU** metric shows the total time that Integration Procedure-specific code took to execute

Please note that, just like in a DataRaptor, the **Apex CPU** metric cannot exceed 10,000ms, or you will exceed the governor limit and your app will throw an exception.

Execution times in OmniScripts

Unlike DataRaptors and Integration Procedures, the system does not track execution times for OmniScripts unless you ask it to. Likely, this is easy to enable.

To turn on the time tracking for an OmniScript, in the OmniScript properties on the **Setup** tab, check the **Enable Tracking** checkbox, as shown in *Figure 3.3*:

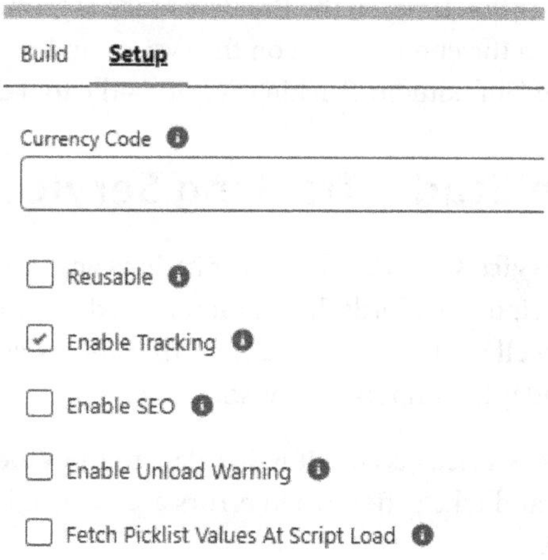

Figure 3.3 – An overview of enabling tracking in OmniScript

Once enabled, OmniScript will measure the time spent by each element. Time taken by each of the steps is now collected and added to the **Preview** window as a `vlocityTracking` JSON node. See *Figure 3.4*:

```
▼ vlcTimeTracking:  Object
    OmniScriptSessionToken:  "c21ae8ca-0efc-4bfd-b137-22830b82fc32"
    DataRaptorExtractAction2: 1935
    DataRaptorExtractAction3: 384
    DataRaptorExtractAction1: 241
    RemoteAction1: 187
    RemoteAction2: 115
    RemoteAction3: 97
    IntegrationProcedureAction1: 267
```

Figure 3.4 – An overview of OmniScript step timing shown in JSON

As you can see, OmniScript Data JSON now contains a new node called `vlocityTracking`—the OmniScript Data JSON node, containing execution times for each OmniScript action element.

> **Note**
>
> Please note that OmniScript time tracking does consume system resources, so it is only recommended for debugging purposes, and, therefore, Salesforce recommends keeping OmniScript time tracking disabled in production.
>
> OmniScript time tracking will also not work when OmniScripts are run off-platform on third-party websites via *OmniOut*. See the Salesforce documentation (`https://help.salesforce.com/s/articleView?id=sf.os_omniout_43469.htm`) for more information on OmniOut.

Well, the ability to measure execution times in the **Preview** mode is great, but how about measuring these times in production, when the end users are on the system and we're not in the office? In the next section, we will look at the OmniStudio Tracking Service—the tool designed to do exactly that.

Exploring the OmniStudio Tracking Service

The **OmniStudio Tracking Service** saves details of user actions across various components of the OmniStudio platform: OmniScripts, FlexCards, Integration Procedures, and more. The data includes the time taken by actions as well as the data outcomes. This allows you to monitor application performance, data integrity, and other important statistics.

I like the OmniStudio Tracking Service because it writes data to the **Vlocity Tracking Entry** object so that we can then analyze it and take action when errors are logged. Let's see how to enable and configure the Tracking Service.

Enabling tracking for OmniStudio

To enable the OmniStudio Tracking Service to begin tracking, go to **Setup> Omni Interaction Configuration**, and then click on **New Omni Interaction Configuration**.

Enter one of the following event triggers in the **Name** field depending on what you would like to track:

- OmniScripts: `Track_OmniScript`
- Integration Procedures: `Track_IntProc`
- FlexCards: `Track_CardFramework` or `Track_CardPreview`

For an example, see *Figure 3.5*:

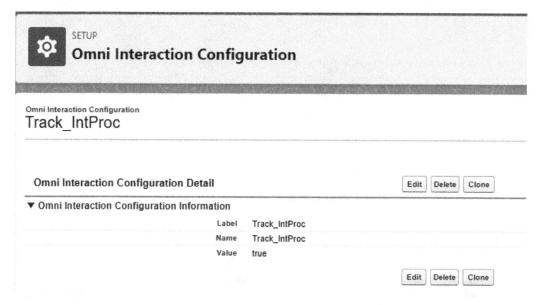

Figure 3.5 – An overview of an Omni Interaction Configuration entry

You can then enable tracking for specific events for each of the component types by creating event trigger entries. The event trigger entry name contains the trigger name from the list discussed earlier in this section, followed by the name of the event you would like to track. For example, to track the time taken by OmniScript steps, create a `StepActionTime` event that will trigger entries for OmniScripts, and then create a `Track_OmniScript_StepActionTime` trigger.

> **Note**
>
> Event trigger names differ between *OmniStudio Standard* and *OmniStudio for Vlocity*. While OmniStudio for Vlocity offers some of the original Vlocity features that are not available in OmniStudio Standard, the latter uses standard Salesforce objects and, therefore, is faster. Virtually all of the new OmniStudio installations I'm seeing now are OmniStudio Standard, so this is why this section is also using the OmniStudio Standard version of event trigger names.
>
> You can tell that you are running the OmniStudio Standard version if your **Omni Interaction Configuration** page in Salesforce **Setup** (where we were adding event triggers in this section) has the `TheFirstInstalledOmniPackage` entry.
>
> For more information on the differences between OmniStudio Standard and OmniStudio for Vlocity, see the following Salesforce documentation page: `https://help.salesforce.com/s/articleView?id=sf.os_differences_between_omnistudio_and_omnistudio_for_vlocity.htm`

You can narrow it down to specific OmniScripts, Integration Procedures, and so on by using the name of the component as your trigger name, prepended by the word `Track`. For instance, to track an Integration Procedure with a type of `RatingCalculation` and sub-type of `GetRating`, use the following trigger name: `Track_RatingCalculation_GetRating`.

When an Integration Procedure you track calls another Integration Procedure, events in that Integration Procedure you call will also be tracked.

I've enabled the `StepActionTime` trigger for OmniScripts and Integration Procedures in my sample org, and that produced the following tracking entries shown in *Figure 3.6*:

		Tracking... ↑∨	Created Date ∨	Event Name ∨	Data
44	☐	IntProc	2023-11-16, 6:37 a.m.	Error	{"SalesforceSessionToken":"96a523d1944dedfb341630a59310962a
45	☐	IntProc	2023-11-16, 7:01 a.m.	StepActionTime	{"SalesforceSessionToken":"96a523d1944dedfb341630a59310962a
46	☐	IntProc	2023-11-16, 7:01 a.m.	StepActionTime	{"SalesforceSessionToken":"96a523d1944dedfb341630a59310962a
47	☐	IntProc	2023-11-16, 7:01 a.m.	Error	{"SalesforceSessionToken":"96a523d1944dedfb341630a59310962a
48	☐	IntProc	2023-11-16, 7:02 a.m.	StepActionTime	{"SalesforceSessionToken":"96a523d1944dedfb341630a59310962a
49	☐	IntProc	2023-11-16, 7:02 a.m.	StepActionTime	{"SalesforceSessionToken":"96a523d1944dedfb341630a59310962a
50	☐	IntProc	2023-11-16, 7:02 a.m.	Error	{"SalesforceSessionToken":"96a523d1944dedfb341630a59310962a
51	☐	OmniScript	2023-07-26, 9:19 a.m.	StepActionTime	{"Timestamp":"2023-07-26T13:19:42.660Z","SalesforceSessionToke
52	☐	OmniScript	2023-07-26, 9:19 a.m.	StepActionTime	{"Timestamp":"2023-07-26T13:19:39.098Z","SalesforceSessionToke
53	☐	OmniScript	2023-07-26, 9:31 a.m.	StepActionTime	{"Timestamp":"2023-07-26T13:31:38.183Z","SalesforceSessionToke
54	☐	OmniScript	2023-07-26, 9:09 a.m.	StepActionTime	{"Timestamp":"2023-07-26T13:09:11.801Z","SalesforceSessionToke
55	☐	OmniScript	2023-07-26, 9:09 a.m.	StepActionTime	{"Timestamp":"2023-07-26T13:09:08.471Z","SalesforceSessionToke
56	☐	OmniScript	2023-07-26, 9:09 a.m.	StepActionTime	{"Timestamp":"2023-07-26T13:09:09.385Z","SalesforceSessionToke

Figure 3.6 – An overview of Vlocity tracking entries list

Each tracking entry contains the event name and the data that was captured during the event:

Figure 3.7 – An overview of a sample tracking entry

The events you can track vary by component. For example, for OmniScripts, you can capture `StepActionTime` and `Outcome` tracking events.

`StepActionTime` captures the elapsed time along with the step and OmniScript details, and the `Outcome` event collects the outcome configured for the **Done Action** element.

Look up the OmniStudio Tracking Service in the OmniStudio documentation for a full list of tracking events for OmniScripts, Integration Procedures, and FlexCards:

`https://help.salesforce.com/s/articleView?id=sf.os_vlocity_tracking_service.htm`

You can also add custom fields to collect any additional info that you might like to track. The following section shows the steps involved in creating and configuring a custom field.

Adding custom fields to event tracking

To include a custom data point in your tracking info, simply add them in the **Tracking Custom Data** section as follows:

- In the **Procedure Configuration** page of an Integration Procedure
- In the **Setup** tab of an OmniScript
- In the **Setup** panel of a FlexCard (at the time of this writing this section, this is only available when running OmniStudio for Vlocity)

For example, I've added a `customKey` data point to an Integration Procedure that is collecting an account name:

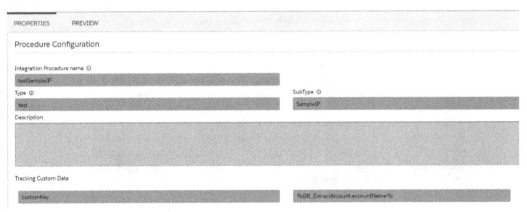

Figure 3.8 – An overview of tracking a custom data entry in an OmniScript

This value will be visible in the corresponding step (the tokens and IDs are hidden for brevity):

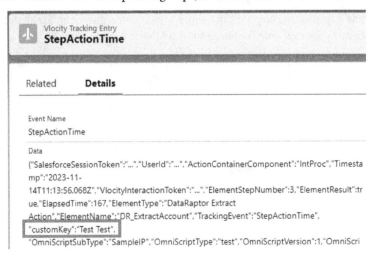

Figure 3.9 – An overview of custom data added to JSON

> **Note**
>
> Please note that while **Vlocity Tracking Entry** objects are also created for some errors (see *Figure 3.10*), they are not created for limits-type errors such as the **Apex CPU** time limit exceeded. So, this type of error will not be captured.

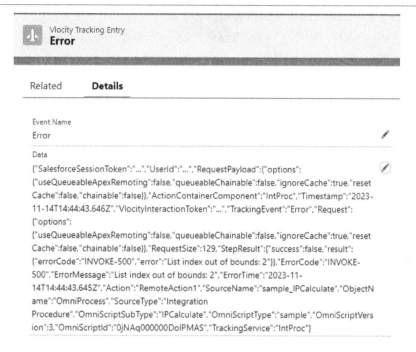

Figure 3.10 – An overview of error info captured in a Vlocity Tracking Entry object

> **Note**
>
> The content of the `Data` field contains an unformatted JSON string and may not be easy to grasp. Copying and pasting its content into a JSON formatting tool of your choice may make it easier to work with. In addition to desktop, there are a lot of free online JSON formatting tools; just search for `JSON formatter online` to find them.

With that, we conclude our exploration of the Vlocity Tracking Service. We can now collect information on errors and user actions along with the time they take—all while our systems are running unattended.

In the following sections, we will be looking at other Vlocity tools for capturing errors and at good old Salesforce trace logs, which often come in handy for measuring performance and debugging Vlocity solutions.

Collecting stats and errors

Earlier in this chapter, we looked at the built-in performance monitoring facilities in OmniStudio as well as the Vlocity Tracking Service. These are the go-to tools for getting performance-related data. Now, what do we do when things are not working as expected, when our code breaks, or when we need to do some quick troubleshooting? In the following section, we will look at tools we can use to dig in and find bugs and reasons for sub-standard performance that are hiding deep below the surface.

Let's begin with every developer's go-to tool: **Salesforce debug logs**. Let's see how debug logs can come in handy when debugging OmniStudio issues.

Salesforce debug logs

Debugging OmniStudio solutions at times can be very straightforward, while at other times it can be difficult. Let me share a couple of tricks we like to use to locate the offending component when troubleshooting errors for our clients. Let's look at a couple of scenarios, and I'll show you the tricks I'm talking about.

> **Note**
>
> Even though this section discusses standard Salesforce platform features that may not be new and specific to OmniStudio, using them can often be indispensable. This is why I would rather be boring here while bringing these to your attention than leave you trying to hopelessly find this key error information inside OmniStudio only, while it is readily available in the old and *boring* parts of the platform.

I've created a simple **Remote Action**—an Apex class that is called from an Integration Procedure—that produces an **Apex CPU** time limit exception by running a simple math calculation in a loop. See *Figure 3.11*:

```
1  global with sharing class SampleIPController implements omnistudio.VlocityOpenInterface2 {
2      global Object invokeMethod(String methodName, Map<String,Object> inputMap,Map<String,Object> outMap, Map<String,Object> options) {
3          if (methodName == 'calculate')
4              calculate(inputMap,outMap,options);
5
6          return true;
7      }
8      global void calculate(Map<String,Object> inputMap,Map<String,Object> outMap, Map<String,Object> options){
9          Decimal sum = 0.0;
10         for (Integer i = 0; i < 5000000; i++){
11             sum += i;
12             sum = sum * sum;
13             sum = math.sqrt(sum);
14         }
15         outMap.put 'result', sum ;
16     }
17 }
```

Figure 3.11 – An overview of a sample Remote Action class

And here's the Remote Action element, invoking the preceding class from an Integration Procedure:

RA_Calculate Remote Action

Element Name ⓘ

RA_Calculate

Remote Class

SampleIPController

Remote Method

calculate

Figure 3.12 – An overview of a Remote Action element in an Integration Procedure

We can see the error when we simply preview the Integration Procedure:

Errors/Debug Output

> Debug Log

✓ Errors

```
[
  "Apex CPU time limit exceeded",
  {
    "statusCode": 400,
    "type": "exception",
    "tid": 10,
    "ref": false,
    "action":
"omnistudio.OmniScriptDesignerController",
    "method": "testIntegrationProcedure",
    "message": "Apex CPU time limit exceeded",
    "where": "",
    "data": {
```

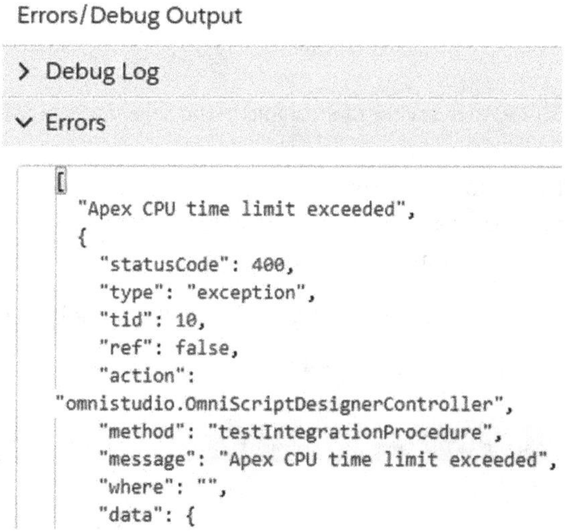

Figure 3.13 – An overview of an error message in the Integration Procedure Preview mode

Now, what if this error happens only in a specific scenario, for certain users, and on a specific record, and the code works fine otherwise? When this happens, you won't be able to catch this error in the **Preview** pane as there will be no error when you simply preview your Integration Procedure.

In a case such as this, you would be trying to replicate the error while looking at Salesforce debug logs. But will the log just tell you that the CPU time exception happened at the RA_Calculate step of testIntegrationProcedure? Unfortunately, it won't.

The good news, though, is that you can trace these exceptions to the Integration Procedure they are coming from by tracking back in the Salesforce log, looking for the query just before the CPU exception. Refer to *Figure 3.14*:

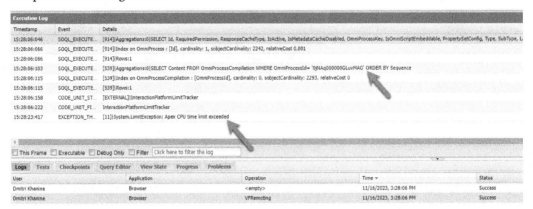

Figure 3.14 – An overview of error info in the Salesforce trace log

Here, we can see the WHERE `OmniProcessId=` `'0jNAq000000GLuvMAG'` clause. At the time of this writing, `OmniProcess` is an undocumented internal OmniStudio object that stores information about Integration Procedures and OmniScripts.

Querying it for the `OmniProcessId` value brings back the offending Integration Procedure:

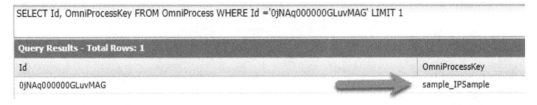

Figure 3.15 – An overview of query results for the OmniProcessId value

Now, let's look at another example. We can throw a common `List index out of bounds` error with a simple statement like the one shown on *line 1* of the following screenshot:

```
List<Account> accs = [select Id, Name from Account LIMIT 1];
System.debug(accs[2].Name);
```

Figure 3.16 – An overview of a code snippet that throws a List index out of bounds error

Sure enough, this throws an exception when we preview our sample Integration Procedure that is running the preceding Apex code in a Remote Action:

```
{
  "success": false,
  "result": {
    "errorCode": "INVOKE-500",
    "error": "List index out of bounds: 2"
  }
}
```

Figure 3.17 – An overview of an error in the Integration Procedure Preview mode

Again, an error of this sort would be sporadic and would not show up on the Integration Procedure preview, so we would need to look at Salesforce debug logs to find it.

This time, we could try setting our DebugLevel parameter to FINEST:

Change DebugLevel

Add   Remove

DebugLevel	DB	Callouts	ApexCode
SFDC_DevConsole	FINEST	FINEST	FINEST

Figure 3.18 – An overview of setting the Salesforce DebugLevel parameter

Then, try to find the Apex method that was called last before the error occurred:

SOQL_EXECUTE...	[914]|Aggregations:0|SELECT Id, RequiredPermission, ResponseCacheType, IsActive, IsMetadataCacheDisabled, Om
SOQL_EXECUTE...	[914]|Index on OmniProcess : [Id], cardinality: 1, sobjectCardinality: 2242, relativeCost 0.001
SOQL_EXECUTE...	[914]|Rows:1
SOQL_EXECUTE...	[539]|Aggregations:0|SELECT Content FROM OmniProcessCompilation WHERE OmniProcessId= '0jNAq000000GLuvl
SOQL_EXECUTE...	[539]|Index on OmniProcessCompilation : [OmniProcessId], cardinality: 0, sobjectCardinality: 2293, relativeCost 0
SOQL_EXECUTE...	[539]|Rows:1
CODE_UNIT_ST...	[EXTERNAL]|InteractionPlatformLimitTracker
CODE_UNIT_FI...	InteractionPlatformLimitTracker
METHOD_ENTRY	[4]|01pAq000001DaRh|SampleIPController.calculate(Map<String,ANY>, Map<String,ANY>, Map<String,ANY>)

Figure 3.19 – An overview of an error log showing the last method called prior to the error

Well, hope you found those helpful. And now, there's just one more question that we did not answer here—how would we look at the logs if the error was only happening to live production users at random times when we cannot be physically present to look at Salesforce debug logs?

Collecting debug logs in production

The following section explains how we can get the Salesforce platform to collect debug logs for us when we're not physically there to look at them.

Begin by going to **Setup** > **Debug Logs**. Here, we would need to create a new trace flag that will instruct the Salesforce platform to collect specific information for specific users for the specified period:

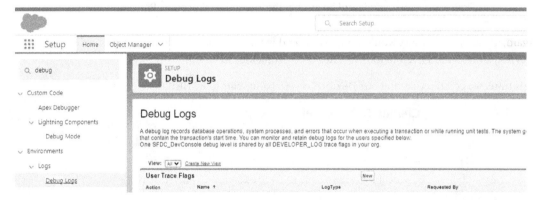

Figure 3.20 – An overview of the Salesforce debug logs tool

What are Salesforce debug log trace flags?

Trace flags instruct the Salesforce platform to collect the information we need in a debug log. They include all necessary details such as debug levels, start and end time, the user, Apex class, trigger, or an automated process whose actions will be logged.

Click the **New** button and select the user who is seeing the error we would like to catch and the debug level by using the lookup buttons. Finally, set start and expiration dates. Refer to *Figure 3.21*:

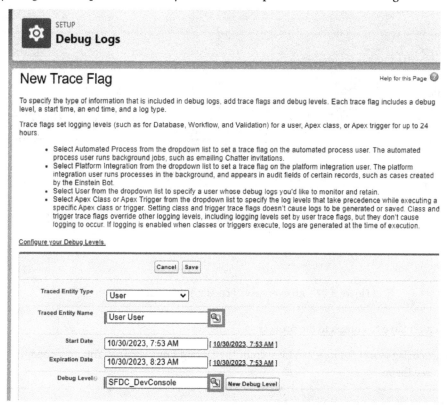

Figure 3.21 – An overview of adding a new trace flag

We can also create a new debug level and specify the level of detail we would like to see for each of the platform components. See *Figure 3.22* (to get to this screen, simply press the **New Debug Level** button on the previous screen):

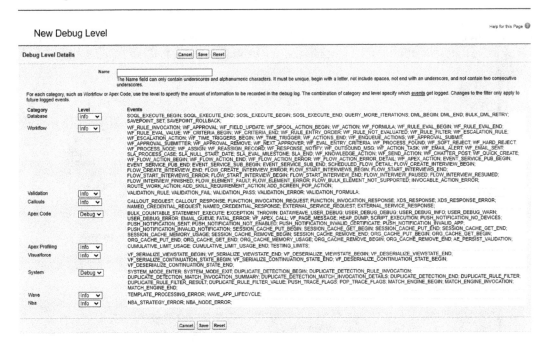

Figure 3.22 – An overview of creating a new debug level

Finally, click on **Save** to complete the process.

Once the trace flag is set, the logs can be seen in the **Debug Logs** section. You may need to refresh the page to see them:

Figure 3.23 – An overview of Salesforce debug logs listing

Also, since the amount of info dumped on logs can be massive, we can further filter it down by creating a trace flag for a specific Apex class, Apex trigger, an automated process, or a Platform Integration instead of a user when creating the new trace flag.

For example, we can set a trace flag for a specific class and use a different debug level (see *Figure 3.24*):

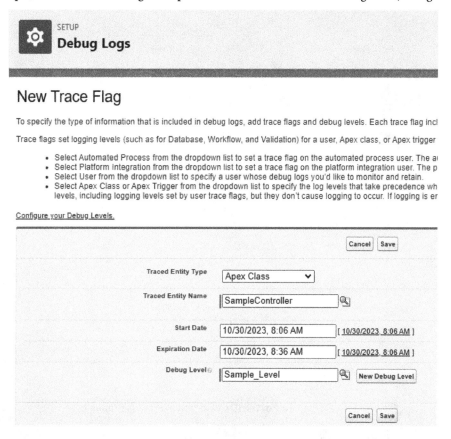

Figure 3.24 – An overview of setting up a class-level new trace flag

Now, while Salesforce trace logs are the go-to tools for debugging, the **Process Profiler** tool in IDX Workbench may come in handy for a quick check on the performance of specific OmniStudio components in your solution.

Process Profiler in IDX Workbench

The **Process Profiler** tool is included with IDX Workbench—a free desktop application offering helpful features for deployment, tracking code changes, and more. To get IDX Workbench, search for `Install IDX Workbench` or follow this link: `https://help.salesforce.com/s/articleView?id=sf.os_install_idx_workbench.htm`

Once installed, you will be able to access the **Process Profiler** tool, which works just like Salesforce trace logs. You set the start and end times for when you would like your monitoring to take place. Then, you also select a Salesforce org and the specific component that you want **Process Profiler** to monitor. See *Figure 3.25*:

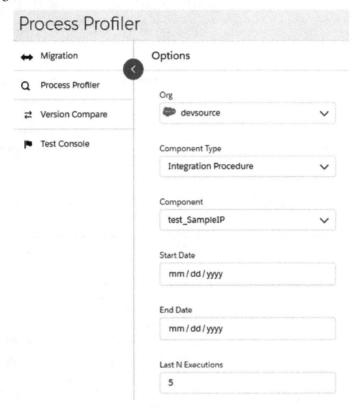

Figure 3.25 – An overview of the IDX Workbench Process Profiler tool

Once tracking is enabled, the following entries are produced, showing you the times taken by individual steps:

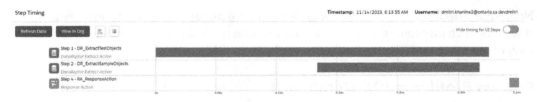

Figure 3.26 – An overview of an OmniScript step timing chart in IDX Workbench

While the IDX Workbench **Process Profiler** tool is a quick and useful tool for checking performance, it is not going to help you capture detailed error information. For this task, I suggest you look at **Vlocity Error Log**.

Vlocity Error Log

If you are running the Winter '20 or later releases of the OmniStudio for Vlocity edition, you can have the system write your **Integration Procedure** errors to the **Vlocity Error Log Entry** object. This tool is handy because it automatically captures errors that may otherwise be very difficult to log, considering that an Integration Procedure may be running asynchronously, and the error message may not make it all the way to the end-user screen.

Another good thing about using this service is that it logs full input data that was sent to the Integration Procedure step that has just failed. Having the input data in addition to error information may make it much easier to troubleshoot.

Now, this may or may not be available in your installation, so to see if it is, check if you have the **Vlocity Error Log Entry** object. If you do, you can enable logging by setting the `ErrorLoggingEnabled` custom setting under **General Settings** to `true`.

Since it does take a few steps to enable and configure, and online documentation (at the time of this writing) does not provide detailed instructions, I've included detailed step-by-step instructions for this on the book's companion site at `https://maximumvlocity.com/`.

Now if you don't have the **Vlocity Error Log** feature available in your org, you can always gather error info into a custom object. This may especially come in handy when you are making callouts to external services out of your Integration Procedures. We all know that these calls often like to fail at the worst possible time, such as in the middle of a long weekend or in rare circumstances (for example, when a specific customer profile is being sent out), so knowing the exact data that was sent out and the response you got may save you hours if not days of troubleshooting.

And that's a wrap for this section as well. We looked at the general-purpose troubleshooting tools made available by the Salesforce platform and how we can use them to find bugs in our OmniStudio components and custom code. We also looked at **Process Profiler** in IDX Workbench and **Vlocity Error Log**—tools that may come in handy in our quest to achieve maximum performance of our OmniStudio apps.

Summary

Well, that was a lot of information! We learned how to measure basic execution times in the **Preview** pane and with OmniScript time tracking. We covered the more sophisticated OmniStudio Tracking Service. Then, we went on to learn about debugging OmniStudio solutions, collecting error and performance info with the **Process Profiler** tool in IDX Workbench, and capturing errors with **Vlocity Error Log**.

We have now seen the go-to tools for measuring the performance of OmniStudio apps, tools we can use before, during, and after we've implemented improvements. These tools can give us a glance at performance when needed, and we can implement ongoing monitoring for errors and performance issues in our implementations.

In the next chapter, we will be looking at load testing—tools and techniques designed to simulate a specific real-life load on an OmniStudio implementation—so that you can be sure it will keep working fine when crowds show up.

4

An Introduction to Load Testing

In the previous chapter, we were looking at the go-to tools and techniques for measuring OmniStudio performance. In this chapter, we will look at load testing: tools, tips, and best practices available for simulating real-life load on the system. This will help us measure its capacity, performance, and scalability and get ready to handle expected customer demands.

In this chapter, you will learn about the following:

- Why should you consider running a load test on your OmniStudio app?
- How to load-test—critical information you will need during planning and execution
- Popular tools—available options and a hands-on introduction to Selenium and JMeter, the popular open source load-testing tools

We have a lot of ground to cover in this chapter, so let's go ahead and begin by looking at why and how to plan and run load testing.

> **Note**
> Salesforce is a multitenant platform, so any kind of heavy load or stress testing needs to be coordinated with them by contacting Salesforce Support. The term *load testing* as used in this chapter refers to a type of performance testing done by simulating your app's expected current or future load in a sandbox environment.

Technical requirements

To follow along with this chapter, you will need access to an OmniStudio installation. If you don't have one handy, you can always request your free trial development environment from the Salesforce Developers site, which is (at the time of this writing) available at `https://developer.salesforce.com/free-trials`. Once on the site, head over to **Industry-Based Trials** and get yourself a trial org for the industry of your choice.

Why and how to do load testing

I often like to ask my clients if they are sure how their application will perform when the target number of users are logged in at the same time. Will their app become unbearably slow or continue to meet targets on page load time? Will it break when people start using it concurrently? Will the data get corrupted, or will it run out of resources or hit governor limits after a few hours of heavy use? And lastly, how many more users can we accommodate with the current setup?

If you are not 100% sure about your answer to any of these questions, you really should add load testing to your release schedule. Since a lot of OmniStudio applications are business-critical and so easy to point and click to add logic to your OmniScripts, DataRaptors, and Integration Procedures, you will need to be certain that none of this logic will slow your system down to a crawl when you least expect it.

To answer this question for yourself and sleep well throughout the night, I suggest you consider using the tools and techniques described in this chapter.

General considerations

Let's start by looking at common but not-so-obvious gotchas that are very important to review before you run your load testing.

Planning for data issues

If you have access to the dataset your system will use, I suggest the first thing you do is get a full or partial-copy sandbox created with a fresh copy of a complete set of your real production data. Or, have a copy of your real-life data loaded onto an adequate capacity sandbox. If you have the actual production data, I suggest you use it for the load test.

Yes—it may be tempting to generate your own test data just for the load test, and there are many solid data generation tools available that would create perfect life-like data. But please hear me out. I still strongly recommend running your load test on your real production data. Yes—you may want to mask some sensitive fields if you must so that you are not posing security risks. Yes—I don't want you sending test emails to your real-life customers (and Salesforce masks emails in sandboxes just for that purpose), but experience has taught me this—the data itself can cause a ton of issues under the load, and it may be very difficult to replicate this with the test data that you are planning to generate.

I've seen our customers encounter some records with more characters in certain fields than their code reasonably expected. Some records had bad or unexpected values or characters, and some were linked to the wrong parent, which caused the code to enter an endless loop.

Testing with all your actual real-life data will give you a chance to hit all these hidden rocks before your most important customer hits them at the worst possible time—during critical end-of-the-month processing or when your team is out of the office for a long weekend!

Identifying key personas

Personas are the roles or the types of business users of your system. For an insurance claims portal, this could be an adjustor who is handling the claim, an applicant submitting it, or a claim administrator who oversees issuing the payment and overall coordination. It's easy to make your load-testing scenarios too complex. This can easily make the whole thing cost-prohibitive and prompt your management to skip load testing altogether.

So, here, as always, the 80/20 rule applies, and your top 20% of the most active or the most important business users would generate 80% of the load that you would want to simulate. 20% of the most important use cases would account for 80% of your system's business value. For example, if your app is open to the public and uses *OmniOut* to serve your customers, they may be your most important persona, and you need to plan to load-test your public site first.

Whatever the case might be, you will most likely need to limit the scope of your load testing, so think of key scenarios, personas, and use cases to focus on.

Your stats may be skewed

And lastly, I want to bring up this point. If you need to know the exact number of customers your system will be able to handle and the exact response time at a specific data/load condition, these numbers may be very difficult to obtain.

You will need a very precise load-test setup to get this kind of data. You will also need to be using a cloud-based load-testing tool and run the test on your actual production org, not on the sandbox. Testing on production brings up its own bowl of wax when you will need to coordinate your load testing with Salesforce, as their other customers may be affected.

The good news, though, is that with the 80/20 rule applied, neither of these is required if all you need is to just get an idea of the kind of load your system is equipped to handle and make sure that nothing bad happens when the end-user crowds are going to come.

When testing a full sandbox, remember that sandbox performance may vary. It may also be very different from production, and the performance may differ significantly between sandboxes. This is because your sandboxes may be hosted on different infrastructures within Salesforce. Even if the infrastructure is similar, the overall load on their servers may differ, and so may the network conditions.

So, do not rely on exact metrics, but test your app for ballpark response times and overall scalability. Compare with the simple *Hello World* app to see the impact that your business logic has on your app's performance.

Another thing that may affect your numbers is your test setup. You may want to *test your setup first before testing your app*. Make sure your network, the hardware you are planning to run your load-testing tools on, and the remaining setup are fast enough. The software you are using for generating the load may pose significant stress on your infrastructure, so it may not generate enough requests per minute. So, you may need to scale your testing infrastructure either vertically by beefing up your hardware and/or horizontally by running your testing software on multiple computers.

Lastly, because of the demand that testing tools are posing on the machines they're running on, reported response times and throughput data may not be accurate. You can opt for a more complex setup with dedicated machines that will take your measurements or measure the performance on the server using the data created during tests.

Oh—and please remember to run your tests multiple times and look at the average numbers. And yes—you need to retest after applying fixes!

Now that we've looked at all these important considerations, let's look at the tools we have available for planning and executing our load tests.

Salesforce Performance Assistant

No matter what your objectives are, Salesforce has a wealth of good information and helpful tools in stock for you. Search for `performance` in **Setup** to load the **Performance Assistant** tool.

You will be taken to the learning resources and tools you might find useful when preparing for your load test and coordinating with Salesforce when testing in production. And then, finally, the **Analyze and Optimize** section presents tools such as *The Page Optimizer Chrome Extension*, *Trailhead* resources, and other relevant information.

The following screenshot shows *step 3* of the **Prepare** stage of **Performance Assistant**:

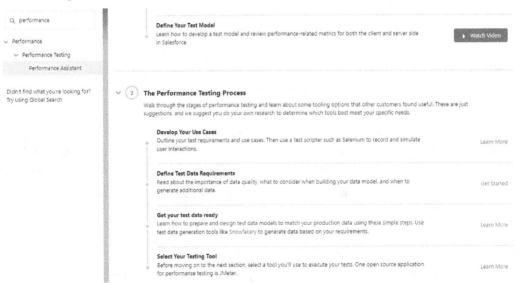

Figure 4.1 – An overview of Salesforce Performance Assistant

Well, that concludes our preparations! You've learned the key reasons why organizations choose to invest in a load test, how to get it done without breaking the bank, how to plan for data issues and identify key persons, and other important things you need to be aware of before and during your load testing. We've also looked at the handy Salesforce **Performance Assistant** tool—a good source of information for planning, implementation, and more.

With these critical insights, you should be able to avoid typical pitfalls and get the most value out of your investment in a load test. They should also afford you a good night's sleep since you will see your app handling the expected load instead of just hoping or expecting it to do so.

In the following section, we will get a feel of what may be involved in deploying and using the popular tools for running your own load tests.

Running your load test

While there is no shortage of load-testing tools available—and you can even create your own simple app using your scripting language of choice that will place the load on your OmniStudio system—in this section, we will be using the two most popular free open source load-testing tools: *Selenium* and *JMeter*. These are not just some of the more popular options. They represent two different approaches to load testing: the *thin client* in the case of JMeter and the *full browser client* in the case of Selenium.

While JMeter focuses on server-side HTTP-level testing, Selenium is a browser-based tool that simulates user activity by automating the browser. Because of its thin client architecture, JMeter is commonly used for performance and load testing, while Selenium could be your tool of choice when you need to assess both client- and server-side performance, which may be the case when testing OmniScripts and **Lightning Web Components** (**LWCs**). Selenium can also do a ton of other things, from automated unit and integration testing to **user interface** (**UI**) testing, in addition to load testing.

> **Note**
>
> Selecting the right load-testing tool is very important because the tools' capabilities and testing styles of each of the tools can be very different. The tool you select needs to match the type of interaction that your most important persona is having with your app.
>
> For instance, if your app is exposing a service layer that another app is consuming via the API, your testing would also be best conducted at the API level, so a low-level tool such as JMeter would best serve your purpose.
>
> On the other hand, if your app is providing guided user interactions with OmniScripts or OmniOut, your UI JavaScript layer will need to be included in your testing, and a browser automation tool such as Selenium may be your best bet.

Looking at both approaches will help you select an appropriate tool or tools depending on your app and the scenarios you are looking to load-test. Let's explore the steps involved in setting up and testing with these. Follow along on your system to get your hands dirty, or just look at the screenshots to get a feel for the steps involved.

Let's start by creating a sample OmniScript that we will be subjecting to load testing. Here's the **EditPersonInformation** sample OmniScript:

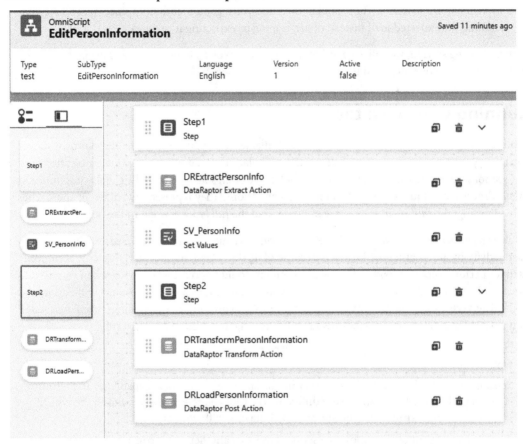

Figure 4.2 – An overview of a sample OmniScript for load testing

It consists of two steps. In the first step, the user enters a person's identifier, which is then used by a DataRaptor to load personal information:

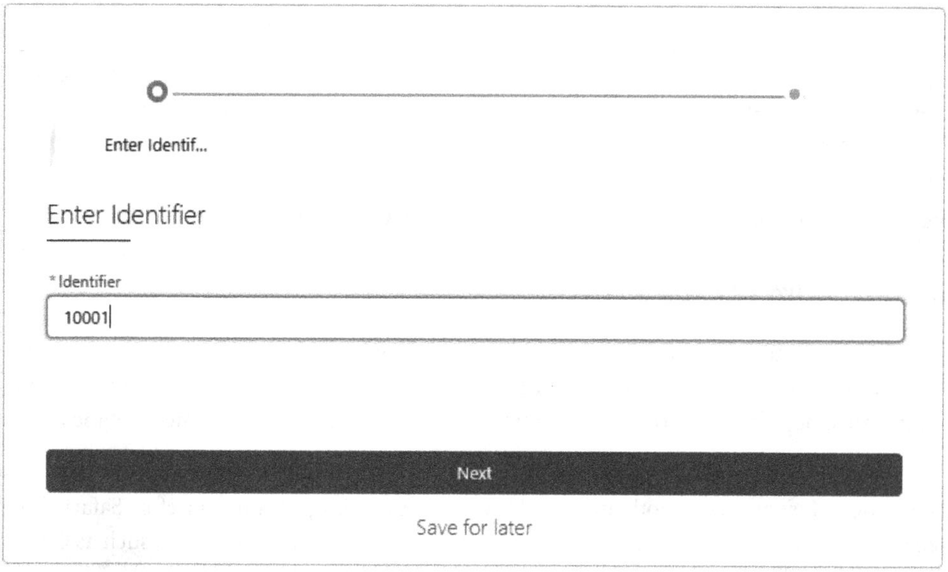

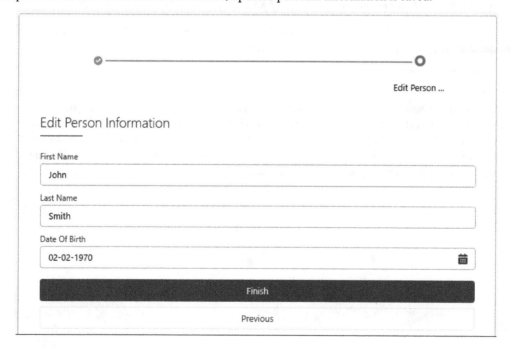

Figure 4.3 – An overview of a sample OmniScript: the Enter Identifier step

In the second step, the user can review and modify the information that was loaded in the previous step. Once the user clicks the **Finish** button, updated personal information is saved:

Figure 4.4 – An overview of a sample OmniScript: the Edit Personal Information step

> **Note**
>
> We place our OmniScript on a public community page so that we can simulate the testing of a public site. This will also keep our JMeter test setup simple by not having to include the login flow in our testing.

Let's begin by implementing a simple load-testing scenario with Selenium.

Using Selenium for load testing

Selenium is an open source suite of tools and libraries; however, the most used Selenium tool is *WebDriver*. Where load testing is concerned, the *TestNG framework* (`https://testng.org/`) is one of the most popular tools for running tests in multiple threads, which comes in handy.

Selenium WebDriver allows a script to control (or automate) the web browser natively, as if a user would be using it. It supports a good number of browsers, including Chrome, Firefox, Safari, Opera, and even the legacy Internet Explorer. You can use several programming languages, such as C#, Java, JavaScript, Python, PHP, and more.

We can also control the browser on a remote machine using *Selenium Server*. However, for our purposes, we will keep things simple and run Selenium WebDriver locally.

The following example uses Java with JDK 21 running on Windows. We will use Eclipse v2023-09 as our **integrated development environment** (**IDE**) and Google Chrome as our web browser.

Begin by downloading *Selenium ChromeDriver*, the web driver for Google Chrome. ChromeDriver is available at `https://chromedriver.chromium.org/downloads`.

> **Note**
>
> The version of ChromeDriver should match the version of Chrome installed on your machine. It will not work if the versions do not match. To prevent Chrome from continually updating and versions getting out of sync, you may want to go to the **Version Selection** page on the ChromeDriver page (see *Figure 4.5*) and download **Chrome For Testing**—the flavor of Chrome built for web app testing and automation use cases.

Figure 4.5 – An overview of a ChromeDriver version selection link

Next, we need to install our testing framework, **TestNG for Eclipse**. Go to **Help** > **Eclipse Marketplace** and search for testng, then install it (you will need to restart Eclipse after the installation is complete):

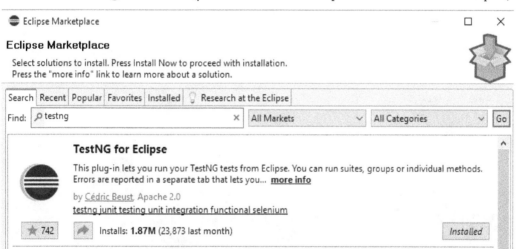

Figure 4.6 – An overview of downloading the TestNG framework in Eclipse

Next, we will use *Apache Maven* to simplify our dependency management. Let's begin by creating a Maven project in Eclipse and then add dependencies for Selenium and TestNG. In Eclipse, go to **File** > **New** > **Project,** and then select **Maven Project**. Then, check the **Create a simple project** checkbox (see *Figure 4.7*):

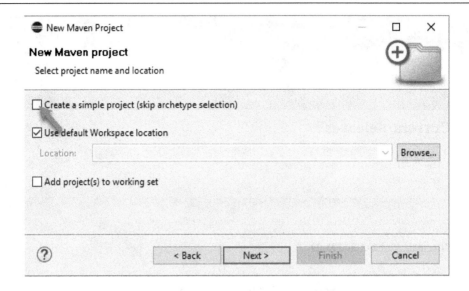

Figure 4.7 – An overview of creating a Maven project

Click **Next** and then fill in the **Group Id**, **Artifact Id**, and **Name** fields with values of your choice, then click **Finish**:

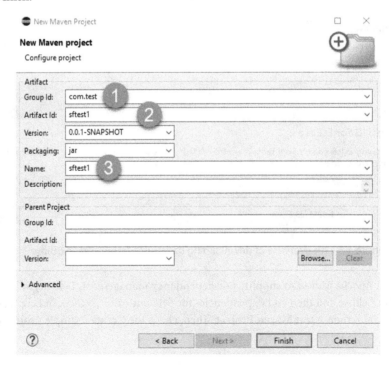

Figure 4.8 – An overview of completing the Maven project properties

Once the project is created, proceed to edit the `pom.xml` file and add a `dependencies` node with `org.seleniumhq.selenium` and `org.testng`, as shown next:

```
<dependencies>
  <dependency>
    <groupId>org.seleniumhq.selenium</groupId>
    <artifactId>selenium-java</artifactId>
    <version>4.13.0</version>
  </dependency>
  <dependency>
    <groupId>org.testng</groupId>
    <artifactId>testng</artifactId>
    <version>7.8.0</version>
    <scope>test</scope>
  </dependency>
</dependencies>
```

> **Note**
> If you see a `Downloading external resources is disabled. Cannot find the declaration of element 'project'` error in your Maven project, replacing `http://` with `https://` will allow Maven to continue.

Next, we need to create our `WebDriverFactory` class. We will use it to instantiate WebDriver and keep it in a thread-local variable. Right-click on your project in the **Project Explorer** pane, go to **New** > **Class**, then populate it with the following code:

```
import org.openqa.selenium.WebDriver;
import org.openqa.selenium.chrome.ChromeDriver;

public class WebDriverFactory {
    private static final WebDriverFactory instance =
        new WebDriverFactory();
    public static WebDriverFactory getInstance()
    {
        return instance;
    }
    private static final ThreadLocal<WebDriver> driver =
        ThreadLocal.withInitial(() -> new ChromeDriver());
    public WebDriver getDriver(){
        return driver.get();
    }
    public void close(){
        driver.get().quit();
```

```
        driver.remove();
    }
}
```

Finally, create a TestNG test class implementing our testing scenarios. Right-click on your project in the **Project Explorer** pane, and go to **TestNG > Create TestNG class** (see *Figure 4.9*):

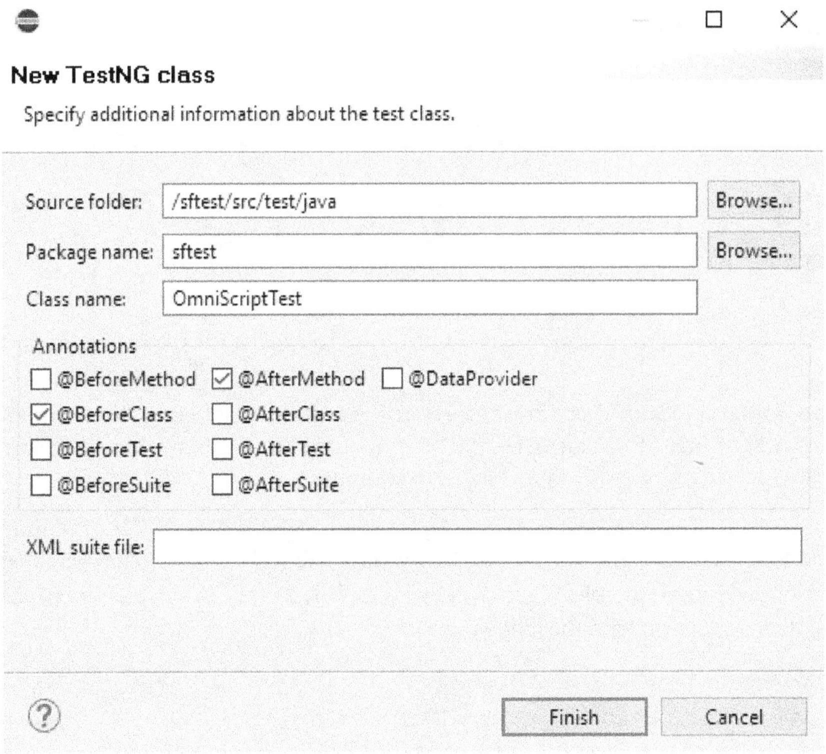

Figure 4.9 – An overview of creating a TestNG test class

Our TestNG test class uses Selenium high-level commands to simulate a user browsing the web. We can write code that will open web pages, manipulate fields, and simulate clicks on the buttons we want. This class also contains simple calls to instantiate and close WebDriver sessions by implementing TestNG lifecycle callbacks with @BeforeClass, @Test, and @AfterMethod annotations.

@*BeforeClass or @BeforeTest annotations*

`@BeforeClass` and `@BeforeTest` TestNG annotations are used to set up and initialize the data as required—before the test session and before each individual test. Next is a sample callback used to specify the path to the ChromeDriver executable:

```
@BeforeClass(alwaysRun = true)
public void setUp() throws Exception {
  System.setProperty("webdriver.chrome.driver","c:\\chromedriver.exe");
}
```

@*AfterMethod annotation*

The `@AfterMethod` annotation marks a callback that is responsible for clearing resources and closing the test session. For example, the following callback invokes the `close` method of the `WebDriverFactory` class that we presented earlier in this section:

```
@AfterMethod
public void after(ITestResult testResult) throws IOException {
  WebDriverFactory.getInstance().close();
}
```

@*Test annotation*

The TestNG `@Test` annotation marks the main test method where all the browser automation is taking place. It also specifies the following testing parameters:

- `invocationCount` defines the number of times the method should be invoked across all concurrent sessions
- `threadPoolSize` specifies the number of concurrent sessions that will be running our test to simulate multiple users accessing the app at the same time

> **Note**
>
> While it is easy to simulate multiple users hitting our page by increasing the `threadPoolSize` parameter, the number of threads is limited by the resources of the local machine that runs our load test. Each thread runs a new instance of the browser, consuming significant amounts of RAM and CPU.

Following is a sample test method that opens a Salesforce org:

```
@Test(invocationCount = 2,threadPoolSize = 2)
public void openOrg() {
    WebDriver driver = WebDriverFactory.getInstance().getDriver();
    driver.get("https://dev-ed.develop.lightning.force.com/");
}
```

The next section provides more information on the test method implementation.

Test method implementation

A **test method** contains the logic we need to manipulate the browser to simulate desired user behavior. We use Selenium high-level commands that are designed to make browser manipulation easy and intuitive. For instance, you can load web pages using the `get` method of the `WebDriver` class and clear or populate form fields with `clear` and `sendKeys` methods.

Since some page elements may not be available immediately, we can ask WebDriver to wait until they are loaded and added to the page. Selenium has three different waiting strategies:

- *Explicit wait* instructs WebDriver to wait until a certain condition occurs before continuing
- *Implicit wait* causes WebDriver to wait for a specified time
- *Fluent wait* directs WebDriver to periodically check it becomes available for up to a specified period

Each of these is represented by a class. For instance, if we use the `FluentWait` class, we will need to define how long we need to wait for a certain condition and how frequently we want WebDriver to check if the condition has occurred. We may also choose to ignore specific types of exceptions while waiting, such as `NoSuchElementException`, when searching for an element on the page.

The following sample code block navigates to a Salesforce instance, populates the login form, clicks the **Login** button, and then waits for the login operation to complete:

```
WebDriver wd = WebDriverFactory.getInstance().getDriver();
wd.get("https://test-dev-ed.develop.lightning.force.com/");
wd.findElement(By.id("username")).clear();
wd.findElement(By.id("username")).sendKeys("test@test.com");
wd.findElement(By.id("password")).clear();
wd.findElement(By.id("password")).sendKeys("Secret123");
wd.findElement(By.id("Login")).click();

Wait<WebDriver> wait = new FluentWait<>(wd)
        .withTimeout(Duration.ofSeconds(120))
        .pollingEvery(Duration.ofMillis(5000))
        .ignoring(NoSuchElementException.class);
```

```
wait.until(
    ExpectedConditions.presenceOfElementLocated(
        By.cssSelector("input[type='search']")
    )
);
```

In this case, we are waiting for the presence of an element located by its CSS selector. We can also select by name or by XPath. For instance, to locate an XPath of the **Enter Identifier** field in our test OmniScript, right-click on the field and select **Inspect**. Then, right-click on the selected HTML element in the **Elements** pane of **Chrome Inspector** and select **Copy > Copy full XPath**, as shown in *Figure 4.10*:

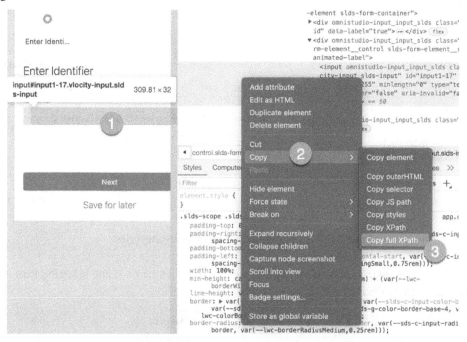

Figure 4.10 – An overview of retrieving an element's XPath using Chrome Inspector

Now, here's what a simple TestNG test class may look like. This class loads an index page, populates a field with a sequential number, proceeds to the next step, and then clicks the **Finish** button:

```
Run All
public class OmniScriptTest {
    public static String endpoint = "...";
    protected String chromeDriverPath = "...";
    public AtomicInteger index = new AtomicInteger(0);

    @BeforeClass(alwaysRun = true)
    public void setUp() throws Exception {
        System.setProperty("webdriver.chrome.driver", chromeDriverPath);
    }

    @Test(invocationCount = 1,threadPoolSize = 1)
    Run | Debug
    public void testOS() {
        int threadIndex = index.addAndGet(1);
        System.out.printf("Thread Index : %s%n", threadIndex);
        WebDriver driver = WebDriverFactory.getInstance().getDriver();

        driver.get(endpoint);
        Wait<WebDriver> wait1 = new FluentWait<>(driver)
                .withTimeout(Duration.ofSeconds(5))
                .pollingEvery(Duration.ofMillis(1000))
                .ignoring(NoSuchElementException.class);
        WebElement identifierElem = wait1.until(ExpectedConditions.presenceOfElementLocated(By.xpath("//
        identifierElem.clear();
        identifierElem.sendKeys(String.valueOf(10000 + threadIndex));
        WebElement nextButton = driver.findElement(By.xpath("//html//body//webruntime-app//lwr-router-co
        nextButton.click();
        WebElement finishButton = wait1.until(ExpectedConditions.presenceOfElementLocated(By.xpath("//ht
        finishButton.click();
    }

    @AfterMethod
    public void after(ITestResult testResult) throws IOException {
        WebDriverFactory.getInstance().close();
    }
}
```

Figure 4.11 – An overview of a sample TestNG test class

Finally, you can run your TestNG class at any time by right-clicking on it and selecting **Run As** > **TestNG Test**, as shown in *Figure 4.12*:

Figure 4.12 – An overview of running a TestNG class in Eclipse

The results will then be printed out on the console:

```
PASSED: testOS

=================================================
    Default test
    Tests run: 1, Failures: 0, Skips: 0
=================================================


=================================================
Default suite
Total tests run: 1, Passes: 1, Failures: 0, Skips: 0
=================================================
```

Figure 4.13 – An overview of a sample output of a TestNG class

And that is it! We have now seen all the steps required to simulate user behavior: load pages, wait for certain elements to appear, click on links and buttons, and analyze the resulting page content. We've also seen how TestNG allows us to run our class multiple times, using the invocationCount and threadPoolSize annotation parameters.

In the next section, we will be looking at JMeter, another popular load-testing tool, which uses a completely different approach to test implementation.

Load testing with JMeter

Apache JMeter is another popular open source testing framework. Unlike Selenium, though, JMeter uses its own HTTP client, which can be a benefit as well as a drawback. It is a benefit because it has a much smaller memory and CPU footprint, so you can simulate 30 concurrent users with the same resources that you will need to run 3 concurrent browser sessions with Selenium. Many times, you don't need the full browser with its JavaScript support, such as when testing an API layer.

On the other hand, the fact that JMeter is not running full browser clients can also be a disadvantage—for instance, when you need to test your client-side logic such as an LWC or a custom JavaScript object.

Also, unlike Selenium, JMeter runs in its own desktop Java application. This application allows you to record tests as JMeter scripts. When recorded, they show up on the left pane of the interface. As you run your tests in JMeter, it creates various reports and graphs visualizing the results.

Out-of-the-box JMeter includes a lot of sample test templates, so it is easy to create new tests. And if those are not enough, there are over 100 plugins available on jmeter-plugins.org, implementing additional logic, protocols, visualizations, and more.

Let's go ahead and create a simple test that has JMeter record our activity directly from the browser.

Recording a test script

For JMeter to be able to record our activity in the browser, we will need to configure our browser to use the JMeter proxy server, which, by default, runs on `localhost` port `8888`:

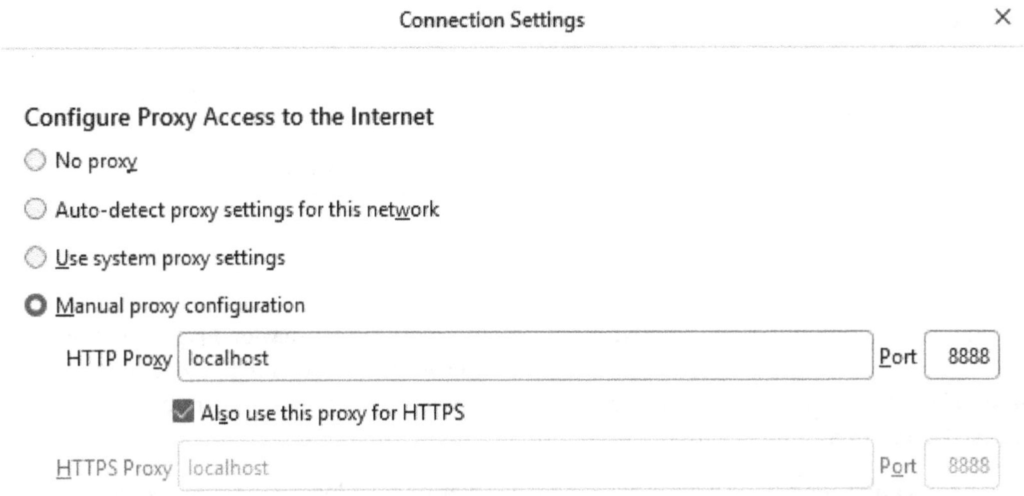

Connection Settings   ✕

Configure Proxy Access to the Internet

◯ No proxy

◯ Auto-detect proxy settings for this network

◯ Use system proxy settings

⦿ Manual proxy configuration

HTTP Proxy | localhost | Port | 8888

☑ Also use this proxy for HTTPS

HTTPS Proxy | localhost | Port | 8888

Figure 4.14 – An overview of configuring your browser to use the JMeter proxy server

Once the HTTP proxy is configured, we can proceed with recording the tests.

The following steps seem elaborate but only take about 5 minutes to complete. Here's what it takes to record a test with JMeter:

1. Press the **Templates** button on the toolbar (see *Figure 4.15*):

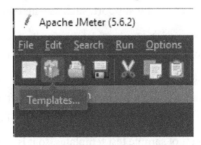

Figure 4.15 – An overview of the JMeter toolbar

2. Select **Building an Advanced Web Test Plan**, then press **Create**:

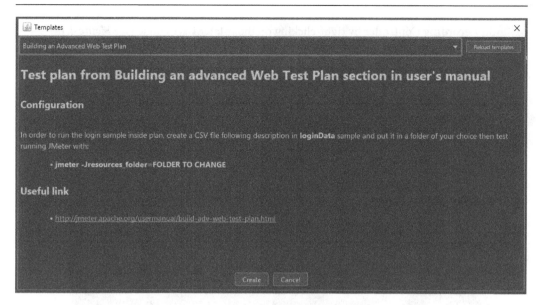

Figure 4.16 – An overview of creating a test plan

3. Optionally, remove the **Home Page, Changes**, and **BugDetail Page** items under **JMeter Users** by right-clicking and selecting **Remove**. Then, disable the **HTTP Request Defaults** and **Login** items by right-clicking and selecting **Disable**:

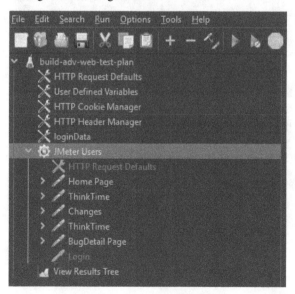

Figure 4.17 – An overview of configuring the JMeter Users node

4. Add **Recording Controller** by right-clicking on the **JMeter Users** node (see *Figure 4.18*):

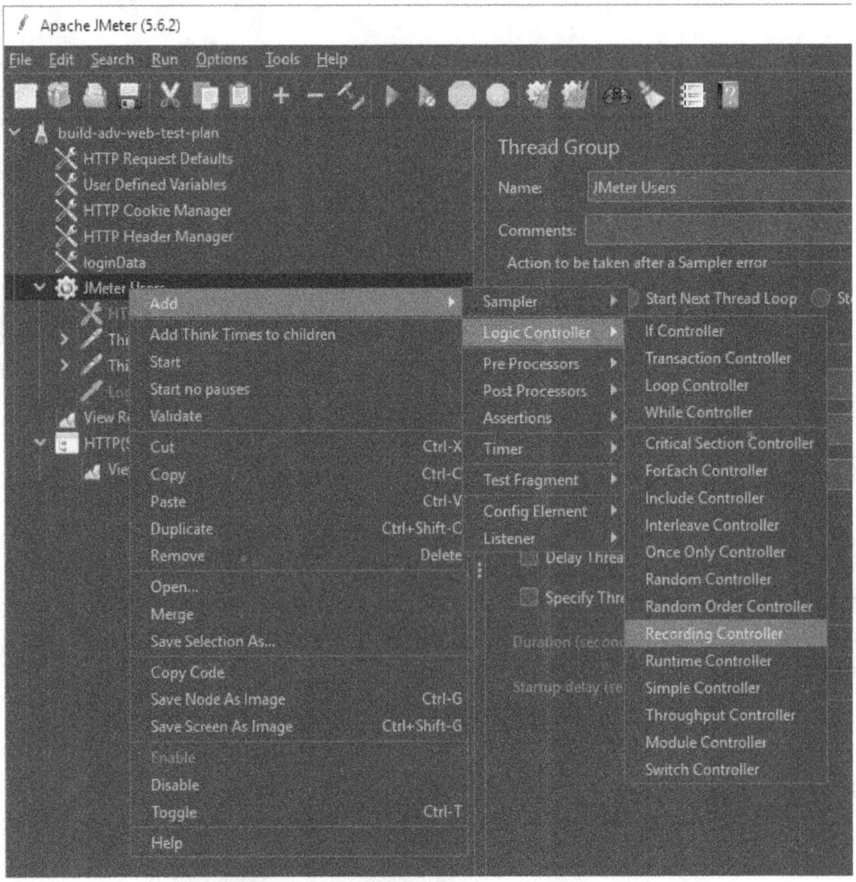

Figure 4.18 – An overview of adding Recording Controller

5. Now, add **HTTP(S) Test Script Recorder** by right-clicking on the **Non-Test**

6. **Elements** node (see *Figure 4.19*):

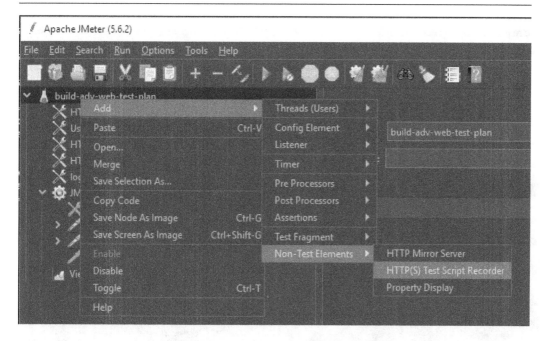

Figure 4.19 – An overview of adding HTTP(S) Test Script Recorder

7. Now, right-click on **HTTP(S) Test Script Recorder** and add **View Results Tree**:

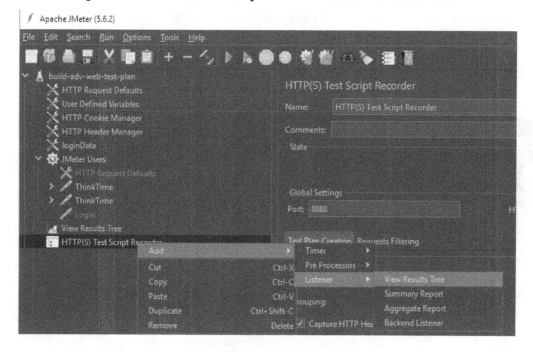

Figure 4.20 – An overview of adding View Results Tree

We're now ready to record our test! Select **HTTP(s) Test Script Recorder** in the tree view on the left and click the **Start** button (see *Figure 4.21*).

> **Note**
>
> Before recording your test, you may want to exclude images, CSS, and other files that may not be relevant for testing your application. To do so, on the **Requests Filtering** tab in the **Recording Controller** window, click on **Add Suggested Excludes** (see *Figure 4.21*).

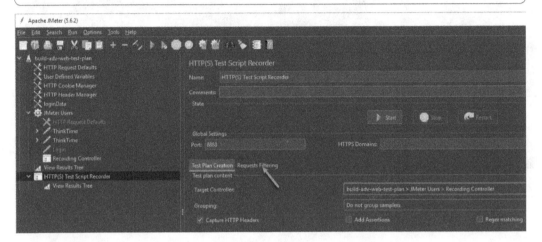

Figure 4.21 – An overview of HTTP(S) Test Script Recorder: clicking on Requests Filtering

When you start recording a test script for the first time, JMeter will generate an SSL certificate (see *Figure 4.22*):

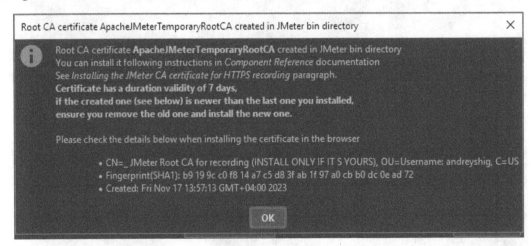

Figure 4.22 – An overview of a JMeter SSL certificate notice

Please import it into the browser to allow JMeter to make HTTPS connections.

> **Note**
>
> Importing the JMeter certificate into Chrome is more complicated, so, for the sake of simplicity, I've used Firefox as my browser during this demonstration. To import a certificate into Firefox, go to **Settings** > **Certificate Manager** and then press the **Import...** button.

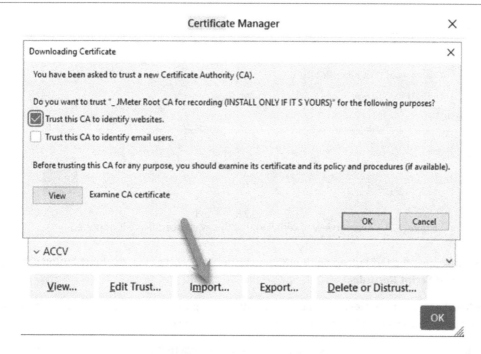

Figure 4.23 – An overview of importing an SSL certificate into Firefox

Once imported, you should see the JMeter certificate added under the **Authorities** tab in **Certificate Manager**:

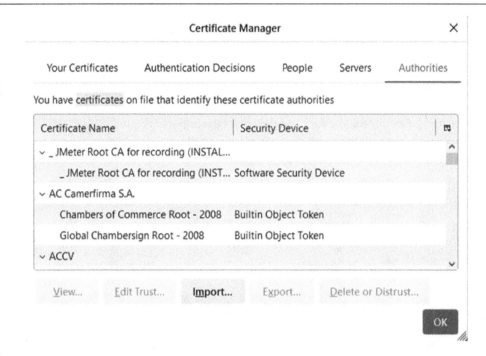

Figure 4.24 – An overview of verifying that the JMeter certificate is imported

You can now press the **OK** button on the JMeter certificate alert (or click the **Start** button again in **HTTP(S) Test Script Recorder**).

This will bring up the **Recorder: Transactions Control** dialog where you can specify the transaction name (or the test case name) that you are about to record (see *Figure 4.25*).

And there you have it! JMeter is now recording your browser activity. Everything you do in Firefox from now on will become a part of your recorded test script until you press the **Stop** button in the **Recorder: Transactions Control** dialog:

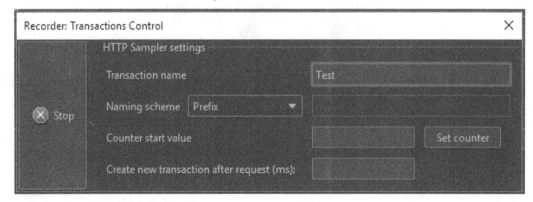

Figure 4.25 – An overview of the Recorder: Transactions Control dialog

Your test script is now recorded! In the next section, we will use it while simulating concurrent users and then look at the results.

Running the test script

Once the test script is recorded, we can run it by clicking the **Run** button on the main toolbar. This will bring up a dialog where we can specify thread group parameters, which represent our virtual users.

We can specify the number of threads or virtual users who will be executing our recorded test cases, the ramp-up period or the time JMeter will take to get the target number of threads running, and the loop count, which represents the number of times each thread will run our test cases:

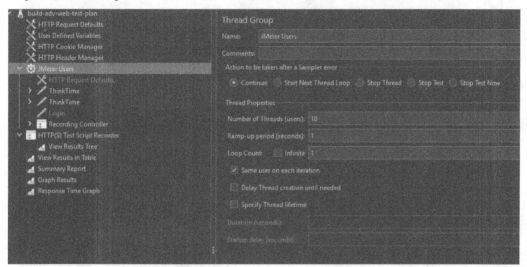

Figure 4.26 – An overview of the JMeter Thread Group dialog

We can also add various reports and graphs to see the results. In JMeter, this is accomplished by adding *listeners* (see *Figure 4.27*):

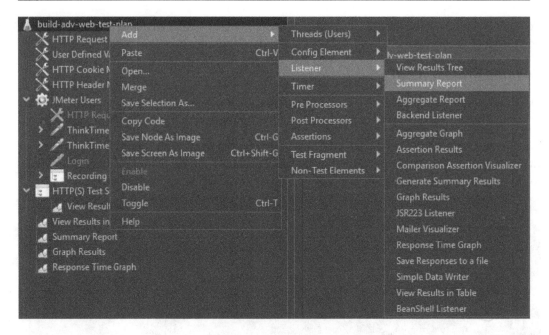

Figure 4.27 – An overview of adding a JMeter listener

The following screenshot shows the **Summary Report** dialog, which shows the URLs we requested (in the **Label** column) along with the stats, such as the number of requests sent (**# Samples**), min, max, and average response time, errors, and other collected statistics:

Label	# Samples	Average	Max	Error %	Throughput	Received KB/sec	Sent KB/sec	Avg. Bytes
/samplec/-279	30	105	457	0.00%	6.2/min	1.14	0.05	11219.9
/samplec/webruntime...	30	228	870	0.00%	6.2/min	0.08	0.10	906.8
/samplec/webruntime...	30	200	530	0.00%	6.2/min	0.07	0.10	666.3
/samplec/webruntime...	30	243	604	0.00%	6.2/min	0.10	0.11	974.2
/samplec/webruntime...	30	194	443	0.00%	6.2/min	0.07	0.10	651.3
/samplec/webruntime...	30	164	430	0.00%	6.2/min	0.07	0.10	707.3
/samplec/webruntime...	30	164	256	0.00%	6.2/min	0.06	0.11	693.3
/submit/firefox-deskt...	30	141	298	0.00%	6.2/min	0.08	0.28	630.5
/submit/activity-strea...	30	114	220	0.00%	6.2/min	0.08	0.16	807.3
/samplec/webruntime...	30	110	219	0.00%	6.2/min	0.07	0.62	640.3
/samplec/webruntime...	30	287	446	0.00%	6.2/min	0.07	0.14	737.3
/samplec/-291	30	18	106	0.00%	6.3/min	1.14	0.05	11163.3
/samplec/webruntime...	30	168	327	0.00%	6.2/min	0.06	0.10	622.3
/samplec/webruntime...	30	164	312	0.00%	6.2/min	0.07	0.10	646.3
TOTAL	420	166	870	0.00%	1.4/sec	3.13	2.12	2222.6

Figure 4.28 – An overview of the JMeter summary report

Or you can choose to display the same set of results as a graph (see *Figure 4.29*):

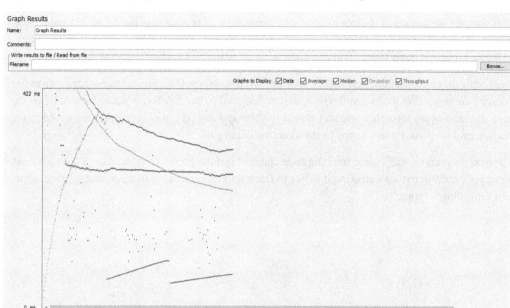

Figure 4.29 – An overview of the JMeter graph results

Once again, we were looking at Selenium and JMeter as examples. They may or may not fit your bill, and that is perfectly fine as there is no shortage of load-testing tools.

Among the other most popular choices is *Mercury LoadRunner*, a commercial tool that has been around for ages. It is now owned by OpenText, and they offer it as a cloud service. (We have a step-by-step demo of using Mercury LoadRunner with OmniStudio on this book's companion site, https://maximumvlocity.com/.)

Running your load-testing tool in the cloud offers the added benefit of not having to take your network and your hardware capacity into consideration, thus bringing you more accurate results. Recording and running tests would also be a little more user-friendly with the LoadRunner tool, but it doesn't have the same plugin library as JMeter and, in the long run, the effort needed to record tests might be quite similar. So, the choice of tool may also be a matter of preference.

And now this concludes our review of load-testing tools. We've set up a sample app and seen what's involved in using Selenium and JMeter in simple load scenarios. So, you should now have a good feel for the time and effort as well as the how-to involved in getting a load test up and running. Having this knowledge will make it easier to plan and execute or manage the planning and execution of a load test.

Summary

In this chapter, we answered the question of why skipping load testing may not be such a good idea. We then went on to review important considerations for planning and executing your load test. Finally, we looked at open source and commercial tools available for placing a load on our systems.

Armed with this information, you will be well prepared to set up your OmniStudio application for success by ensuring that it can handle the load it is designed to handle. You will also be able to get an idea of the kind of performance you can expect of your app and its critical components, avoid nasty surprises, and keep your users happy in the short and long run.

In the next chapter, we will look at tracking code changes and deployment—tools that cast a safety net around your daily activities—making it easier to track and reverse our daily code and configuration to our OmniStudio apps.

5

Tracking Code Changes and Deployment

Now that you've established your performance baseline and have your monitoring tools ready to go, I bet you can't wait to start slashing seconds off your app screens. Before you make any code changes, though, let me suggest that you please be sure to review this chapter first.

It's easy to break things, especially when your app is complex, and especially when your app was built with high-level point-and-click tools such as OmniStudio! The information presented in this chapter will make it easy for you to see exactly what has been updated and allow you to reverse any specific change you made.

In this chapter, we will cover the following topics:

- Seeing how to use the out-of-the-box export and import tools and understand their limitations

- Learning how to use the all-powerful and omnipresent **Vlocity Build** tool

- Understanding when we must rely on **Salesforce Developer Experience (SFDX) Command-Line Interface (CLI)** tool

- Looking at IDX Workbench and other OmniStudio configuration management tools that may come in handy

Let's begin by looking at the out-of-the-box tools for export and import—the built-in ones—so that you can start using them right off the bat.

Technical requirements

To follow along with this chapter, you will need access to an OmniStudio installation. If you don't have one handy, you can always request your free trial development environment from the Salesforce Developers site, which is (at the time of this writing) available at `https://developer.salesforce.com/free-trials`.

Once on the site, head over to **Industry-Based Trials** and get yourself a trial org for the industry of your choice.

You will also need to install Node.js as it is required for using the **Vlocity Build** tool. If you don't have Node.js installed on your system, head over to `https://nodejs.org/en/download` to download it.

Using the out-of-the-box export and import tools

If you haven't used the out-of-the-box export and import tools of OmniStudio, here's a quick introduction. Let's begin by exporting a DataRaptor.

> **Note**
>
> It's always a good idea to export or clone a DataRaptor before you are about to touch it in any way. At the time of this writing, DataRaptors, unlike OmniScripts and Integration Procedures, do not have versions in most OmniStudio installations. And because they are point-and-click tools, it is often hard to see what has changed and easy to inadvertently break things. I've also noticed developers break OmniScripts by *fixing* DataRaptors—changing them to fit one OmniScript without realizing that other OmniScripts or Integration Procedures are using them. So, it's very important to see what has changed and be able to go back to the previous state of your DataRaptors.

The out-of-the-box **export and import tools** are easy to use. They provide a quick way of exporting and then importing OmniStudio components using a proprietary JSON file format. Child components are exported along with their parents. Just click the **Export** button on the top right of an **OmniStudio DataRaptor** screen (see *Figure 5.1*):

Figure 5.1 – An overview of exporting a DataRaptor

The export tool will proceed to create a DataPack—a JSON file containing the export. The first step of the export also allows you to deselect some of the components. In our case, the DataPack only contains one component—our DataRaptor—so we can simply proceed to the next step:

Figure 5.2 – An overview of the Export DataPack screen

The next step takes us to the **Review DataPack Export** screen, which shows the components you are about to export:

Figure 5.3 – An overview of the Review DataPack Export screen

You are then taken to the final screen of the export where (if you were keeping the default values in the dialog) you will be able to download your DataPack as soon as you hit **Done** (see *Figure 5.4*):

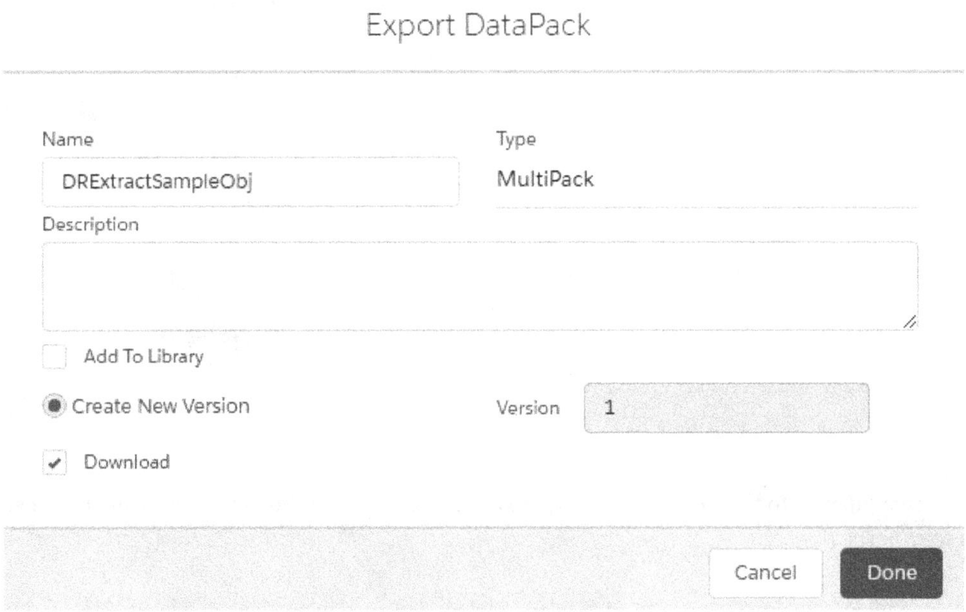

Export DataPack

Name   Type

DRExtractSampleObj   MultiPack

Description

☐ Add To Library

◉ Create New Version   Version   1

☑ Download

Cancel   Done

Figure 5.4 – An overview of the final step in the Export DataPack screen

The import of a DataRaptor is equally simple. Assuming you have an export created with the **Export** button before, all it takes to import is a click on a corresponding **Import** button (see *Figure 5.5*):

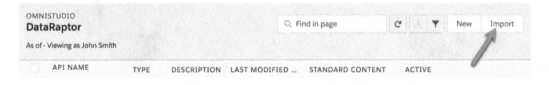

Figure 5.5 – An overview of importing a DataRaptor

Next, you will need to select the DataPack file (see *Figure 5.6*):

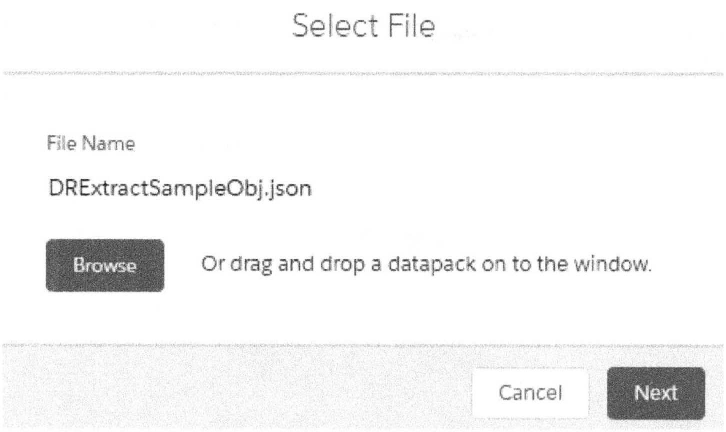

Select File

File Name

DRExtractSampleObj.json

Browse   Or drag and drop a datapack on to the window.

Cancel   Next

Figure 5.6 – An overview of the Select File screen

Now, select the components you would like to import (see *Figure 5.7*):

Select Items to Import

Figure 5.7 – An overview of the Select Items to Import screen

Review your items one more time in the **Review Items to Import** screen (see *Figure 5.8*):

Review Items to Import

Figure 5.8 – An overview of the Review Items to Import screen

And that is it! You should now see your components (or the new versions that you have imported) added to your system:

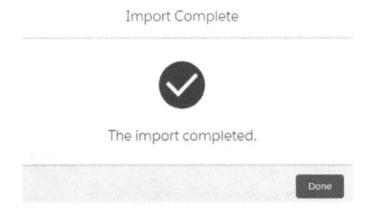

Figure 5.9 – An overview of import completion confirmation

Well, that was quick and easy. Now, let's look at a slightly more complicated scenario.

Exporting Integration Procedures and OmniScripts

The steps involved in exporting Integration Procedures and OmniScripts are the same, but let's follow them briefly to understand an important point about the out-of-the-box *export tool*.

Let's export an Integration Procedure containing Apex-based *Remote Actions* and child Integration Procedures (see *Figure 5.10*):

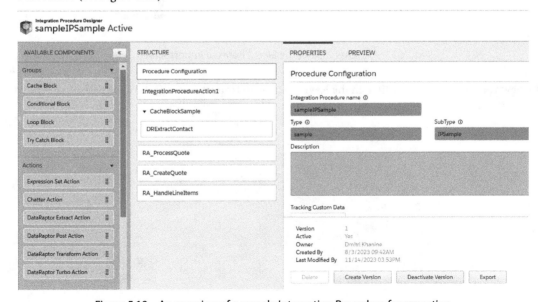

Figure 5.10 – An overview of a sample Integration Procedure for exporting

After clicking the **Export** button, the platform mentions that *Apex classes* will not be included with the export. It will, however, suggest exporting the child Integration Procedure:

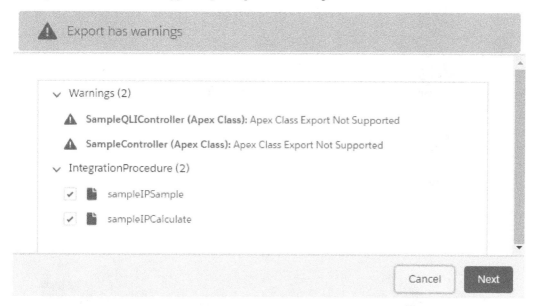

Figure 5.11 – An overview of the export warnings screen

The **Review DataPack Export** step is the same as we've seen before:

Figure 5.12 – An overview of the Integration Procedure Review DataPack Export screen

And so is the final **Export DataPack** step (see *Figure 5.13*):

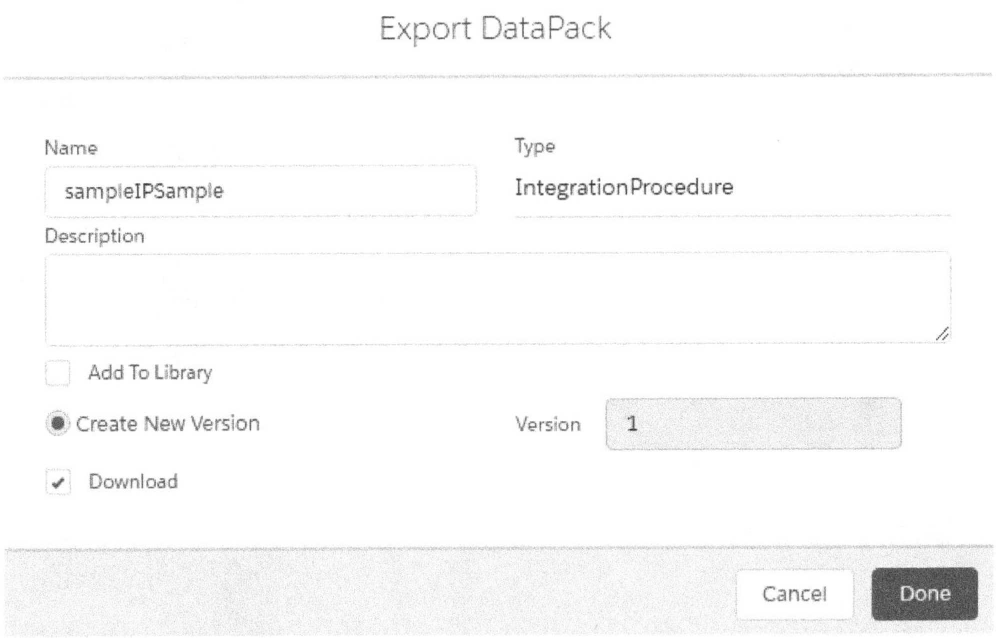

Export DataPack

Name

sampleIPSample

Type

IntegrationProcedure

Description

☐ Add To Library

⦿ Create New Version

Version | 1

✔ Download

Cancel   Done

Figure 5.13 – An overview of the Integration Procedure Export DataPack screen

The export is now complete. And now, let's look at the corresponding steps required to import the Integration Procedure we just exported.

Begin by clicking the **Import** button just as before:

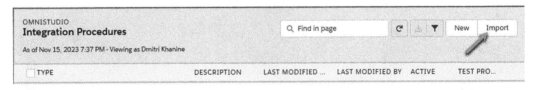

Figure 5.14 – An overview of importing an Integration Procedure

After selecting the DataPack JSON file, the **Import** screen shows the same warning we just saw during the export—the OmniStudio export tool does not import or export Apex classes, so you would need to export and import those yourself:

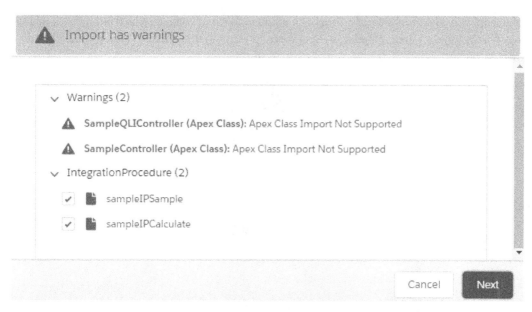

Figure 5.15 – An overview of the import warnings screen

However, there are no surprises on the **Review Items to Import** screen:

Figure 5.16 – An overview of the Review Items to Import screen

And finally, we're looking at a familiar **Import Complete** confirmation dialog box, but there's a slight difference this time around. Integration Procedures and OmniScripts need to be activated after the import is complete, so the import tool offers to activate them for you:

Figure 5.17 – An overview of the Import Complete screen

Finally, let's take a quick look at exporting and importing OmniScripts. You will see why I'm insisting on showing you these steps in a second.

OmniScripts have their **Export** option hidden in a drop-down menu on the right. This is the first option, though (see *Figure 5.18*):

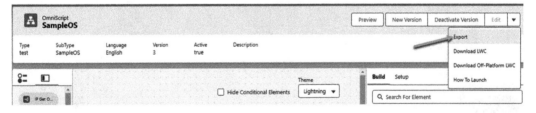

Figure 5.18 – An overview of exporting an OmniScript

Once clicked, it shows you a list of components you are about to export. Along with the OmniScript itself, there are the child components that are being used inside the OmniScript—the DataRaptors in our case—but there could also be child OmniScripts, Integration Procedures, and their child Integration Procedures. We're also being warned that, since we chose to use an Apex class in this OmniScript, its export is our responsibility:

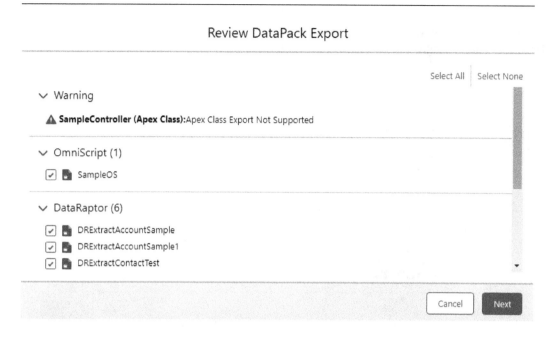

Figure 5.19 – An overview of an OmniScript export: review and warnings screen

There is, once again, no surprise on the **Review DataPack Export** screen:

Figure 5.20 – An overview of the Review DataPack Export screen

No surprises either on the **Export DataPack** screen except for the fact that the **Type** value of the DataPack is now changed to **OmniScript** (see *Figure 5.21*):

Figure 5.21 – An overview of the OmniScript Export DataPack screen

To import an OmniScript along with all its dependencies, we can now click on the **Import** button on the **OmniScripts** page:

Figure 5.22 – An overview of importing an OmniScript

Preview and optionally select the components you would like to import, as shown in *Figure 5.23*:

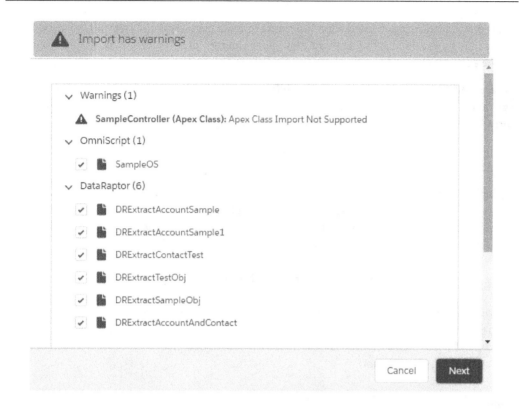

Figure 5.23 – An overview of an OmniScript import warnings screen

And, after going past the familiar **Import Preview** dialog, get the **Import Complete** confirmation again, offering to activate our newly imported OmniScript (or the new OmniScript version) and its dependent components.

> **Have you noticed?**
>
> While OmniStudio's built-in import and export tools are quick and easy to use, they do come with a significant disadvantage—all the components are exported as part of a single DataPack, producing one large JSON file.

Placing all the dependent components inside a single DataPack may be okay when all you need is to migrate an OmniScript from one sandbox to another sandbox, but you will have a hard time using it to track changes in a team setting. Just like Salesforce's own *Change Sets*, this is a good ad hoc tool for moving code and creating emergency copies, but I don't recommend using this for larger projects, especially when multiple developers are involved. It is also not a good idea to deploy your code to production using the built-in import and export tools as they cannot be integrated into a DevOps process.

Imagine that you are using an Integration Procedure in more than one OmniScript and that you had to change the Integration Procedure or a DataRaptor. You then exported one of these OmniScripts using the export tool.

If you are now going to import your other OmniScript extracts into the system, it will overwrite your Integration Procedure, replacing it with the old version. This is because it will use the version that was exported as a dependency of the second OmniScript, making you lose your recent changes.

So, in the following sections, we will be looking at more robust and source-control-friendly code and configuration tracking tools.

Now, that's a wrap for the out-of-the-box export and import tools. We have learned how and when to use them, as well as the limits of using them that we need to be aware of. Knowing these will allow us to extract maximum value out of these handy **Export** and **Import** buttons you will see everywhere in the OmniStudio components.

Extracting metadata with the Vlocity Build tool

The **Vlocity Build** tool is the newer, industry-standard tool that addresses the shortcomings of the built-in export and import tool. Just like the SFDX CLI tool, it integrates with a variety of products and tools, and it is DevOps friendly. (If you need help with SFDX, please search for `Salesforce CLI Command Reference`.)

> **Note**
>
> Metadata support differs between *OmniStudio Standard* and *OmniStudio for Vlocity*. While OmniStudio for Vlocity offers some of the original Vlocity features that are not available in OmniStudio Standard, the latter uses standard Salesforce objects and, therefore, is faster.
>
> If you are running OmniStudio Standard, you can enable **Metadata** API support by going to **Setup** > **OmniStudio Settings**. Once enabled, you will be able to retrieve and deploy OmniStudio standard objects (FlexCards, OmniScripts, DataRaptors, and Integration Procedures) using the SFDX CLI and the Force.com Migration Tool.
>
> Now, while most of the new OmniStudio installations are OmniStudio Standard, some orgs still run OmniStudio for Vlocity, and you will need to use the **Vlocity Build** tool to retrieve and deploy OmniStudio components there. This is why this section is covering the **Vlocity Build** tool that works with both OmniStudio editions.
>
> You can tell that you are running the OmniStudio Standard edition if your **Omni Interaction Configuration** page in Salesforce **Setup** has the `TheFirstInstalledOmniPackage` entry. For more information on the differences between *OmniStudio Standard* and *OmniStudio for Vlocity*, see the following Salesforce documentation page: `https://help.salesforce.com/s/articleView?id=sf.os_differences_between_omnistudio_and_omnistudio_for_vlocity.htm`.

The **Vlocity Build** tool places each type of OmniStudio component neatly into its own folder (see *Figure 5.24*):

This PC › UserProfile (D:) › Vlocity ›

Name	Date modified	Type
ContentVersion	11/15/2023 6:51 PM	File folder
DataRaptor	11/15/2023 6:51 PM	File folder
DocumentTemplates	11/15/2023 6:51 PM	File folder
FlexCard	11/15/2023 6:51 PM	File folder
IntegrationProcedure	11/15/2023 6:51 PM	File folder
OmniScript	11/15/2023 6:51 PM	File folder
vlocity-temp	11/15/2023 6:51 PM	File folder
VlocityBuildErrors.log	11/15/2023 6:51 PM	Text Document
VlocityBuildLog.yaml	11/15/2023 6:51 PM	Yaml Source File

Figure 5.24 – An overview of the metadata exported with the Vlocity Build tool

Then, in each folder, you will see a sub-folder containing the metadata for just that component. For instance, here's how the folder containing DataRaptors may look:

This PC › UserProfile (D:) › Vlocity › DataRaptor

Name	Date modified	Type
DRExtractAccountAndContact	11/15/2023 6:51 PM	File folder
DRExtractAccountSample	11/15/2023 6:51 PM	File folder
DRExtractAccountSample1	11/15/2023 6:51 PM	File folder
DRExtractContactTest	11/15/2023 6:51 PM	File folder
DRExtractPersonInformation	11/15/2023 6:51 PM	File folder
DRExtractQuoteById	11/15/2023 6:51 PM	File folder
DRExtractQuoteLineItems	11/15/2023 6:51 PM	File folder
DRExtractQuotes	11/15/2023 6:51 PM	File folder
DRExtractSampleObj	11/15/2023 6:51 PM	File folder

Figure 5.25 – An overview of DataRaptors exported with the Vlocity Build tool

Each component's folder contains individual JSON files, representing its logical chunks. For instance, there are three JSON files describing our sample DataRaptor: `DataPack`, `Items`, and `Inputs`. For OmniScripts, there would be JSON files for each step, so when you add a step to an OmniScript, a new JSON file will be added, and it will be easy to see what has changed when you compare it with the previous version in your source control:

This PC › UserProfile (D:) › Vlocity › DataRaptor › DRExtractTestObj

Name ^	Date modified	Type	Size
☐ DRExtractTestObj_DataPack.json	11/15/2023 6:51 PM	JSON File	2 KB
☐ DRExtractTestObj_Items.json	11/15/2023 6:51 PM	JSON File	10 KB
☐ DRExtractTestObj_SampleInputJson.json	11/15/2023 6:51 PM	JSON File	1 KB

Figure 5.26 – An overview of a sample DataRaptor extract

Let's have a glance at the JSON files. The `DataPack.json` file predictably contains general DataRaptor properties such as the `Active` flag, its name, and the names of the other JSON files describing our DataRaptor:

```
DRExtractTestObj_DataPack.json
11        "InputParsingClass": "",
12        "InputType": "JSON",
13        "IsActive": false,
14        "IsAssignmentRulesUsed": false,
15        "IsDeletedOnSuccess": false,
16        "IsErrorIgnored": false,
17        "IsFieldLevelSecurityEnabled": false,
18        "IsNullInputsIncludedInOutput": false,
19        "IsProcessSuperBulk": false,
20        "IsRollbackOnError": false,
21        "IsSourceObjectDefault": false,
22        "IsXmlDeclarationRemoved": false,
23        "Name": "DRExtractTestObj",
24        "Namespace": "",
25        "OmniDataTransformItem": "DRExtractTestObj_Items.json",
26        "OutputParsingClass": "",
27        "OutputType": "JSON",
28        "OverrideKey": "",
29        "PreprocessorClassName": "",
30        "PreviewJsonData": "DRExtractTestObj_SampleInputJson.json",
31        "PreviewOtherData": "",
32        "PreviewSourceObjectData": "",
```

Figure 5.27 – An overview of the DataRaptor DataPack.json file fragment

The `Items.json` file describes the inputs and the outputs (see *Figure 5.28*). Again, the format is designed to be source-control friendly, so if you were to, for instance, update the name of a Salesforce field you were extracting, there would only be a one-line difference when you did a version compare, so it would be easy to see the changes:

```
DRExtractTestObj_Items.json
 1    [
 2        {
 3            "FilterGroup": 0,
 4            "FilterOperator": ">",
 5            "FilterValue": "'500'",
 6            "GlobalKey": "DRExtractTestObjCustom608",
 7            "InputFieldName": "Index__c",
 8            "InputObjectName": "Test_Obj__c",
 9            "InputObjectQuerySequence": 1,
10            "IsDisabled": false,
11            "IsRequiredForUpsert": false,
12            "IsUpsertKey": false,
13            "Name": "DRExtractTestObj",
14            "OmniDataTransformationId": {
15                "Name": "DRExtractTestObj",
16                "VlocityDataPackType": "VlocityMatchingKeyObject",
17                "VlocityMatchingRecordSourceKey": "OmniDataTransform/DRExtractTestObj",
18                "VlocityRecordSObjectType": "OmniDataTransform"
19            },
20            "OutputCreationSequence": 0,
21            "OutputFieldName": "result",
22            "OutputObjectName": "json",
23            "VlocityDataPackType": "SObject",
24            "VlocityRecordSObjectType": "OmniDataTransformItem"
25        },
26        {
```

Figure 5.28 – An overview of the DataRaptor Items.json file fragment

---

Working with the Vlocity Build tool and other tools

The **Vlocity Build** tool is the go-to tool I've seen on a lot of recent OmniStudio implementations. It is designed to be used together with SFDX and is also in conjunction with other popular configuration management tools such as Copado, GitHub, Bitbucket Pipelines, and IDX Workbench.

Let's now look at the steps involved in exporting and importing OmniStudio components using the **Vlocity Build** tool.

Downloading the Vlocity Build tool

The **Vlocity Build** tool is a free open source tool and can be downloaded from its GitHub page, available at https://github.com/vlocityinc/vlocity_build.

This page also contains extensive documentation. The tool is written as a Node.jsmodule, so you will need to install Node.js prior to installing the **Vlocity Build** tool.

Once you have Node.js installed, just type the following in your Node.js command prompt:

```
npm install --global vlocity
```

This will install the **Vlocity Build** tool, and you can verify the installation by typing the following:

```
vlocity help
```

And that is all it takes to install the **Vlocity Build** tool. In the following sections, we will go through the steps of using it.

Running the Vlocity Build tool

It only takes two parameters to export or import any number of OmniStudio components with the **Vlocity Build** tool: a `Manifest` YAML file and an *SFDX org alias*. (If you need help with SFDX, please search for `Salesforce CLI Command Reference`.)

The `Manifest` YAML file specifies the OmniStudio components we need to export or import. It may list specific components, as in this sample `Manifest` file:

```
manifest:
    - DataRaptor/DRExtractSampleObj
    - IntegrationProcedure/test_SampleIP
    - OmniScript/test_SampleOS_English
```

Or it may list entire classes of components. For instance, the following `Manifest` file will extract all OmniScripts, Integration Procedures, DataRaptors, and FlexCards in the system:

```
queries:
    - OmniScript
    - IntegrationProcedure
    - DataRaptor
    - FlexCard
```

Once the `Manifest` file is ready, we can run the **Vlocity Build** tool to export or deploy our component metadata, as shown in the following sections.

> **Note**
>
> In this section, we're looking at examples of using the **Vlocity Build** tool by hand. This allows us to focus on the tool itself and keeps things simple. In a real-life project situation, it's best to run a **Vlocity Build** tool as part of your **continuous integration** (**CI**) flow or your DevOps process. For instance, Bitbucket and GitHub offer CI automation tools that can be used to include the **Vlocity Build** tool in your CI pipeline.

Exporting Vlocity metadata

To export the OmniStudio components, simply run the following command:

```
vlocity packExport -job [path] [manifest] .yaml -sfdx.username
[username]
```

If our `Manifest` file is in `d:/velocity`, its name is `VlocityBuildLog.yaml`, and my SFDX org alias is `myOrg`, the command will look like this:

```
vlocity packExport -job d:/vlocity/VlocityBuildLog.yaml -sfdx.username
myOrg
```

> **Note**
>
> Please note the period in the `sfdx.username` parameter. After typing legacy SFDX commands such as `sfdx force:source:retrieve`, it is very tempting to put a colon there. However, that will result in an error, and your Vlocity command will not run.

If all goes well, the **Vlocity Build** tool displays some stats after the run is completed:

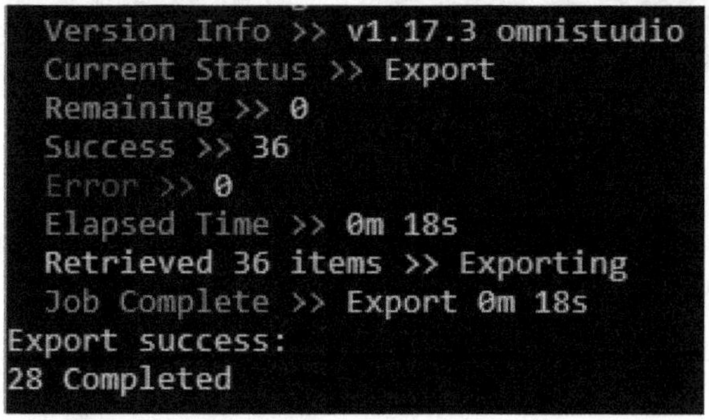

```
Version Info >> v1.17.3 omnistudio
Current Status >> Export
Remaining >> 0
Success >> 36
Error >> 0
Elapsed Time >> 0m 18s
Retrieved 36 items >> Exporting
Job Complete >> Export 0m 18s
Export success:
28 Completed
```

Figure 5.29 – An overview of the Vlocity Build tool export confirmation

By default, your component metadata will be placed in the same folder as your `Manifest` file. You can override that by adding a `projectPath` parameter inside your `Manifest`, file as in this example:

```
projectPath: ./vlocity
```

When the `extract` command is complete, you are ready to commit extracted metadata to GitHub, Bitbucket, or another source control of your choice.

Deploying Vlocity metadata

Deploying extracted OmniStudio component metadata is equally simple. It also uses the same `Manifest YAML` file. The command is simply this:

```
vlocity packDeploy -job [path] [manifest].yaml -sfdx.username
[username]
```

If our `Manifest` file is in `d:/vlocity`, its name is `VlocityBuildLog.yaml`, and my SFDX org alias is `myOrg2`, the command will look like this:

```
vlocity packDeploy -job d:/vlocity/VlocityBuildLog.yaml -sfdx.username
myOrg2
```

Again, if all goes well, you will be greeted with a `Deploy success` message and some quick stats:

```
Version Info >> v1.17.3 omnistudio 238.2
Current Status >> Deploy
Remaining >> 0
Success >> 3
Error >> 0
Elapsed Time >> 0m 28s
Migrated 3 items >> Deploying
Job Complete >> Deploy 0m 28s
Deploy success:
3 Completed
```

Figure 5.30 – An overview of the Vlocity Build tool deployment success message

And there you have it. You are now able to export and deploy OmniStudio components in a source-control-friendly format using the **Vlocity Build** tool.

Finally, let me share a command that may come in handy for generating your `Manifest YAML` file for the first time.

Generating a Vlocity Manifest

When implementing the **Vlocity Build** tool for the first time, you will need to create a `Manifest YAML` file containing all your OmniStudio components. Yes—you can, of course, just use the `queries:` syntax and have the tool export everything there is, but this approach may bring unwanted results. Why?

Each time a developer creates a test DataRaptor or a sample OmniScript to play around or to test some code, these test components will make it into your source control and, later, to your production org if your `Manifest YAML` file matches any OmniStudio component out there.

This is why I always advise my clients to have specific component names listed in the `Manifest YAML` file. Each time a developer adds a new component—if this is meant to be eventually deployed to production—they will need to add its name to the `Manifest` file. That way, you will not get any unwanted components promoted to higher environments, and your systems will stay clean.

However, when you are implementing the **Vlocity Build** tool for the first time, it may be easier to generate a `Manifest YAML` file and then prune it by hand rather than type it up from scratch. Use the following command to generate your initial `Manifest` file, containing every single Vlocity metadata component in the system:

```
vlocity packGetAllAvailableExports --nojob -sfdx.username [username]
```

This will create a file called `VlocityBuildLog.yaml`, which will save all the results in a format that you can move to your YAML job file. *Figure 5.31* shows what that may look like:

```
manifest:
  - DataRaptor/DRGetAccountDetails
  - DataRaptor/DRSaveAccountDetails
  - DataRaptor/DRExtractTestObj
  - DataRaptor/DRTurboExtractTestObj
  - DataRaptor/DRExtractQuoteLineItems
  - DataRaptor/DRLoadQuoteLineItem
  - DataRaptor/DRExtractQuoteById
  - DataRaptor/DRTransformSample
  - DataRaptor/DRExtractAccountSample
  - DataRaptor/DRLoadPersonInformation
  - DataRaptor/DRTransformPersonInformation
  - DocumentTemplates/Quote Document Template
  - FlexCard/SampleFlexCard
  - FlexCard/SampleCard
  - IntegrationProcedure/sample_IPCalculate
  - IntegrationProcedure/sample_IPSample
  - OmniScript/docGenerationSample_fndMultiDocxLwc_English
  - OmniScript/docGenerationSample_fndSingleDocxLwc_English
  - OmniScript/docGenerationSample_fndSingleDocxServersideLwc_English
  - OmniScript/test_EditPersonInformation_English
  - OmniScript/test_SampleOS_English
```

Figure 5.31 – An overview of a sample VlocityBuildLog.yaml file

And that is it for the **Vlocity Build** tool. We've learned how to download, install, and use the **Vlocity Build** tool to extract and deploy OmniStudio metadata. We've seen how it makes it source-control friendly and how easy it is to make it a part of a CI solution. This knowledge affords a significant power to track virtually every tiny change in any of your OmniStudio components.

In the next section, we will take a brief look at Salesforce's own SFDX CLI tool. Why? Continue reading to find out.

Using Salesforce's SFDX tool

Do you remember how the out-of-the-box export tool did not export and import Apex classes that were used in Remote Actions? The same is true for the **Vlocity Build** tool. And just like the Apex classes, you will also need to export and deploy any custom **Lightning Web Components** (**LWCs**) you will be creating for inserting into your OmniScripts and your FlexCards.

Now, as you probably know, just like the **Vlocity Build** tool uses a `Manifest YAML` file, the SFDX CLI tool also requires the list of components you would like to extract or deploy, and it will also need the org alias. The difference is that the SFDX job file is in XML format and uses a different syntax. For instance, the following `package.xml` file lists two LWCs:

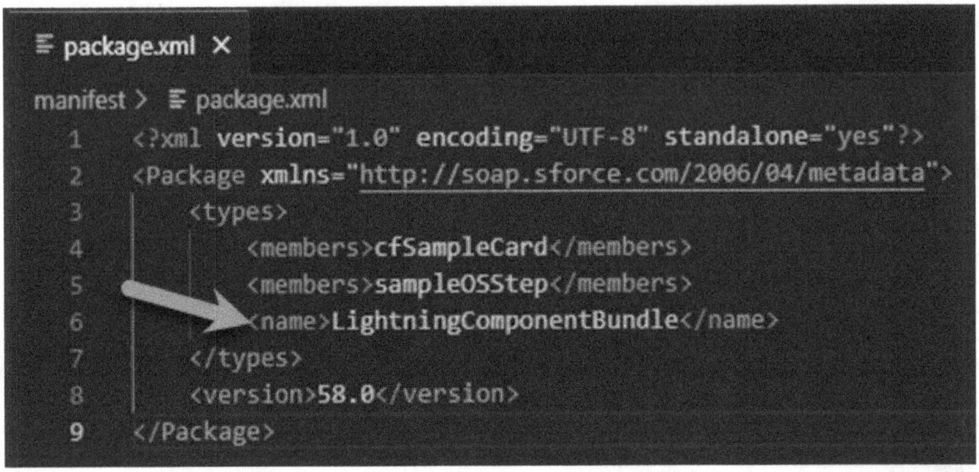

Figure 5.32 – An overview of a sample package.xml file

To retrieve these LWCs using the SFDX tool, run the following command:

```
sf project retrieve start --manifest [path]package.xml --target-org
[org alias]
```

This produces the following output:

Figure 5.33 – An overview of an extract output of the SFDX tool

You would need to run it from your Salesforce project directory.

Unlike the **Vlocity Build** tool, though, there are a lot of **graphical user interface** (**GUI**) tools available for running the SFDX commands with one click, including the Salesforce official extensions for **Visual Studio Code** (**VS Code**) available at https://developer.salesforce.com/tools/vscode.

Well, that is the end of our quick look at Salesforce's SFDX CLI tool. We saw when and how you may need to use it and learned about Salesforce extensions for VS Code, available for making the SFDX tool easier for you to run. You now have the missing link that allows you to export and deploy your complete end-to-end solution, including OmniStudio and core Salesforce components.

In the next section, we will look at other OmniStudio configuration management utilities and standalone tools that may come in handy in your daily workflow.

Other OmniStudio configuration management tools

There are other tools worth mentioning besides the out-of-the-box export and import tools and the **Vlocity Build** tool. So, let's review them here in case you might like to explore them further.

Salesforce Vlocity Integration VS Code extension

This free VS Code extension (built by `curlybracket-nl`) is a useful GUI for the **Vlocity Build** tool (`https://marketplace.visualstudio.com/items?itemName=curlybracket.vlocode`). Once installed, it allows you to browse OmniStudio components and extract them with one click. So, you don't have to create or update a `YAML file` and type commands.

To add it to your VS Code, just search for `Vlocity` in **Visual Studio Marketplace** and install the extension (see *Figure 5.34*):

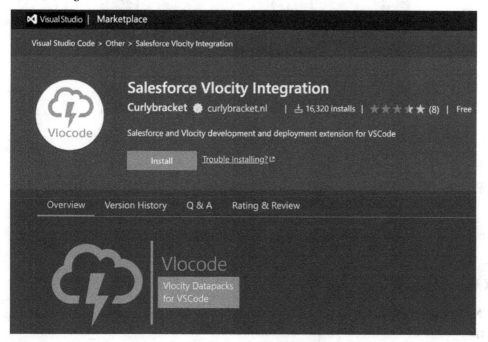

Figure 5.34 – An overview of installing the Salesforce Vlocity Integration extension

Once installed and connected to your org, you should be able to see the DataPacks and extract the required versions of components. You may want to do this when you are about to change them or when you need to commit them to source control:

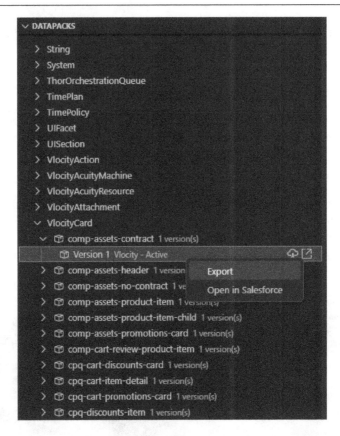

Figure 5.35 – An overview of extracting metadata with Vlocity VS Code extension

> **Note**
>
> While this extension saves time and is great when it works, at the time of this writing, I see developers struggle to make the recent builds of the extension connect to their orgs. If it does not work for you, just use the command-line version of the **Vlocity Build** tool.

IDX Workbench

IDX Workbench is a free desktop application offering helpful features for tracking OmniStudio and **Enterprise Product Catalog (EPC)** data and components.

To get IDX Workbench, search for `Install IDX Workbench` or follow this link: `https://help.salesforce.com/s/articleView?id=sf.os_install_idx_workbench.htm`

Once installed, you will be able to, among other things, visually compare versions and migrate the versions between environments. Let's look at the steps involved.

> **Note**
>
> Even though IDX Workbench is a lot more advanced than the built-in import and export tools, it too should not be considered a replacement for a proper DevOps/CI code management solution.

After IDX Workbench is installed, it offers to connect to the source and target Salesforce orgs. You will then be able to extract selected OmniStudio components from the source org and deploy them to the target:

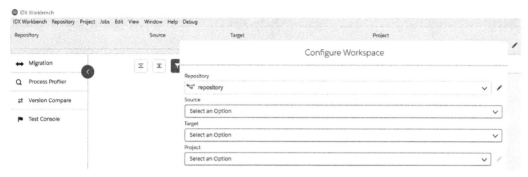

Figure 5.36 – An overview of the IDX Workbench Configure Workspace screen

Figure 5.37 shows the DataPacks selection screen, which allows you to select OmniStudio/Vlocity components, such as DataRaptors and OmniScripts, and Salesforce components, such as Apex classes and LWCs:

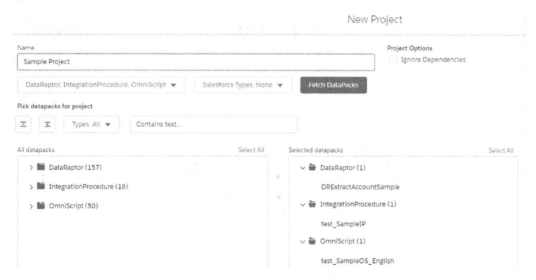

Figure 5.37 – An overview of selecting metadata for export in IDX Workbench

The next sections show how selected DataPacks can be migrated and kept in sync across orgs.

Migrating DataPacks

Once the project is set up, you can then migrate selected metadata using the **Migration** section on the left, as shown in *Figure 5.38*:

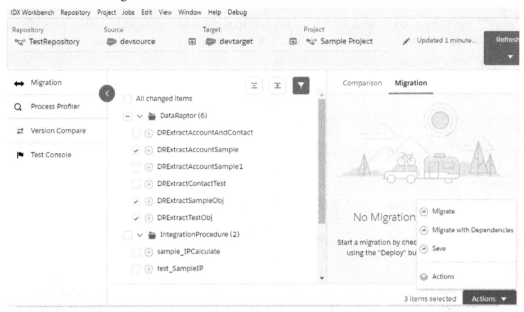

Figure 5.38 – An overview of the IDX Workbench Migration tool

In addition to initial migration, IDX Workbench allows you to track changes and push updated metadata over to the target org:

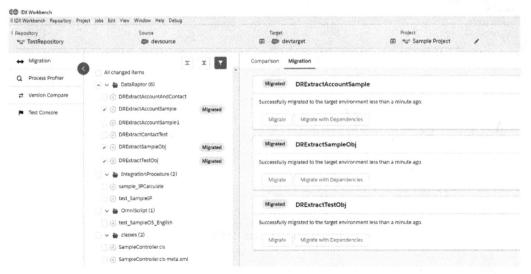

Figure 5.39 – An overview of an IDX Workbench incremental migration

This incremental migration makes it easy to keep multiple environments in sync and simplifies quality assurance by flagging metadata components that have changed. Similar to how it can identify changes in metadata components you have initially migrated with the help of IDX Workbench, it can also identify changes by comparing two separate orgs. Head over to the next section to learn more.

Comparing versions

IDX Workbench also offers a handy visual tool to compare OmniStudio components. You can select the org, component type, components, and versions you would like to compare (see *Figure 5.40*):

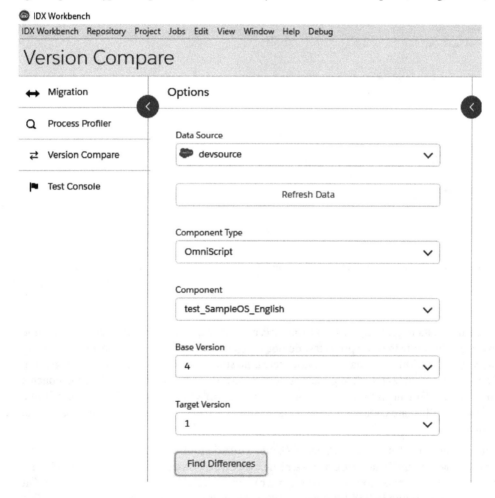

Figure 5.40 – An overview of the IDX Workbench Version Compare screen

Once you click the **Find Differences** button, you will see code and property changes that took place between the versions you selected. For instance, *Figure 5.41* shows the new LWC added to an OmniScript:

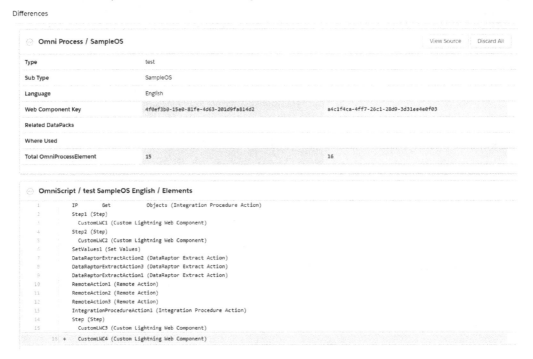

Figure 5.41 – An overview of Version Compare: the changes detected screen on IDX Workbench

> **Note**
>
> While metadata migration, **Version Compare**, and other IDX Workbench features may come in extremely handy in small projects, I do not see clients with larger development teams using them very often. This is primarily because there is no straightforward source control integration. I can't advise strongly enough to get all your OmniStudio (and Salesforce) metadata components committed to GitHub, Bitbucket, or another source control of your choice. There's a lot of value in having up-to-date copies and full change history or, better yet, using your source control to drive CI.
>
> On another note, *Trailhead* (https://trailhead.salesforce.com/content/learn/modules/omnistudio-architecture/meet-omnistudio?trail_id=build-guided-experiences-with-omnistudio) suggests that there is a Git repository integration in IDX Workbench. While I have not seen that feature at the time of this writing, if you'd like to use IDX Workbench with a source control, it may be worth checking periodically and see if the Git integration feature has been added.

CI tools

CI is a practice when each new metadata component committed to the source control triggers an automated build. This validates or deploys the code to the next environment and runs Salesforce unit tests, thus performing the first stage of quality assurance. This also makes sure that one developer's work does not break any of the existing code. There are a few popular Salesforce CI solutions that support OmniStudio. *Copado* seems to be a very popular choice among our larger client organizations; however, it can be costly. I also see many clients use SFDX and the **Vlocity Build** tool with a lot of industry-standard CI tools such as Jenkins and the new CI features of GitHub and Bitbucket Cloud. A deeper review of CI tools is outside the focus of this book.

Now, that concludes our brief review of other configuration management tools and utilities. We've seen the Vlocity VS Code extension, providing a handy GUI for the **Vlocity Build** tool, IDX Workbench, offering migration and version comparison features, and touched upon CI tools. These tools may come in very handy in your daily code management tasks.

Summary

And that is the end of this chapter. We looked at omnipresent out-of-the-box export and import tools, their best use, and their limitations. We then continued to look at the **Vlocity Build** tool: the powerful workhorse of OmniStudio configuration management. We also touched on Salesforce's own SFDX CLI tool, which we frequently need to use together with the **Vlocity Build** tool, and then concluded our journey with a couple of helpful utilities.

You now have the tools to export and deploy your OmniStudio metadata components. Before making changes, you can now commit your code to a source control of your choice so that it will be easy to see exactly what has changed and who has changed it. You will then be able to undo any changes quickly.

In the next chapter, we will begin our quest for maximizing the performance of our OmniStudio applications by looking at async execution options—the first and the easiest for trying configuration changes.

Part 3:
Best Practices for
Improving Performance

You are now familiar with the layers and key components of Vlocity OmniStudio, have got your hands dirty with the sample app, and have learned how to test the performance of your OmniStudio implementation and its individual components. In this final part of this book, we will review the best practices, tips, and tricks to achieve better performance at multiple levels.

By the end of this part, you will be able to diagnose common performance problems in your application components. You will also learn how to measure the improvement you can expect from the common best practices and use them to tune your application components for maximum performance.

This part has the following chapters:

- *Chapter 6, Options for Async Execution*
- *Chapter 7, Understanding Caching*
- *Chapter 8, Non-Selective Queries and Data Skew*
- *Chapter 9, Improving the Performance of the Service Layer*
- *Chapter 10, Improving the Performance of the Presentation Layer*
- *Chapter 11, DataRaptor Formula Performance Considerations*
- *Chapter 12, OmniStudio Performance Anti-Patterns*

Options for Async Execution

At last, we're ready to dive into performance optimizations! All the prep work is done; we are now tracking our code and configuration changes and can go back to the previous version at any time; we have our performance stats and know exactly which metrics we're trying to improve. So, let's start improving our app's performance. The best place to start is the area where a simple configuration change may produce a massive performance impact with just a few clicks. Will this be the case with your app? Let's look at the OmniStudio async execution options and how they can be applied.

In this chapter, you will learn the following:

- Why to consider async code execution
- Three quick, configuration-based ways to bypass governor limits in Integration Procedures
- How to call Integration Procedures from Apex and **Lightning Web Components** (**LWC**)
- Four ways to run async code on the Salesforce platform and how it can benefit your OmniStudio app

Let's jump in to find out more.

Technical requirements

To follow along with this chapter, you will need access to an OmniStudio installation. If you don't have one handy, you can always request your free trial development environment from the Salesforce Developers site, which is (at the time of this writing) available at `https://developer.salesforce.com/free-trials`. Once on the site, head over to **Industry-Based Trials** and get yourself a trial org for the industry of your choice.

Why to consider async code execution

In *Chapter 3, Evaluating the Performance of an OmniStudio Implementation*, we looked at tools for measuring the performance of OmniStudio applications. Have you had a chance to give them a try? If so, did you identify any areas for improvement?

When you have identified a performance issue in one of your app's components and removing it is not an option, you have two choices. You can either tune this component, make it run faster, or you can allow it to continue running slowly but allow your users to continue without having to wait. The first option is usually more involved—and we will be looking at several ways to increase the performance of OmniStudio components in the following chapters. On the other hand, allowing the component to run in the background may only take a couple of clicks to accomplish.

Not all components can run in the background, but if we're dealing with an Integration Procedure or an Integration Procedure Action step in an OmniScript, all we need to do is change the value in its **Invoke Mode** setting in the **Integration Procedure Action Properties** screen (see *Figure 6.1*):

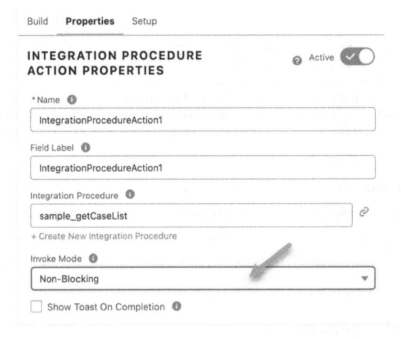

Figure 6.1 – An overview of the Invoke Mode setting

We have three options available in the **Invoke Mode** dropdown:

- **Default**: The **user interface** (**UI**) will be blocked, and the user will see a spinner until the Integration Procedure Action is complete.

- **Non-Blocking**: The Integration Procedure Action will run asynchronously, so the user will be able to continue down their path. Data JSON and UI elements will be updated when the Action is complete.

- **Fire and Forget**: The Integration Procedure Action will run asynchronously, and there will be no update made to the Data JSON and the UI when the Action completes. You will, however, still see a response in the debug console.

While the **Non-Blocking** option may be a great choice for long-running calculations and callouts, the **Fire and Forget** mode may work great for replicating data to external systems. Both options free the end user from having to wait for the long-running operation to be completed, making them more productive and your system more responsive and a pleasure to use. (We have a step-by-step demo of using the **Non-Blocking** invoke mode for calling an Integration Procedure early in the OmniScript on this book's companion site, `https://maximumvlocity.com/`.)

Now, what if your Integration Procedure is running out of resources, hitting the CPU time, the number of queries, or other governor limits? Continue to the next section to find out.

Async configuration options for Integration Procedures

As with almost everything on the Salesforce platform, an Integration Procedure, including all its actions, by default is running in a single transaction. And every transaction must stay within governor limits. Because all the code running on the Salesforce platform needs to play well in a multitenant environment, the platform strictly enforces governor limits to make sure that no shared resources are monopolized or abused—intentionally or unintentionally.

So, if an Integration Procedure hits any of the governor limits by, say, running more than 100 SOQL queries or taking longer than 10 seconds of CPU time (at the time of this writing), Salesforce terminates the transaction, and the Integration Procedure fails.

The good news, though, is that we can configure an Integration Procedure to start a new transaction each time it is about to hit a governor limit. This feature is called **chaining**, and when this happens, the OmniStudio platform stores the interim results, starts a new transaction, and lets the Integration Procedure continue from where it has left off.

Another bit of good news is that it is easy to configure an Integration Procedure to take advantage of the chaining feature. The following sections provide the details.

Chainable

The **Chainable** feature instructs the OmniStudio platform to watch the resource use during the Integration Procedure execution. If at the end of any of the Integration Procedure actions the use of any one of the resources specified in the **Chainable Configuration** section of the **Integration Procedure Configuration** pane reaches the specified limit (see *Figure 6.2*), *chaining* takes place, and the execution continues in a new transaction:

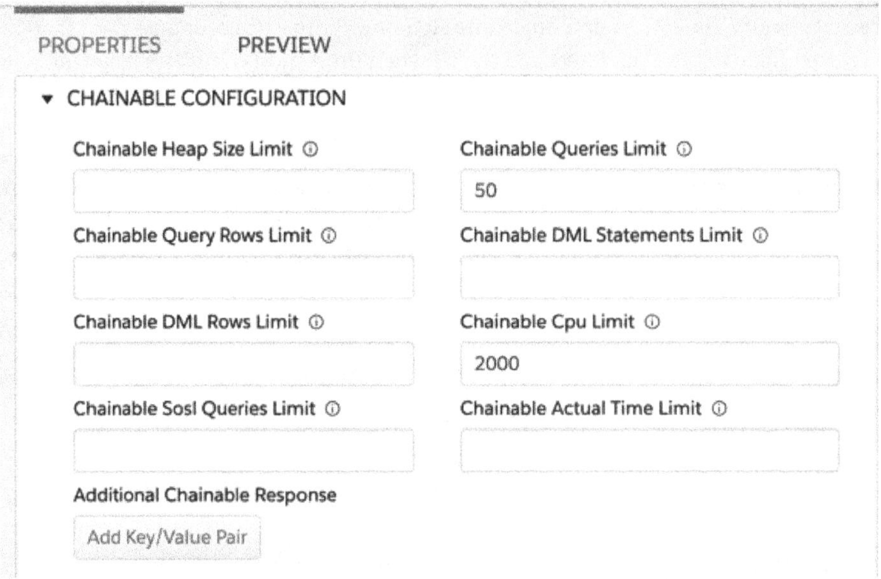

Figure 6.2 – An overview of the Chainable Configuration section

> **Note**
>
> The platform is only checking for limits on resources where values are specified in the **Chainable Configuration** section. For example, because there is no value specified in the **Chainable Sosl Queries Limit** field in the bottom left of the screen shown in *Figure 6.2*, if the number of SOSL queries exceeds the governor limit, no chaining will take place and the Integration Procedure will fail.

If no limits out of the ones specified in the **Chainable Configuration** section are hit during the Integration Procedure execution, it will continue to run in a single transaction.

> **Note**
>
> Each transaction out of the ones created by the **Chainable** option in Integration Procedures is subject to *synchronous Apex governor limits* (https://developer.salesforce.com/docs/atlas.en-us.salesforce_app_limits_cheatsheet.meta/salesforce_app_limits_cheatsheet/salesforce_app_limits_platform_apexgov.htm).
>
> To go up to a higher *asynchronous Apex limit* (https://developer.salesforce.com/docs/atlas.en-us.salesforce_app_limits_cheatsheet.meta/salesforce_app_limits_cheatsheet/salesforce_app_limits_platform_apexgov.htm), use the setting described in the *Queueable Chainable setting* section.

Here are some of the current synchronous governor limits in place at the time of this writing, which you can use as guidelines for populating the fields in the **Chainable Configuration** section:

- **Chainable Heap Size Limit:** The amount of shared memory used to store data during the transaction. The maximum is 6 MB.

- **Chainable DML Rows Limit:** The maximum number of records affected by **Data Manipulation Language (DML)** statements, including the ones in the approval process and Recycle Bin operations. The maximum is 10,000.

- **Chainable Queries Limit:** The maximum number of SOQL queries run inside the transaction. The maximum is 100.

- **Chainable CPU Limit:** The maximum CPU time used on the Salesforce servers. The maximum is 10,000ms or milliseconds.

Once one or more limits are specified, the only thing left is to instruct the system to run the Integration Procedure as chainable. If an Integration Procedure is run by an Integration Procedure Action inside an OmniScript, check the **Chainable** box under the **Remote Properties** section in the **Integration Procedure Action Properties** screen (see *Figure 6.3*):

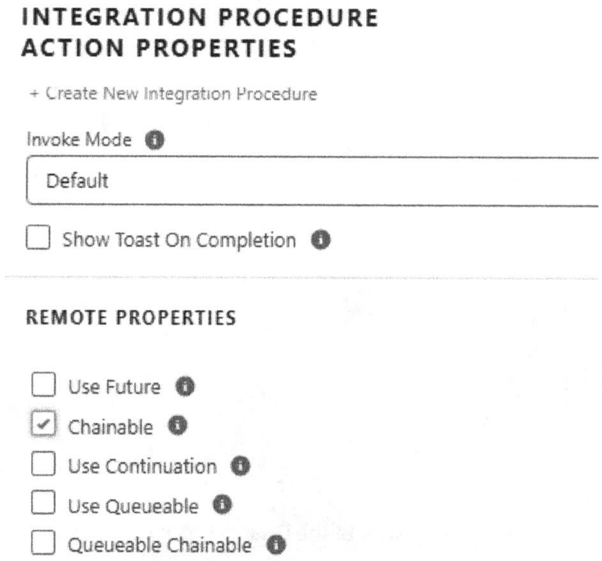

Figure 6.3 – An overview of enabling Chainable in Integration Procedure Action Properties screen

If you are calling your Integration Procedure from a REST API, you will set the **Chainable** option to true. For more information on calling a long-running Integration Procedure from Apex and from an LWC, see the *How to call long-running Integration Procedures from the code* section later in this chapter.

> **Note**
>
> Until the Integration Procedure is invoked with the **Chainable** option, the **Chainable Configuration** setting inside the Integration Procedure will not be used and chaining will not take place.
>
> Also please remember that the system only checks the current resource usage against **Chainable Configuration** at the end of each of the Integration Procedure actions. If any single action alone consumes significant resources and hits governor limits inside the action itself, the Integration Procedure will fail.
>
> If this happens, consider splitting the logic and creating more granular actions. For instance, if a Remote Action is hitting governor limits, consider splitting the logic inside it into multiple steps or, better yet, see if some of the logic inside the Remote Action can be accomplished with Integration Procedure tools.

Finally, there's one more scenario related to **Chainable** configuration. An Integration Procedure can call a child Integration Procedure, which is a great tool for structuring your logic and maximizing reuse. And when a parent Integration Procedure calls a child, it can disable chaining in a child when you check the **Disable Chainable** box in the **Integration Procedure Action** screen inside the parent Integration Procedure (see *Figure 6.4*):

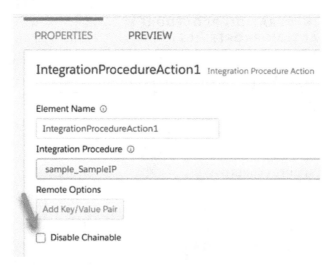

Figure 6.4 – An overview of the Disable Chainable option

Now, why would you want to disable chaining in a child Integration Procedure?

In some scenarios, you may need to force an Integration Procedure to run in a single transaction. For instance, if you are using static variables in an Apex class used in a Remote Action in the parent and child Integration Procedures, starting a new transaction would clear these variable's values, and running in the same transaction would preserve them, so the child Integration Procedure would be able to access the values set by a parent.

However, I would probably advise against such heavy use of Remote Actions unless there is a good reason for it. We have a lot of configuration-based options, and I prefer using them over code-based ones whenever it makes sense.

With all that said, while almost perfect, the **Chainable** Integration Procedure configuration is not without limitations. The next section provides details.

Queueable Chainable setting

While the use of the **Chainable** setting allows long-running Integration Procedures to span transaction boundaries and thus avoid hitting governor limits, in some cases, a chunk of work, such as a callout or a Remote Action, cannot continue in a new transaction. So, even with chaining configured, Integration Procedures may still fail due to a lack of resources.

In addition, certain organizations impose limits on the maximum number of times chaining can occur, so we may have to do more work in each of the chained transactions.

Thankfully, the OmniStudio platform provides an option to accomplish just that—step up to the increased set of governor limits available to each of the chained transactions.

The **Queueable Chainable** setting gets the Integration Procedure running as an Apex Queueable job, and a new job is created each time a chaining occurs. Queueable jobs are asynchronous and, therefore, allow a much higher set of governor limits—in many cases—two times the allowance of their synchronous counterparts.

> **Note**
>
> An Integration Procedure configured to run as **Queueable Chainable** will run slower than the same Integration Procedure configured as **Chainable** because of the asynchronous nature of Queueable jobs it uses to run.

Queueable Chainable settings are just as easy to implement. Begin by setting the value for one or more of the **Queueable Chainable Limits** options under the Integration Procedure **Properties** section (see *Figure 6.5*):

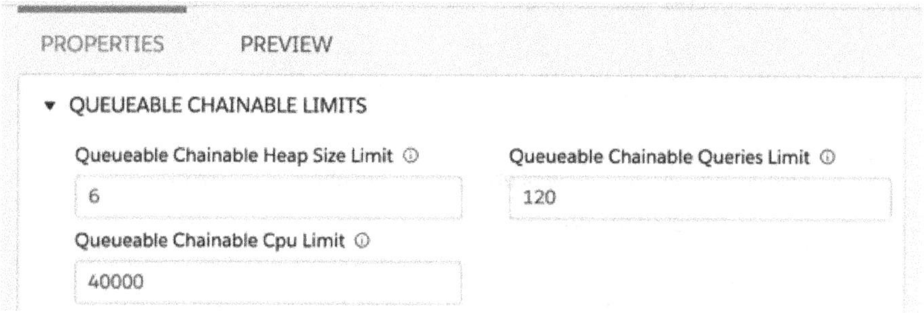

Figure 6.5 – An overview of the Queueable Chainable configuration section

Here are some of the current asynchronous governor limits in place at the time of this writing, which you can use as a guideline for populating the fields in the **Queueable Chainable Limits** section:

- **Queueable Chainable Heap Size Limit**: The amount of shared memory used during transaction processing. The asynchronous limit is 12 MB.

- **Queueable Chainable CPU Limit**: The amount of CPU time a process can take on the Salesforce servers. The asynchronous limit is 60,000ms.

- **Queueable Chainable Queries Limit**: The maximum number of SOQL queries used by the process. The asynchronous limit is 200.

Once one or more of these limits are specified, just as with its **Chainable** counterpart, we need to instruct the system to run the Integration Procedure as **Queueable Chainable**. If an Integration Procedure is run by an Integration Procedure Action inside an OmniScript, check the **Queueable Chainable** box under the **Remote Properties** section in the **Integration Procedure Action Properties** screen (see *Figure 6.6*):

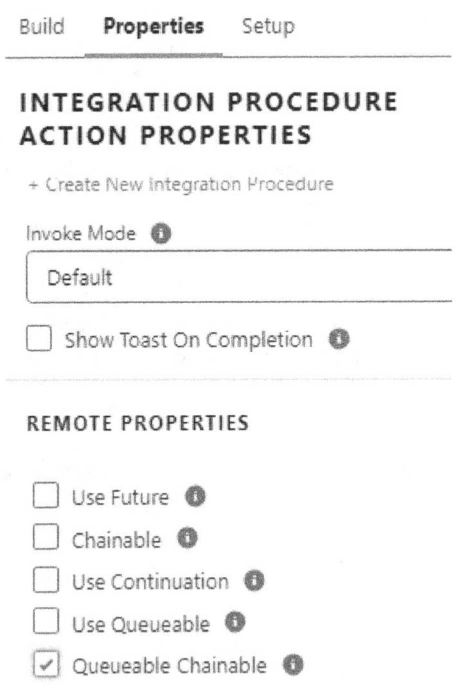

Build   **Properties**   Setup

INTEGRATION PROCEDURE
ACTION PROPERTIES

+ Create New Integration Procedure

Invoke Mode ⓘ

Default

☐ Show Toast On Completion ⓘ

REMOTE PROPERTIES

☐ Use Future ⓘ
☐ Chainable ⓘ
☐ Use Continuation ⓘ
☐ Use Queueable ⓘ
☑ Queueable Chainable ⓘ

Figure 6.6 – An overview of enabling Queueable Chainable in
Integration Procedure Action Properties screen

And if you're calling an Integration Procedure from a REST API, you can set the `queueableChainable` option to `true`.

Finally, there's one more way you can use chaining to avoid hitting governor limits. Continue to the next section to find out.

Chain On Step

The **Chain On Step** option, when selected for a particular Integration Procedure step, forces that step to run in its own transaction. This happens regardless of whether **Chainable** or **Queueable Chainable** limits are configured and whether chaining takes place. This setting is independent and could be a lifesaver in some cases when you need a step to run in a separate transaction.

For example, if your Integration Procedure is doing some data manipulation followed by an HTTP callout, you will not be able to run these in the same transaction due to Salesforce's *uncommitted work* error, as seen here:

```
"error": "You have uncommitted work pending. Commit or rollback before
calling out"
```

When you see this error message, configuring your DML action, such as your DataRaptor Post Action, as **Chain On Step**—see *Figure 6.7*—will allow the Integration Procedure to complete successfully:

Figure 6.7 – An overview of the Chain On Step setting

The **Chain On Step** feature is also a great way to run a child Integration Procedure in parallel. This allows you to run chunks of logic in the background without delaying user interactions. It is like the **Non-Blocking Invoke Mode** setting available in the Integration Procedure Action that we looked at earlier in this chapter.

Well, these were the three options we can use to allow our Integration Procedures to continue running even when they were hitting governor limits before. Without these options in our arsenal, we would've had to rewrite them, splitting them into several chunks and running them individually, preserving the results by hand, and then passing them on to each of the following consecutive steps.

We had to do just that on a project back in the early days of Vlocity, and I can tell you that the quick configuration choices you've just learned could've saved us over a month of custom development!

Speaking of custom development, you can often accomplish tasks with Integration Procedures quite a bit faster than they would otherwise take to do with code. Once the logic is ready, we may need to invoke it from within our existing code base.

That means we are not calling it from an Integration Procedure Action in an OmniScript. So, we will need other means of letting the Integration Procedure know to run as **Chainable** or **Queueable Chainable**. And again, the designers of the OmniStudio platform have made this easy for us. Continue to the next section to find out how.

How to call long-running Integration Procedures from the code

Let's look at what it takes to run a **Chainable** or **Queueable Chainable** Integration Procedure configuration from within the two most popular coding platforms in Salesforce: Apex and LWC.

Calling from Apex

To call an Integration Procedure from Apex, use the `runIntegrationService` method of the `IntegrationProcedureService` class.

This method expects the procedure name, input map, and options map, returning results in the map as well. For example, here's what the call may look like:

```
Map <String, Object> ipOutput =
  (Map <String, Object>) omnistudio.IntegrationProcedureService
    .runIntegrationService(
      'sample_IPCalculate',
      new Map <String, Object>(),
      new Map <String, Object>()
  );
```

This is a basic Integration Procedure call without specifying **Chainable** or **Queueable Chainable** options. So, an Integration Procedure that might hit governor limits will fail. For example, we have a sample Integration Procedure with multiple Remote Actions that call time-consuming Apex code, as shown in *Figure 6.8*:

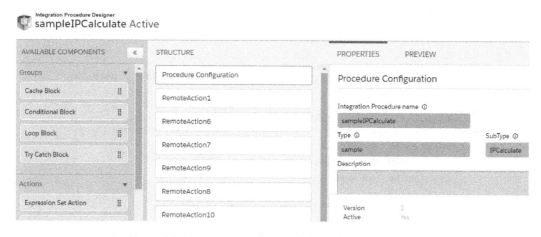

Figure 6.8 – An overview of a sample Integration Procedure

This Integration Procedure fails when we call it via **Preview**, and we will see the same *CPU limit exceeded* error if we call it from Apex without the **Chainable** or **Queueable Chainable** options:

Errors/Debug Output

> Debug Log

∨ Errors

```
[
  "Apex CPU time limit exceeded",
  {
    "statusCode": 400,
    "type": "exception",
```

Figure 6.9 – An overview of an Apex CPU exception in Debug Output

Let's now pass the `queueableChainable` option via an `options` map:

```
Map <String, Object> ipOutput =
  (Map <String, Object>) omnistudio.IntegrationProcedureService
    .runIntegrationService(
      'sample_IPCalculate',
      new Map <String, Object>(),
      new Map<String, Object>{'queueableChainable' => true}
    );
```

The Integration Procedure is now succeeding, and we see several completed Queueable jobs in the **Apex Jobs** panel of our org setup:

Apex Jobs

Monitor the status of all Apex jobs, and optionally, abort jobs that are in progress.

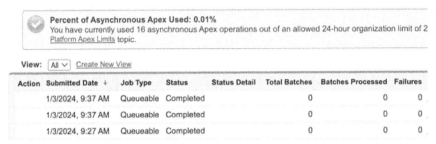

Percent of Asynchronous Apex Used: 0.01%
You have currently used 16 asynchronous Apex operations out of an allowed 24-hour organization limit of 2
Platform Apex Limits topic.

View: [All ∨] Create New View

Action	Submitted Date ↓	Job Type	Status	Status Detail	Total Batches	Batches Processed	Failures
	1/3/2024, 9:37 AM	Queueable	Completed		0	0	0
	1/3/2024, 9:37 AM	Queueable	Completed		0	0	0
	1/3/2024, 9:27 AM	Queueable	Completed		0	0	0

Figure 6.10 – An overview of the Apex Jobs screen

Now, what if you need to call an Integration Procedure from an LWC? Check the following section to see how.

Calling from an LWC

The code for calling an Integration Procedure from an LWC is very similar to its Apex counterpart discussed in the previous section. Here is a screenshot showing a simple JavaScript class that calls an Integration Procedure specifying a `queueableChainable` flag:

```
import { LightningElement, api } from "lwc";
import { OmniscriptBaseMixin } from "omnistudio/omniscriptBaseMixin";
import { getNamespaceDotNotation } from "omnistudio/omniscriptInternalUtils";
import { OmniscriptActionCommonUtil } from "omnistudio/omniscriptActionUtils";

export default class SampleOSStep extends OmniscriptBaseMixin(LightningElement) {
    _actionUtil;
    _ns = getNamespaceDotNotation();

    connectedCallback(){
        this._actionUtil = new OmniscriptActionCommonUtil();
    }

    handleClick(){
        this.callIP();
    }

    callIP(){
        const options = {
            queueableChainable: true
        };
        const ipInput = {};
        const params = {
            input: JSON.stringify(ipInput),
            sClassName: `${this._ns}IntegrationProcedureService`,
            sMethodName: 'sample_IPCalculate',
            options: JSON.stringify(options),
        };
        this._actionUtil
            .executeAction(params, null, this, null, null)
            .then((response) => {
                console.log(response);
            })
            .catch((error) => {
                console.error(error, "ERROR");
            });
    }
}
```

Figure 6.11 – An overview of a sample LWC JavaScript class

Instead of maps, it takes JavaScript objects for the options, parameters, and the response.

Well, we now know how to call Integration Procedures from Apex and LWC. We can now leverage Integration Procedure tools instead of having to manually code things such as external service calls, saving ourselves tons of time and making our configurations easier to maintain.

Now, even with the full power of OmniStudio at our disposal, there will be times when we must fall back on the Salesforce platform behind it. And Salesforce has its own set of tools that make running asynchronous code easy and efficient. Let's take a quick look.

Async execution options in Apex

In this section, we will do a brief review of the options available in the Salesforce platform itself for running code asynchronously. These can come in handy when you need to do a long-running operation inside a Remote Action or when you need to do some work outside of the OmniStudio framework, and in many other cases, thus allowing your business users to continue using the app without having to wait for operations to complete.

Apex @future annotation

The **Apex @future annotation** is a quick way to run a method asynchronously without delaying an Apex transaction. This is also great for making Web Service callouts, separating DML statements, and preventing *mixed save DML* errors, just like we did with the **Chain On Step** Integration Procedure setting earlier in this chapter.

To get an Apex method to run asynchronously, simply add the `@future` annotation before the method, as shown in the following screenshot:

```
1   public class ProcessOpportunityHelper {
2       @future
3       public static void process(String accountId) {
4           List<Opportunity> opps = [select Id, CloseDate from Opportunity where AccountId=:accountId];
5           for (Opportunity opp : opps){
6               opp.CloseDate = opp.CloseDate.addDays(7);
7           }
8           if (!opps.isEmpty())
9               update opps;
10      }
11  }
```

Figure 6.12 – An overview of the static method with the @future annotation

> **Note**
>
> There are some limitations and conditions you need to meet for your method to be able to run as a future method. For instance, it needs to be static, and you cannot pass a **Salesforce Object** (**sObject**) as an argument because it may change between the time you call the method and the time it executes. For more information on future methods, check the following Salesforce documentation page: `https://developer.salesforce.com/docs/atlas.en-us.apexcode.meta/apexcode/apex_invoking_future_methods.htm`.

Once a future method is defined, you call it just like any regular method. For example, to invoke the `process` method shown previously, you can use the following statement:

```
ProcessOpportunityHelper.process('001Hr00001rjcOlIAI');
```

Now, what if you need to get a larger set of governor limits? Queueable Apex offers just that and more, at a cost of slightly increased code complexity.

Queueable Apex

Just as with the `@future` annotation, **Queueable Apex** allows us to run asynchronous operations and benefit from a larger asynchronous set of governor limits. In addition to that, it allows us to check progress and pass complex data types as parameters, and we can chain Queueable jobs!

To run the code as a Queueable job, you will need to implement a `Queueable` interface, as shown in *Figure 6.13*:

```
1  public class ProcessOpportunityQueueable implements Queueable {
2      private String accountId;
3      public ProcessOpportunityQueueable(String accountId){
4          this.accountId = accountId;
5      }
6      public void execute(QueueableContext context) {
7          List<Opportunity> opps = [select Id, CloseDate from Opportunity where AccountId=:accountId];
8          for (Opportunity opp : opps){
9              opp.CloseDate = opp.CloseDate.addDays(7);
10         }
11         if (!opps.isEmpty())
12             update opps;
13     }
14 }
```

Figure 6.13 – An overview of the sample Queueable class

To start a Queueable job, you will need to run `System.enqueueJob`, as shown next. (The call also returns the ID of the Queueable job, so you can optionally check on its completion status.) You can use the same call inside your `execute` method to add another job to the queue and chain your queueable jobs:

```
System.enqueueJob(new
ProcessOpportunityQueueable('001Hr00001rjcOlIAI'));
```

For more information on Queueable Apex, check out its Salesforce documentation page (`https://developer.salesforce.com/docs/atlas.en-us.apexcode.meta/apexcode/apex_queueing_jobs.htm`).

Now, what if you need to process a very large number of records when even the asynchronous governor limits are not enough? In this case, *Batch Apex* may just be the tool you need. Check the next section to find out more.

Batch Apex

Batch Apex allows us to process thousands of records and implement complex logic well beyond what we would otherwise be able to do with a future or even a Queueable job. It does so by splitting a large set of query results into manageable chunks and having our code process them sequentially. You will need to implement the `Database.Batchable` interface, as shown in *Figure 6.14*:

```
1   public class ProcessOpportunitiesBatch implements Database.Batchable<sObject>{
2       public Database.QueryLocator start(Database.BatchableContext BC){
3           return Database.getQueryLocator([select Id, CloseDate from Opportunity where StageName='Prospecting']);
4       }
5       public void execute(Database.BatchableContext BC, List<Opportunity> scope){
6           for (Opportunity opp : scope){
7               opp.CloseDate = opp.CloseDate.addDays(30);
8           }
9           update scope;
10      }
11      public void finish(Database.BatchableContext BC){
12      }
13  }
```

Figure 6.14 – An overview of a sample Batch class

Once the code is in place, to start a batch job, run `Database.executeBatch`, as shown next:

```
Database.executeBatch(new ProcessOpportunitiesBatch(), 100);
```

For more information on Batch Apex, check out its Salesforce documentation page (`https://developer.salesforce.com/docs/atlas.en-us.apexcode.meta/apexcode/apex_batch.htm`).

And finally, there is one more way you can use to run your async logic on the Salesforce platform. Continue to the next section to find out.

Scheduled Apex

If you need some processing to occur repeatedly at specified times, **scheduled Apex** is the tool you need. Implementing the `Schedulable` interface allows you to schedule your Apex job—manually or even automatically from a call to the `System.schedule` method. The following screenshot shows a simple scheduled Apex class:

```
 1  global class ProcessOpportunitySchedulable implements Schedulable {
 2      global void execute(SchedulableContext SC) {
 3          List<Opportunity> opps = [select Id, CloseDate from Opportunity where StageName='Prospecting'];
 4          for (Opportunity opp : opps){
 5              opp.CloseDate = opp.CloseDate.addDays 30 ;
 6          }
 7          if (!opps.isEmpty())
 8              update opps;
 9      }
10  }
```

Figure 6.15 – An overview of a sample Schedulable class

Please note that although scheduled Apex is asynchronous, synchronous governor limits apply to scheduled Apex jobs. To step up to a higher set of limits, have your scheduled code fire off future methods or create Queueable jobs.

To have our class automatically run every day at 1 p.m., go to the **Setup** menu, then type Apex Classes, and finally click on the **Schedule Apex** button, as shown in *Figure 6.16*:

Figure 6.16 – An overview of the Schedule Apex button on the Apex Classes screen

This brings up the **Schedule Apex** page where you can specify the job name, select an Apex class you would like to run, and set your schedule:

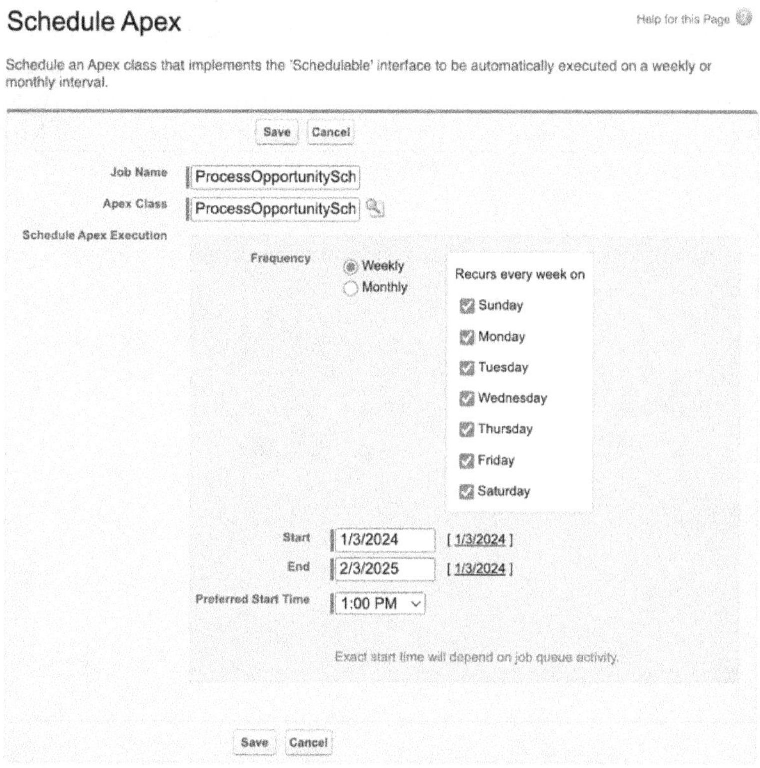

Figure 6.17 – An overview of the Schedule Apex screen

You can also accomplish the same result by running the following statement:

```
System.schedule('ProcessOpportunitySchedulable', '0 0 13 * * ?', new
ProcessOpportunitySchedulable());
```

For more information on scheduled Apex, check out its Salesforce documentation page (https://developer.salesforce.com/docs/atlas.en-us.apexcode.meta/apexcode/apex_scheduler.htm).

Well, that concludes our review of async Apex tools. In this section, we've seen a simple way to fire off async jobs with the Apex @future annotation, the powerful Queueable Apex tool, which takes the same concept to an entirely new level, the mighty Batch Apex tool, which gives us the tools to handle thousands and even millions of records, and the handy scheduled Apex tool, which makes it easy for us to get code running at specific regular points in time, taking care of maintenance tasks for us. Having seen these, you now have a complete set of tools that you can use to get things to run asynchronously, improving the user experience and staying within governor limits.

Summary

And that is a wrap on the options for async execution. In this chapter, we built a case for async code execution and saw when it can be a game changer for our OmniStudio apps. We also explored three quick, configuration-based ways to bypass governor limits in our Integration Procedures and how to invoke our Integration Procedures from Apex and LWC, giving us the power to leverage Integration Procedure tools and saving us hours or even days of development. We then concluded our journey by looking at four ways to run async code on the Salesforce platform itself and how those can benefit our OmniStudio apps.

In the next chapter, we will look at caching—the second way to produce big performance boosts quickly.

Understanding Caching

After async code execution, caching is the second tool that can produce big performance impacts quickly. In some cases, you will be able to see parts of your application performing orders of magnitude faster after just a few clicks. In this chapter, we will explore the caching architecture of OmniStudio and the underlying Salesforce platform and how these can be applied to speed things up.

In this chapter, you will learn about the following:

- The reason why caching is widely used throughout the Salesforce and OmniStudio platforms
- The caching architecture of the core Salesforce platform
- How to use the Salesforce platform cache in Apex to improve performance
- How to use caching with DataRaptors and Integration Procedures to achieve impressive results
- The client-side caching options you can use in your Lightning Web Components

Let's get started!

Technical requirements

To follow along with this chapter, you will need access to an OmniStudio installation. If you don't have one handy, you can always request your free trial development environment from the Salesforce Developers site, which is (at the time of this writing) available at `https://developer.salesforce.com/free-trials`. Once on the site, head over to **Industry-Based Trials** and get yourself a trial org for the industry of your choice.

What's with all the caching?

All of us are familiar with the term **caching**, but how familiar are we with the underlying technology? Are we using it to its full potential? We know that caching is there to improve performance and that we need to clear the cache when the old content is getting stuck. So, when we need to see the most recent version of a page in the web browser, an OmniScript, or a **Lightning Web Component** (**LWC**), we know we need to clear the cache.

While letting the tools take care of the caching for us is perfectly fine, how about a 50x boost for an otherwise slow Remote Action call? Yes, this is not a typo. The next section shows an example of an Integration Procedure where the run time dropped considerably (measured in milliseconds, i.e., ms) from 3,907ms to a mere 63ms after wrapping its long-running step in a **Cache Block**, a simple configuration change that only takes a few clicks to implement.

While this may be an extreme case, significant performance improvements are not uncommon when custom caching is introduced to OmniStudio apps. If any of your system's components rely on expensive-to-retrieve but infrequently updated data, and if those data are more or less frequently used, that component may be a prime candidate for caching. This means that you may be able to achieve a serious boost in that component's performance easily.

Components or external system calls that retrieve product catalogs, geographic information, financial or statistical information, or other infrequently changing data are all good candidates. Saving the results of such operations in temporary storage reduces the need for round trips to the database and your business logic layer.

When Salesforce and OmniStudio are concerned, we have several types of caching available for us to work with. These are as follows:

- **Automatic caching**: It is used implicitly throughout the platforms by Lightning Framework, OmniScripts, Integration Procedures, DataRaptors, and more for structure, metadata, and configuration.

- **Manual caching**: The tools available for developers and administrators to implement custom data caching in Salesforce and OmniStudio apps.

> **Note**
>
> The automatic caching of OmniStudio components is implemented using the **Scale Cache** feature. Scale Cache uses the memory allocated to the **VlocityMetadata Platform Cache** partition. See the *Caching in the Salesforce platform* section for more information on the Salesforce platform cache architecture.

Well, this gives us a better idea of caching and the options we have at our disposal. While automatic caching is already part of the platform and is in place to benefit all apps, learning our options and applying the manual caching options to our apps can offer great performance improvements, so let's review them in the next section.

Manual caching options

Let's look at the options we have available for adding cache features to our apps. Let's begin with the core Salesforce platform.

> **Note**
>
> The Salesforce and OmniStudio caching options described may not work as expected when running off-platform, for example, with OmniOut. In these scenarios, custom caching may need to be considered.

Caching in the Salesforce platform

The Salesforce platform provides a dedicated memory space for caching your app's complex calculations, long-running queries, API calls, and other types of components returning infrequently changing data. At the time of writing, the memory size available for different org editions is as follows:

- **Enterprise edition**: 10 MB by default
- **Unlimited and Performance editions**: 30 MB by default, but you can request more cache space by contacting Salesforce support

To prevent any single app from monopolizing the entire cache, this space is divided into partitions. For instance, you can create a separate partition for caching products. OmniStudio defines two partitions called **VlocityMetadata** and **VlocityAPIResponse**. Go to **Setup|Platform Cache** to update the partition sizes and create partitions:

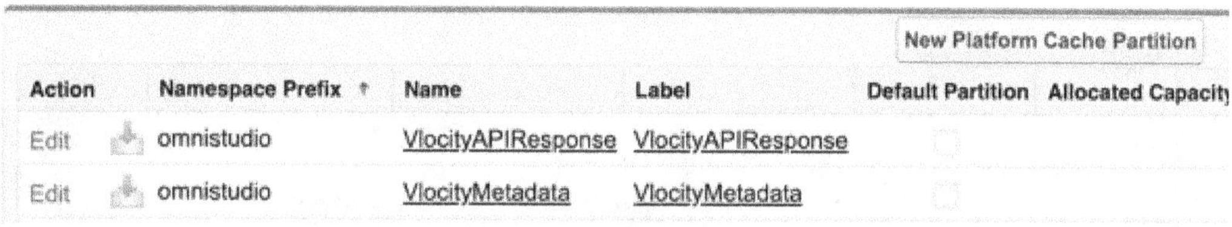

Action	Namespace Prefix ↑	Name	Label	Default Partition	Allocated Capacity
Edit	omnistudio	VlocityAPIResponse	VlocityAPIResponse		
Edit	omnistudio	VlocityMetadata	VlocityMetadata		

Figure 7.1 – An overview of the screen showing Platform Cache partitions

Each partition, in turn, is also divided into two separate cache spaces: Session and Org. The **Session cache** stores the data that is unique for each user's logged-in session. This data is also only available to this individual user and no one else. The **Org cache** is shared and visible to all users in the org. The following screenshot shows the **Session Cache Allocation** and the **Org Cache Allocation** for the **VlocityMetadata** partition of a sample org:

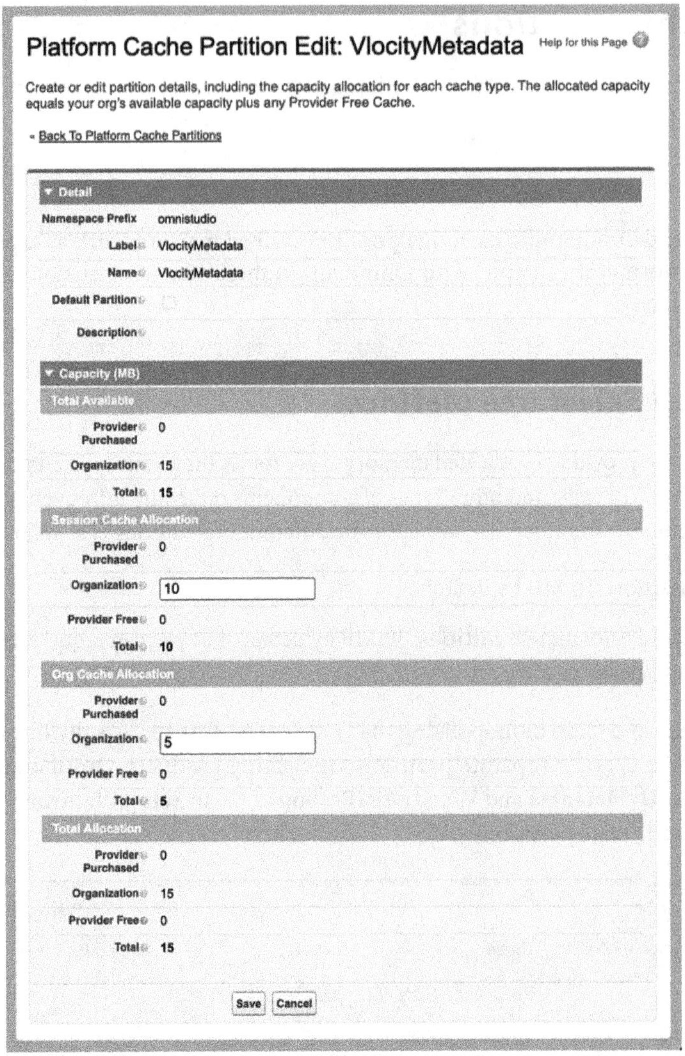

Figure 7.2 – An overview of the Platform Cache partition edit screen

> **Note**
>
> The data in the cache are stored as name-value pairs, and each individual item cannot exceed 100 KB. You may want to check out the article called *Platform Cache Best Practices* (`https://developer.salesforce.com/docs/atlas.en-us.apexcode.meta/apexcode/apex_platform_cache_best_practices.htm`) for more limits and advanced tips.

Now, let's look at a simple app showing how we can use Salesforce Platform Cache from Apex.

Sample app

The following simple Apex class adds up the numbers to simulate a long-running calculation. Its `calculate` method takes a number as an argument. It also implements the `calculateWithCache` method that checks if the result of `calculate` for a given argument is already present in the cache. If it is, the cached version is returned. If not, it runs the calculation and puts the result into the cache:

```
 1  ▾ public class SampleCalculationHelper
 2  ▾     public static Decimal calculate(Integer count){
 3            Decimal sum = 0.0;
 4  ▾         for (Integer i = 0; i < count; i++){
 5                sum += i;
 6            }
 7
 8            return sum;
 9        }
10  ▾     public static Decimal calculateWithCache(Integer count){
11            String cacheKey = 'local.myPartition.' + count;
12            if (Cache.Org.contains(cacheKey))
13                return (Decimal)Cache.Org.get(cacheKey);
14  ▾         else{
15                Decimal res = calculate(count);
16                Cache.Org.put(cacheKey, res);
17                return res;
18            }
19        }
20    |
```

Figure 7.3 – An overview of a sample Apex class for testing Platform Cache

Now, let's look at the performance when we run both methods using **Developer Console**. I ran each of the methods three times to get consistent benchmarks.

When calling the `calculate` method that does not use Salesforce Platform Cache (see *Figure 7.4*), we get the following run times: 3,458ms, 2,856ms, and 3,027ms.

Enter Apex Code

```
1    Long t1 = DateTime.now().getTime();
2    System.debug(SampleCalculationHelper.calculate(100000));
3    Long t2 = DateTime.now().getTime();
4    System.debug(t2-t1);
```

Figure 7.4 – An overview of running the calculate method

Now, when calling the `calculateWithCache` method (see *Figure 7.5*), the run times are 3,373ms, 14ms, and 13ms!

Enter Apex Code

```
1   Long t1 = DateTime.now().getTime();
2   System.debug(SampleCalculationHelper.calculateWithCache(100000));
3   Long t2 = DateTime.now().getTime();
4   System.debug(t2-t1);
```

Figure 7.5 – An overview of running the calculateWithCache method

Wow! We got our calculation to run over 250 times faster after allowing it to use the Platform Cache! Now, let's look at the manual caching options in OmniStudio.

Caching options in DataRaptors

If your **Extract** or **Transform** type DataRaptor runs a computationally expensive query or logic that produces infrequently updated data, then DataRaptor may benefit from caching. It is easy to configure; simply specify the **Salesforce Platform Cache Type**—the Session Cache or the Org Cache (see the *Caching in the Salesforce platform* section for more information)—and the **Time To Live In Minutes** values. See *Figure 7.6*:

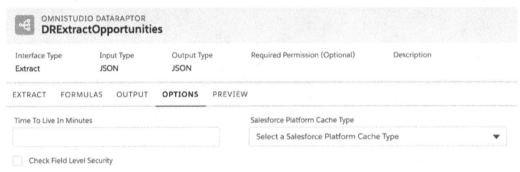

Figure 7.6 – An overview of the cache configuration pane of DataRaptor

You can then test your DataRaptor with and without caching by checking or clearing the **Ignore Cache** box on the **Preview** window, as shown in *Figure 7.7*:

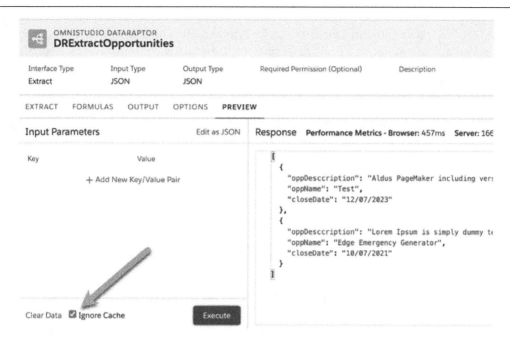

Figure 7.7 – An overview of the Ignore Cache checkbox on the DataRaptor preview pane

While caching the response of DataRaptor is easy, more flexible caching options may be required for the task at hand at times. These are available in **Integration Procedures**.

Cache blocks in Integration Procedures

The OmniStudio makes it easy for us to add caching to any step of an Integration Procedure. Simply add a **Cache Block** to your **Structure** panel, and then drag in the actions that you want to include into the block, as shown in *Figure 7.8*:

Figure 7.8 – An overview of the Cache Block in an Integration Procedure

You will need to specify **Salesforce Platform Cache Type** as Session or Org cache (see the *Caching in the Salesforce platform* section for more information), **Time To Live In Minutes**, which specifies how long the data remains in the cache, and then **Cache Block Output**, which is the key/value pairs that you would like to place into the cache.

Let's give it a try. *Figure 7.9* shows a Remote Action class implementing the same simple calculation we used to test Salesforce Platform Cache; only, in this case, I'm hardcoding the maximum value for simplicity:

```
1  global with sharing class SampleIPController implements Callable {
2      public Object call(String action, Map<String, Object> args) {
3          Map<String, Object> input = (Map<String, Object>)args.get('input');
4          Map<String, Object> output = (Map<String, Object>)args.get('output');
5          Map<String, Object> options = (Map<String, Object>)args.get('options');
6
7          return invokeMethod(action, input, output, options);
8      }
9      global Object invokeMethod(String methodName, Map<String,Object> inputMap,Map<String,Object> outMap, Map<String,Object> options) {
10         if (methodName == 'calculate')
11             calculate(inputMap,outMap,options);
12
13         return true;
14     }
15     global void calculate(Map<String,Object> inputMap,Map<String,Object> outMap, Map<String,Object> options){
16         Decimal sum = 0.0;
17         for (Integer i = 0; i < 100000; i++){
18             sum += i;
19         }
20         outMap.put('result', sum);
21     }
22 }
```

Figure 7.9 – An overview of a sample Remote Action with a long-running calculation

> **Note**
>
> You can test your Integration Procedures with and without cache by specifying the value for the `ignoreCache` variable in the **Options** panel in the bottom right of the Integration Procedure **Preview** window (see *Figure 7.10*). Another useful option is `resetCache`, which forces the fresh data into the cache, so this may come in handy for testing the cache itself.

Let's begin by setting the `ignoreCache` to `true` when previewing the Integration Procedure:

Figure 7.10 – An overview of the Integration Procedure Preview Options panel

Without caching, we can see a server-side run time of 3,907ms (see *Figure 7.11*):

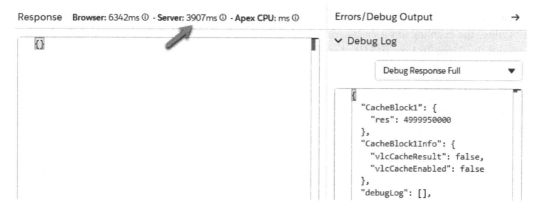

Figure 7.11 – An overview of an Integration Procedure run without caching

Now, let's allow **Cache Block** to do its work. Setting `ignoreCache` to `false` results in a server-side run time of only 63ms (see *Figure 7.12*):

Figure 7.12 – An overview of an Integration Procedure run with caching

While slightly longer than running our calculation in pure Apex, wrapping it in **Cache Block** still results in impressive time-saving.

Now, let's look at another, even simpler, way to add caching to an Integration Procedure.

Caching the response of the entire Integration Procedure

In some cases, the entire Integration Procedure (or the IP's **top-level data**) can be a good candidate for caching, and enabling this is even easier in this case. Simply specify the **Salesforce Platform Cache Type** and the **Time To Live In Minutes** values (refer to the *Cache blocks in Integration Procedures* section for more information). See *Figure 7.13*:

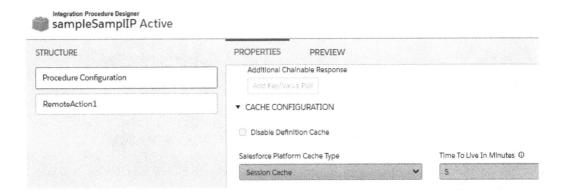

Figure 7.13 – An overview of the Cache configuration pane of an Integration Procedure

You can then test your Integration Procedure with and without caching by specifying the `ignoreCache` parameter in the **Options** panel of the **Preview** window, as shown in the previous section.

In the next section, we will look at the tools available for the client-side caching of the Apex method results in our LWCs.

Caching with the Lightning Wire service

When calling Apex methods from an LWC, we can have the Lightning framework cache so that these methods return. Lightning Wire service saves the data on the client side, so no Platform Cache resources are consumed.

If your Apex method is computationally expensive or involves a long-running query or a callout, this will allow it to run these less frequently, making your app more responsive. However, even when your code runs relatively fast, avoiding a server round trip may improve performance, especially for users on slow and unreliable networks. So, if the data returned by your Apex method is relatively static, consider marking your method as **Cacheable**.

All it takes is adding `cacheable=true` to your `@AuraEnabled` Apex method annotation. *Figure 7.14* shows a simple code snippet with two test methods that we have marked as Cacheable: a computationally expensive `calculate` method, which we used earlier in this chapter, and a quick `getName` method that runs a simple query:

```apex
public class SampleController
    @AuraEnabled(cacheable=true)
    public static Decimal calculate(){
        Decimal sum = 0.0;
        for (Integer i = 0; i < 100000; i++){
            sum += i;
        }
        return sum;
    }
    @AuraEnabled(cacheable=true)
    public static String getName(){
        String name = [select Name from Account limit 1]?.Name;
        return name;
    }
}
```

Figure 7.14 – An overview of marking the Apex method as cacheable

Here's a sample LWC calling our `calculate` and `getName` methods. As you can see, there's no difference between calling a Cacheable and a regular Apex method when using the LWC wire service:

```javascript
import getName from '@salesforce/apex/SampleController.getName'

export default class SampleCmp extends OmniscriptBaseMixin(LightningElement) {
    @api stepName;

    @wire(calculate)
    calc({ error, data }) {
        console.log('calc');
        if (data) {
            console.log(data);
        } else if (error) {
            console.log(error);
        }
    }

    @wire(getName)
    onGetName({ error, data }) {
        console.log('onGetName');
        if (data) {
            console.log(data);
        } else if (error) {
            console.log(error);
        }
    }
}
```

Figure 7.15 – An overview of a sample LWC using the Lightning Wire service

> **Note**
>
> Unlike the OmniStudio and the Apex code when using the Platform Cache, there is no set cache duration when using a Lightning Wire service, as it is managed by the framework. If you need your component to flush the cache and request the data from the server, call the `refreshApex()` method. To refresh the cache in our sample LWC shown in *Figure 7.15*, we could call `refreshApex(this.calc)`.

Now, what if you want more control over your client-side caching? Continue to the next section to see some options.

Custom caching on the client side

When we're not using the Lightning Wire service or when we simply need more control over the cache duration, we can use cookies for local and session storage in our component's JavaScript code. Manipulating these from an LWC is as easy as it would be from any JavaScript method. *Figure 7.14* shows a simple LWC, which illustrates the setting and retrieving the values for cookies and local and session storage in the browser:

```javascript
import { LightningElement, api} from "lwc";
import { OmniscriptBaseMixin } from "omnistudio/omniscriptBaseMixin";

export default class SampleCmp extends OmniscriptBaseMixin(LightningElement) {
    @api stepName;

    connectedCallback(){
        console.log(this.stepName);
        if (this.stepName === 'Step1'){
            document.cookie = 'cookie1=Test';
            sessionStorage.setItem('item','Test1')
            localStorage.setItem('item','Test2');
        }
        else {
            console.log(document.cookie);
            console.log(sessionStorage.getItem('item'));
            console.log(localStorage.getItem('item'));
        }
    }
}
```

Figure 7.16 – An overview of a sample LWC updating and retrieving cookies and local and session storage data

You can also see these values in your browser's development tools, making it easier to debug your cache management code. Here's the value we've just put into the session storage, as seen from the **Application** tab in Chrome DevTools:

Figure 7.17 – An overview of a session storage inspector in Chrome DevTools

Notice the LSKey prefix added by the Lightning framework. This is to make sure each LWC's data remains separate.

> **Note**
> Since the Synchronous Governor Limit for Apex heap size is 6 MB, and the data come from the server in a URL encoded form, the maximum size of a single JSON item you can receive from the server would be about 4 MB. This gives you a lot of flexibility for caching when compared to the 100 KB maximum size of the server-side Platform Cache item.

That wraps up our review of configurable caching options. We learned about the caching architecture of the core Salesforce platform and how to use it in Apex. Next, we reviewed how to use caching with DataRaptors and Integration Procedures, and finally, we looked at the client-side caching options you can use in your LWCs. You now have a full set of tools available to achieve massive performance improvements in your app's complex calculations, long-running queries, API calls, and other types of logic that return infrequently changing data.

Summary

In this chapter, we explored the types of caching used in the Salesforce and OmniStudio platforms and the tools and options available for applying them. We also looked at scenarios where applying the caching tools and options would be most beneficial and the magnitude of performance improvement that we may come to expect. With these tools and knowledge under our belt, we should be able to impress our business users, enable them to be more productive, and make their experience with our apps more rewarding.

In the next chapter, we will look at non-selective queries and Data Skew—a frequent cause of the slow-running queries behind our Integration Procedures and DataRaptors—and the corresponding tools and best practices for improving performance.

8

Non-Selective
Queries and Data Skew

When a DataRaptor or an Integration Procedure is slow, we are often quick to blame it on OmniStudio, while the issue may often originate in the underlying queries we're running. In this chapter, we will look at an example of when a query on an indexed field may run slower than one on a non-indexed field. We will explore the reasons and look at tools we can use for benchmarking and optimizing our queries. So, if a query on your DataRaptor times out, or when your debug log shows a query taking a long time, the tools and techniques described in this chapter may help.

In this chapter, you will learn about the following:

- Why the Salesforce platform is sometimes not able to leverage indexes, even in a query where they were used before

- Factors that make queries in DataRaptors selective and non-selective and how to maintain your query performance as your data volume grows

- How to use the **Query Plan** tool for query optimization

- What is data skew and how does it affect our apps?

Let's begin by looking at a common misconception. Everyone with experience in traditional databases knows that indexes increase performance. So, searching on an index field would be faster than searching on a non-indexed one. Is this still true in Salesforce? Not always. Let's look at a simple test in the following section.

Technical requirements

To follow along with this chapter, you will need access to an OmniStudio installation. If you don't have one handy, you can always request your free trial development environment from the Salesforce Developers site, which is (at the time of this writing) available at `https://developer.salesforce.com/free-trials`. Once on the site, head over to **Industry-Based Trials** and get yourself a trial org for the industry of your choice.

Case study – when an indexed field performs slower than a non-indexed one

Just like other databases, Salesforce maintains indexes on important fields of standard and custom objects to improve performance. However, unlike traditional databases, the Salesforce platform is multitenant, so in some cases, its database behaves differently.

Let's look at a simple custom object. Let's call it `Sample_Obj__c` and let's create 100,000 test records. *Figure 8.1* shows the fields we have created. Please note that the **INDEXED** column shows the fields where the Salesforce platform is maintaining indexes. So, selecting these fields should result in faster queries:

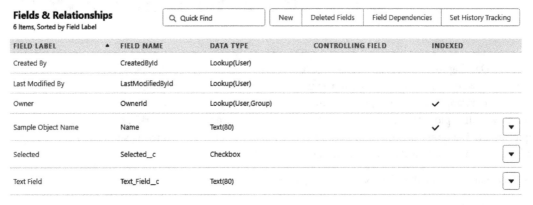

Figure 8.1 – An overview of a sample object for testing a DataRaptor extract

To make this test easy, we will put the same values in the standard `Name` field and the `Text_Field__c` custom object in all records. This way, we can query both fields for the same value and compare query performance.

Let's create a sample DataRaptor extract and add `Sample_Obj__c`. Then, let's begin by running a simple query on an indexed field (see *Figure 8.2*):

Figure 8.2 – An overview of a DataRaptor extract: an indexed query on the Name field

In our test, the query matched one row and ran very fast, taking 436ms on the server (see *Figure 8.3*):

Figure 8.3 – An overview of an indexed query on the Name field test run

Now, let's modify our DataRaptor so that it searches for the same value in a non-indexed field. For that, just change the field in the **Filter** box, as shown in *Figure 8.4*:

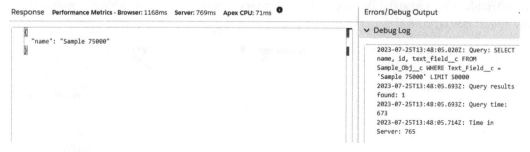

Figure 8.4 – An overview of a DataRaptor extract: a query on a non-indexed field

Let's run this query by switching to the **Preview** mode. The DataRaptor now runs almost two times slower, returning the same row, but it takes 765ms this time since we were searching in a non-indexed field:

Response **Performance Metrics - Browser:** 1168ms **Server:** 769ms **Apex CPU:** 71ms

```
{
    "name": "Sample 75000"
}
```

Errors/Debug Output

∨ Debug Log

```
2023-07-25T13:48:05.020Z: Query: SELECT
name, id, text_field__c FROM
Sample_Obj__c WHERE Text_Field__c =
'Sample 75000' LIMIT 50000
2023-07-25T13:48:05.693Z: Query results
found: 1
2023-07-25T13:48:05.693Z: Query time:
673
2023-07-25T13:48:05.714Z: Time in
Server: 765
```

Figure 8.5 – An overview of a non-indexed query on the test field run

Everything makes sense so far. Let's proceed by searching for a different value inside the same two fields, seeing what will happen when more results are returned. Let's update our DataRaptor to search for Test, which will return 5,000 result rows.

When searching on the indexed `Name` field, the query now takes 826ms (see *Figure 8.6*):

Figure 8.6 – An overview of a test run on the Name field with 5,000 results

Searching on a non-indexed `Text_Field__c` field takes 1,079ms. This time, while still taking longer, the search on a non-indexed field was only 1.3 times longer, a much smaller improvement compared to the nearly 2x better performance in our previous test, when only one row was returned:

Figure 8.7 – An overview of a test run on the Test field with 5,000 results

Finally, let's update the **Filter** expression in our DataRaptor (see *Figure 8.4*) one more time so that we can search for the `TestNonSelective` value in the `Name` field. In our test dataset, this returns 40,000 results. Here's what the DataRaptor **Preview** pane will look like when searching on an indexed `Name` field (see *Figure 8.8*):

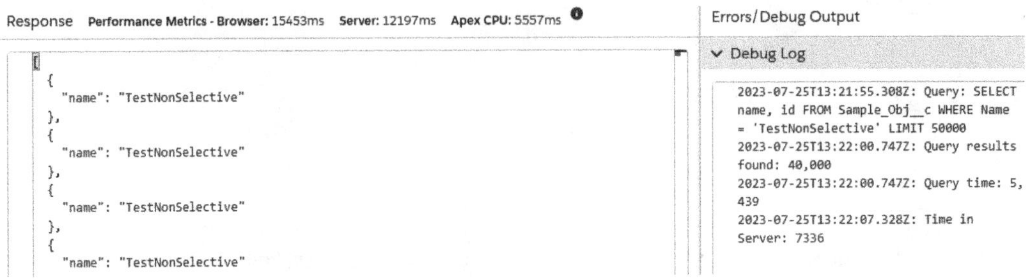

Figure 8.8 – An overview of a sample non-selective query on an indexed field

This time, the query is taking 7,336ms. Now, let's update the **Filter** expression in our DataRaptor one last time and search the same value of `TestNonSelective`, but this time, the search is on a non-indexed `Text_Field__c` field (see *Figure 8.9*):

Figure 8.9 – An overview of a sample query on a non-indexed field with 40,000 results

Wow! This time, the search on a non-indexed field was faster, taking 5,468ms, which is 1.3 times faster than searching for the same value on an indexed field. How is this possible?

As it turns out, in some cases, the queries are unable to leverage indexes, forcing the platform to scan all records in the object and check each to match the filter criteria. This is known as a **full table scan**. This kind of query, causing the system to perform a full table scan, is called **non-selective**.

Conversely, the queries allowing the platform to leverage indexes are called **selective**. Selective queries, in most cases, will perform better than non-selective ones. So, making the query selective would improve the performance and allow it to complete without timing out.

> **Note**
> If the field you need to use in a filter criterion is not indexed, and this is causing performance problems, consider marking it as `External ID` or contact Salesforce Support to create a custom index on that field.

How do we make sure that the platform uses an index for our query and avoids full table scans? Continue to the next section to find out.

Selective and non-selective queries

Two criteria determine if a query will be selective: the total number of records returned and the filter criteria in use. Let's take a closer look at this:

- The number of records returned from the query must not exceed the *selectivity threshold*, which is 10 percent of the total number of records in an object—up to a maximum of 333,333 records for a custom index or 1 million records for a standard index. Standard indexes are maintained on `Name`, `ID`, system datestamp fields, `CreatedById`, `RecordType`, Lookup fields, `Unique`, and `External ID` fields.

- The filter criteria—the `WHERE` clause of the SOQL query—needs to reference a field containing an index and avoid the use of `null` values, negative operators (` != `), wildcards, and text comparison. Using any of these in the `WHERE` clause may cause the system to not use an index.

> **Note**
>
> As we've seen earlier in this section, the same query that used to be selective may become non-selective as the data volume grows or when run in a different org. It is, therefore, extremely important to perform query profiling in a full sandbox containing a copy of all your real-life production data or in the production org itself.

In real life, though, when looking at a complex query that does not perform well, it may be difficult to say which indexes will be used. It may also be difficult to say which indexes might need to be added and what part of the filter criteria will need to be modified to make the query selective. So, how do we go about optimizing this type of query? The next section introduces a helpful tool.

Optimizing queries with the Query Plan tool

Salesforce makes it easy for us to see exactly how indexes will be used by a given query by providing us with the **Query Plan** tool. This tool is available in the Salesforce **Developer Console**. (You can also pass the `explain` parameter when sending a query via the Salesforce REST API to achieve a similar result.)

Let's use the **Query Plan** tool to see if we can get more insight into the behavior of the query we used at the beginning of this section. (More info on the **Query Plan** tool is available at `https://help.salesforce.com/s/articleView?id=000386864&type=1`.)

Begin by enabling the **Query Plan** tool by going to **Help** > **Preferences** in the **Developer Console**. Then, set the **Enable Query Plan** setting to `true` (see *Figure 8.10*):

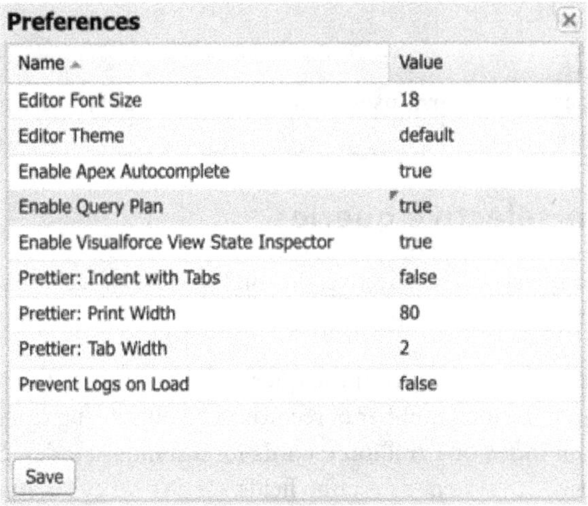

Preferences	✕
Name ▲	**Value**
Editor Font Size	18
Editor Theme	default
Enable Apex Autocomplete	true
Enable Query Plan	true
Enable Visualforce View State Inspector	true
Prettier: Indent with Tabs	false
Prettier: Print Width	80
Prettier: Tab Width	2
Prevent Logs on Load	false

Save

Figure 8.10 – An overview of enabling the Query Plan tool

Once enabled, you will see the **Query Plan** button next to the **Execute** button in **Query Editor**:

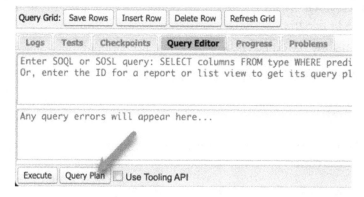

Figure 8.11 – An overview of the Query Plan button

Now, let's type in the first query we used:

```
SELECT name, id, text_field__c FROM Sample_Obj__c WHERE Name = 'Sample
7500' LIMIT 50000
```

When we click the **Query Plan** button, the dialog comes up showing three possible options that the platform would consider for executing our query:

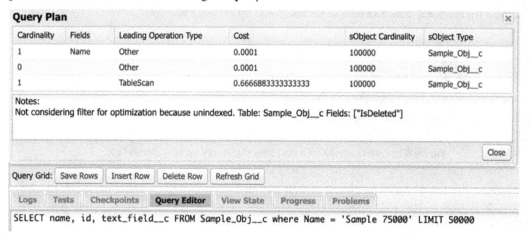

Figure 8.12 – An overview of the Query Plan dialog with details of the first test query

The columns in the table shown in *Figure 8.12* are as follows:

- **Cardinality**: This shows the estimated number of result rows.
- **Leading Operation Type**: This is the operation that the platform will use to run the query. All options except for `TableScan` represent different types of indexes being used.

- **Cost**: This is the most important field showing the relative cost of each option. While the option with the lowest cost is usually selected by the platform, a value greater than 1 means that the query will not be selective.

- **sObject Cardinality**: This shows the estimated number of records in the object to be queried.

- **sObject Type**: This shows the name of the object to query.

The first option is expected to select one record using the platform's internal optimizations on the Name field. This option also shows a much lower internal cost than the full table scan (TableScan) option.

Now, let's look at the query plan of the last test where the query on the indexed field took longer than the one on a non-indexed field:

```
SELECT name, id, text_field__c FROM Sample_Obj__c where Name =
'TestNonSelective' LIMIT 50000
```

The corresponding **Query Plan** window is shown in *Figure 8.13*:

Query Plan

Cardinality	Fields	Leading Operation Type	Cost	sObject Cardinality	sObject Type
42000		TableScan	1.5766666666666667	100000	Sample_Obj__c
10000	Name	Other	1.5766666666666667	100000	Sample_Obj__c
0		Other	1.5766666666666667	100000	Sample_Obj__c

Notes:
Not considering filter for optimization because unindexed. Table: Sample_Obj__c Fields: ["IsDeleted"]

Close

Query Grid: Save Rows   Insert Row   Delete Row   Refresh Grid

Logs   Tests   Checkpoints   **Query Editor**   View State   Progress   Problems

```
SELECT name, id, text_field__c FROM Sample_Obj__c where Name = 'TestNonSelective' LIMIT 50000
```

Figure 8.13 – An overview of a non-selective query on an indexed field

We now see that the estimated number of records returned by the query or **Cardinality** value is 42,000 out of the 100,000 records we're about to query. The **Cost** value is above 1, and the **Leading Operation Type** value of TableScan confirms that the query is not selective.

Finally, let's see what happens when we use the negative operator in our WHERE clause. Let's change it in our first example where the query otherwise was performing at its best:

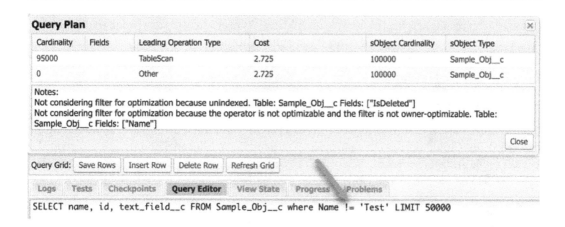

Figure 8.14 – An overview of the Query Plan tool showing the effect of using the negative operator

The **Notes** section now tells us that the *Not Equal* operator we used is not optimizable and, therefore, a table scan will be used. The cost of the query has also increased substantially, so it will most likely perform worse than the other query examples we tested.

Now, this is the end of the section. We saw why the Salesforce platform is not always able to leverage indexes, even when a query has performed well in the past and has not changed. We then learned about selective and non-selective queries and the factors that make our queries selective. Finally, we saw how to use the **Query Plan** tool to get insights and improve performance. These skills will come in handy for getting our extract DataRaptors to perform well now and continue to perform as our data volumes grow.

While looking at common query performance issues, let's look at another frequent source of database trouble that is known to slow down insert and update operations and cause record-locking issues. Continue to the next section to learn more.

Understanding data skew

If you are seeing update operations take a while and/or seeing UNABLE_TO_LOCK_ROW exceptions during inserts or updates, *data skew* issues could be the reason. **Data skew** is a database anti-pattern that occurs when a significant number of records are dependent on one single record. For instance, many Contacts are children of the same Account.

When a child record is then updated, the platform locks the parent to ensure data integrity during the update. Normally, this happens very fast and does not cause any issues. However, as data volumes grow, updating children of the same parent may become very slow and, when done in different threads, some of the updates may fail.

Salesforce recommends keeping the number of child records related to the same parent under 10,000 to avoid performance and locking issues. So, if you must relate many child records to the same parent, create additional parents to keep the number of children under 10,000. You may also want to keep an eye on old records and delete them so that they're not contributing to data skew.

Now, what will happen if you do have more than 10,000 children? Let's look at an example to find out.

I set up a simple object called **Test Object** to act as a parent in our test. I then created another simple object called **Test Child**, which is our child object. I then loaded 50,000 **Test Child** records and pointed them to a single **Test Object** record. I also added a `Total_Cost__c` custom object—the `Roll-up Summary` field on the parent **Test Object** object, summarizing values from all its children:

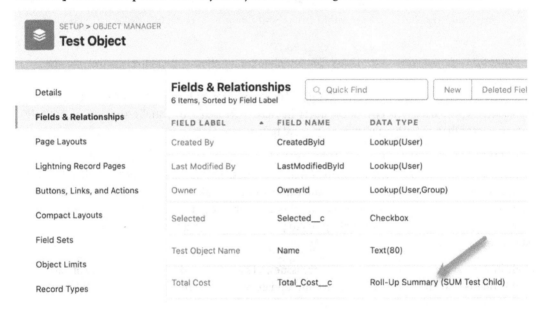

Figure 8.15 – An overview of a Test Object object for creating data skew

Each of the **Test Child** records also contains a sequential index value, making it easy to select and process our test records in batches.

After that, I created `SampleHelper`, a simple Apex class that updates batches of **Test Child** records by incrementing the **Cost** value. Here is the code for the class:

```
public class SampleHelper {
    @future
    public static void updateCost(
        Integer startIndex,
        Integer endIndex
    ) {
```

```
List<Test_Child__c> children = [
    select Cost__c
    from Test_Child__c
    where Index__c >= :startIndex and Index__c < :endIndex
];
for (Test_Child__c t : children){
    t.Cost__c += 1;
}
update children;
    }
}
```

Then, I fired off five concurrent threads of our `SampleHelper` class, each updating 1,000 records using **Execute Anonymous Window** in the **Developer Console**:

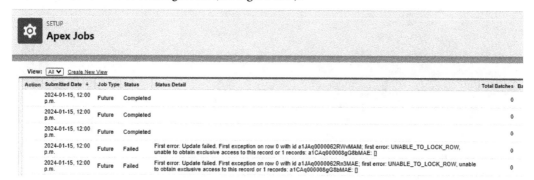

Figure 8.16 – An overview of initiating concurrent record updates

After several tests, I see that the first 3 to 4 batches of 1,000 records update successfully and the last 1 to 2 batches fail due to locking issues (see *Figure 8.17*):

Action	Submitted Date ↓	Job Type	Status	Status Detail	Total Batches	Ba
	2024-01-15, 12:00 p.m.	Future	Completed		0	
	2024-01-15, 12:00 p.m.	Future	Completed		0	
	2024-01-15, 12:00 p.m.	Future	Completed		0	
	2024-01-15, 12:00 p.m.	Future	Failed	First error: Update failed. First exception on row 0 with id a1JAq0000062RWvMAM; first error: UNABLE_TO_LOCK_ROW, unable to obtain exclusive access to this record or 1 records: a1CAq000008gG8bMAE: []	0	
	2024-01-15, 12:00 p.m.	Future	Failed	First error: Update failed. First exception on row 0 with id a1JAq0000062Rn3MAE; first error: UNABLE_TO_LOCK_ROW, unable to obtain exclusive access to this record or 1 records: a1CAq000008gG8bMAE: []	0	

Figure 8.17 – An overview of the results of concurrent record updates

As you see, the recommended maximum of 10,000 child records is not a breaking point. You may be able to get away with a much higher number of records linking up to the same parent without seeing locking or performance issues.

And that is it on data skew. We've seen what it is, when it could happen, and how it affects our apps. This knowledge should help us plan your data model and your logic to avoid record locking and performance issues caused by data skew. This also brings us to the end of the chapter.

Summary

We've just completed our dive into the realm of Salesforce and OmniStudio data issues, looking at common causes of non-selective queries and data skew. We now know why the same DataRaptor may perform differently depending on the data. We saw how Salesforce differs from traditional databases and why its indexes are not always used. We then saw how to use the **Query Plan** tool to keep our queries selective, staying clear of full table scans as much as possible to allow us to keep our queries and our DataRaptors performing at their best—even when our data volumes are growing.

We then looked at data skew issues, locking and performance issues they may cause, and how to avoid them.

In the next chapter, we will look at other causes of sub-standard performance in OmniStudio DataRaptors and Integration Procedures and the best ways to resolve them.

9
Improving the Performance of the Service Layer

In this chapter, we will look at quick, sure-fire ways to spot and improve sub-standard performance in the OmniStudio Service Layer: Integration Procedures and DataRaptors. While at it, we will also explore the limits and the most suitable times to apply each of these best practices.

This chapter also introduces an important approach to optimizing Salesforce Industries solutions by showing you how to test, compare alternatives, and make decisions about your app architecture based on hard numbers. There's no shortage of best practices, and I'm sure that, while working on your OmniStudio projects, you will come up with your own best practices and design patterns as well. Each one of these has its own area of application. While in some scenarios the same best practice may bring massive performance improvements, in other scenarios, it may not perform as well or even be not worth applying.

The good news here is, as we've seen before, OmniStudio makes it easy to measure the performance of its components. (Please refer to *Chapter 3, Evaluating the Performance of an OmniStudio Implementation*, and *Chapter 4, An Introduction to Load Testing*, if you need a refresher on measuring performance and load testing.)

In this chapter, we will cover the following topics:

- Comparing standalone DataRaptors and Remote Actions with those running inside Integration Procedures, looking at their performance and the best areas of application

- Learning how to speed up our Extract DataRaptors by using relationship notation

- Looking at the effect that trimming the response JSON can have on our Integration Procedure and DataRaptor performance

- Comparing Turbo Extract and regular Extract DataRaptors in terms of performance and areas of application

This will be a fun chapter packed with easy-to-follow step-by-step examples. Let's begin by looking at DataRaptors and Remote Actions and compare their performance when running on the client side as part of an OmniScript or a FlexCard and when running on the server as part of the Integration Procedure.

Technical requirements

To follow along with this chapter, you will need access to an OmniStudio installation. If you don't have one handy, you can always request your free trial development environment from the Salesforce Developers site, which is (at the time of this writing) available at `https://developer.salesforce.com/free-trials`. Once on the site, head over to **Industry-Based Trials** and get yourself a trial org for the industry of your choice.

Client or server side?

Standalone DataRaptors run on the client side, while Integration Procedures and DataRaptors run as Integration Procedure Actions run on the server. Due to this, the latter ones should run faster. Virtually every OmniStudio developer knows that. But the real question is, how much faster?

Suppose you have two DataRaptors that you need to call from an OmniScript. Is it worth creating an Integration Procedure and calling your DataRaptors from there so that they run on the server? And if so, when? Let's walk through a simple example to find out.

DataRaptors or an Integration Procedure?

I've created a simple OmniScript that calls two Extract DataRaptors before its first step (see *Figure 9.1*):

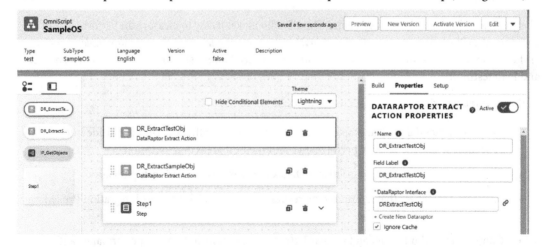

Figure 9.1 – An overview of a sample OmniScript with two DataRaptor Extract Actions

Both DataRaptors perform a simple extract. Here's the first DataRaptor:

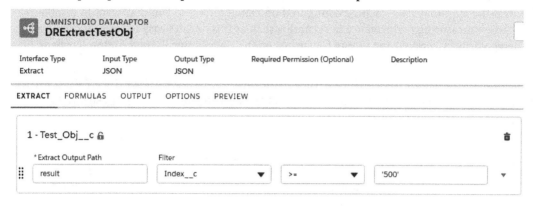

Figure 9.2 – An overview of the first sample DataRaptor

And here's the second:

Figure 9.3 – An overview of the second sample DataRaptor

I enabled time tracking in our sample OmniScript (see *Chapter 3, Evaluating the Performance of an OmniStudio Implementation,* for more information on how to enable time tracking; remember that OmniScript, DataRaptor, and Integration Procedure time-tracking measurements are expressed in ms or milliseconds.

> **Note**
>
> Real-life apps may have caching configured on DataRaptors, so you may want to disable it when measuring performance in scenarios such as this one. It's easy to turn off caching temporarily by checking the **Ignore Cache** box on the **DataRaptor Extract Action** screen or in the DataRaptor **Preview** pane.

When OmniScript runs, the first DataRaptor takes 771ms, and the second one takes 502ms. Refer to the following screenshot:

```
▼ vlcTimeTracking:  Object
    OmniScriptSessionToken:  "4f715e77-52a6-4be9-9a37-b74bce657162"
    DR_ExtractTestObj: 771
    DR_ExtractSampleObj: 502
  ► testObjects:  Array[500]
  ► sampleObjects:  Array[500]
```

Figure 9.4 – An overview of time-tracking values of the sample OmniScript

Now, let's create an Integration Procedure and call our DataRaptors from the DataRaptor Extract Actions inside it. Then, we'll call the Integration Procedure from our OmniScript. This will reduce server round-trips as both our DataRaptors will now run on the server. You can see the updated OmniScript in *Figure 9.5*:

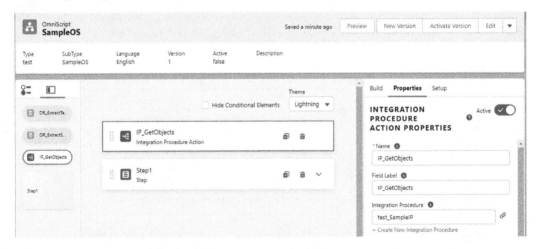

Figure 9.5 – An overview of a sample OmniScript with one Integration Procedure Action

And here's our new Integration Procedure calling our DataRaptors:

Figure 9.6 – An overview of a sample Integration Procedure for running DataRaptors

Now, let's call our OmniScript and see the time-tracking values for the new configuration:

```
▼ vlcTimeTracking:  Object
    OmniScriptSessionToken: "fa8a0801-7d06-49a5-9218-183cae236bb7"
    IP_GetObjects: 960
▼ result:  Object
  ► testObjs:  Array[500]
  ► sampleObjs:  Array[500]
```

Figure 9.7 – An overview of updated time-tracking values of the sample OmniScript

Our new Integration Procedure that includes both DataRaptors is taking 960ms, saving us 313ms or, in our case, achieving about 30% performance improvement.

> **Note**
>
> While testing real-life apps, you may consider turning off caching in Integration Procedures if that may interfere with your testing scenario, just like it would in this sample OmniScript.
>
> While it is easy to pass the `ignoreCache` parameter in the Integration Procedure **Preview** pane (see *Chapter 7, Understanding Caching*, for more information), to test an Integration Procedure called from an OmniScript without caching, we need to turn off **Scale Cache**. See the *Turn Off the Scale Cache* OmniStudio documentation page for steps to disable **Scale Cache** (`https://help.salesforce.com/s/articleView?id=sf.os_turn_off_the_scale_cache_55140.htm`).

So, is it worth running your DataRaptors on the server as part of an Integration Procedure? The answer here is, *it depends*. If your DataRaptors extract a handful of fields and do not have heavy transform logic, running them on the server may not produce a noticeable performance improvement (313ms in our case). But if you are extracting a lot of fields, you may want to repeat the simple test we just did on your own configuration and see the time saving for yourself.

If you don't really need an extra Integration Procedure, it's probably best not to create one—just to keep your system complexity lower and make your application easier to maintain. On the other hand, if any of your DataRaptors would benefit from running asynchronously in the background or could use a bigger set of governor limits, running them inside an Integration Procedure would make these options available. (See *Chapter 8*, *Non-Selective Queries and Data Skew*, for more information on async code execution.)

Now, what about Remote Actions? We use Remote Actions to call OmniStudio services and custom Apex classes, so their logic runs on the server. At the same time, each Remote Action call results in a round-trip to the server, so would it make sense to have our Remote Actions run on the server inside an Integration Procedure to avoid these round-trips? Let's walk through a simple example in the next section and do the comparison.

Integration Procedure or server calls

I've updated our sample OmniScript to run three separate Remote Actions followed by a call to a simple Integration Procedure that runs the same three Remote Actions on the server side (see *Figure 9.8*):

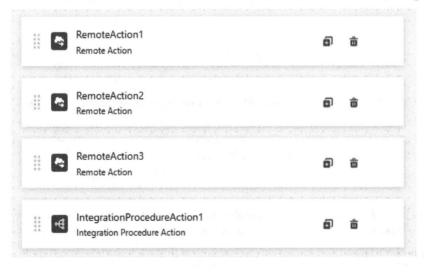

Figure 9.8 – An overview of Remote Actions added to sample OmniScript

Each of the Remote Action calls the same sample long-running calculation that we used in *Chapter 7, Understanding Caching* (see *Figure 9.9*):

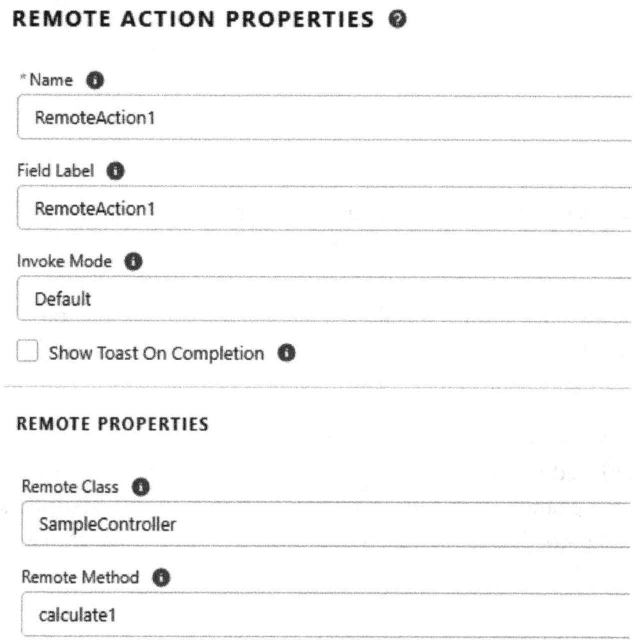

REMOTE ACTION PROPERTIES ❷

* Name ❶

RemoteAction1

Field Label ❶

RemoteAction1

Invoke Mode ❶

Default

☐ Show Toast On Completion ❶

REMOTE PROPERTIES

Remote Class ❶

SampleController

Remote Method ❶

calculate1

Figure 9.9 – An overview of our sample Remote Action properties

And here's our sample Integration Procedure, again, running the same three Remote Actions on the server side:

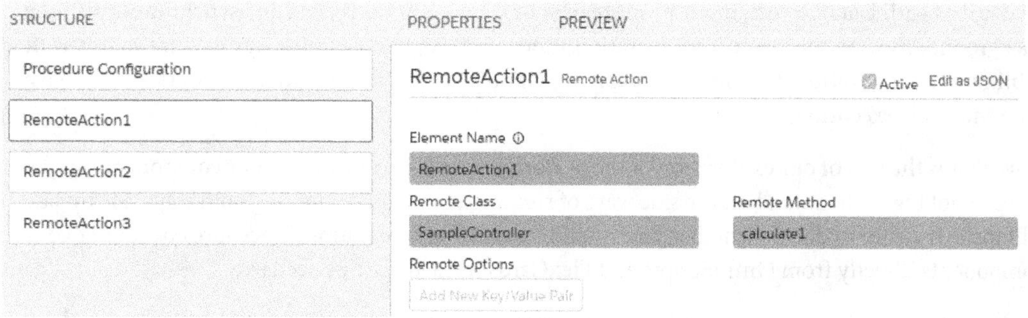

STRUCTURE	PROPERTIES PREVIEW
Procedure Configuration	RemoteAction1 Remote Action ☑ Active Edit as JSON
RemoteAction1	Element Name ⓘ
RemoteAction2	RemoteAction1
	Remote Class Remote Method
RemoteAction3	SampleController calculate1
	Remote Options
	Add New Key/Value Pair

Figure 9.10 – An overview of our sample Integration Procedure with Remote Actions

Running our OmniScript with time tracking on produces the following results:

```
▼ vlcTimeTracking:  Object
    OmniScriptSessionToken:  "48908cc3-60cd-4a63-843b-55a3ef51accf"
    RemoteAction1: 4540
    RemoteAction2: 4288
    RemoteAction3: 4312
    IntegrationProcedureAction1: 10054
  result: 124997.5
```

Figure 9.11 – An overview of time-tracking values for Remote Actions and Integration Procedure

While each Remote Action ran from the OmniScript takes about 4.3 seconds to complete (taking about 13 seconds altogether), the Integration Procedure running all 3 actions only takes about 10 seconds. So, this also results in a 30% improvement, an increase like the one we saw in the *DataRaptors or an Integration Procedure?* section, after moving DataRaptors inside an Integration Procedure.

However, this time, we witnessed a 10 times larger time saving of 3 seconds instead of 0.3 seconds (313ms), which we achieved in the previous section. Therefore, if that were a test conducted on a real OmniStudio app, the change we tested—moving our Remote Actions inside a new Integration Procedure—might well be worth considering. So, it's always best to run a simple test like the one we just did and see for yourself.

> **Note**
>
> Just as we saw in previous chapters, the data may significantly affect the performance. So, when testing to compare client- versus server-side execution times, it is best to do so on a full sandbox with a fresh complete copy of your live production data.

And just as with DataRaptors, if one or more of your Remote Actions can run asynchronously in the background, moving them into an Integration Procedure would be a quick way to achieve this with minimum configuration. (Again, see *Chapter 6*, *Options for Async Execution*, for options you have for async code execution.)

Now, that is the end of our exploration of the performance effects of running our components on the server. Looking at client- and server-side ways of running them and comparing both ways side by side will make it easier to decide whether you should be creating Integration Procedures or calling your components directly from OmniScripts and FlexCards in each specific scenario.

In the next section, let's look at a quick way to speed up some of your Extract DataRaptors and see how easy it is to measure the performance difference this best practice brings.

Comparing relationship notation and multiple extract steps

When working with dependent objects in your Extract DataRaptor, you may need to retrieve records from a parent along with the corresponding values from child objects. There are two ways of getting this done. First, you can extract records from the parent object and each of your child objects, just like you would with any multi-object extract. Second, you can also use a trick called **relationship notation**, which is the equivalent of traversing relationships in SOQL. Relationship notation allows DataRaptors to use child-to-parent relationship queries, traversing the object relationships defined in your Salesforce org.

> **Note**
>
> Only child-to-parent relationship queries are supported in DataRaptors and not parent-to-child relationship queries. See the *Relationship Queries* documentation page (https://developer.salesforce.com/docs/atlas.en-us.248.0.soql_sosl.meta/soql_sosl/sforce_api_calls_soql_relationships.htm) for more information on relationship queries in SOQL.

Let's look at both options and compare them in terms of performance. For this test, I have created a parent object called `Test_Type_c`. Then, it has a first-level child called `Test_SubType_c`, and then `Test_SubType_c`, in turn, has a child called `Test_Item_c`.

Using multiple extract steps

This would be a no-brainer option. We can just throw our objects on the **Extract** tab of a DataRaptor and connect them using **Filter** expressions. Here is how this may look in our test. We would begin by querying for the `Test_Item__c` object, our lowest-level child. We would then use the result to extract rows from its parent and then, finally, use that result to extract from our top-level parent (see *Figure 9.12*):

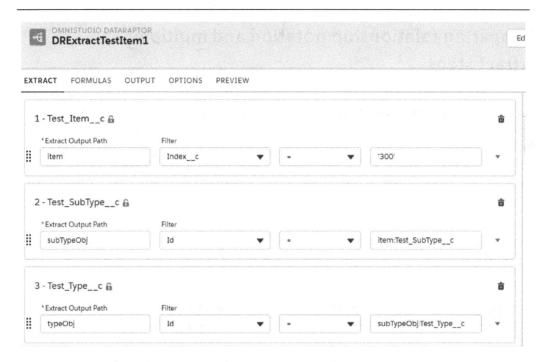

Figure 9.12 – An overview of the Extract tab of the DataRaptor using multiple extract steps

Then, on the **Output** tab, we would simply specify the fields we want. Let's say we want the **Amount** field from Test_Type_c, our top-level parent object, and the **Index** field from Test_Item_c, our lowest-level child:

OMNISTUDIO DATARAPTOR **DRExtractTestItem1**			
Interface Type	Input Type	Output Type	Required Permission (Optional)
Extract	JSON	JSON	

EXTRACT   FORMULAS   **OUTPUT**   OPTIONS   PREVIEW

EXTRACT JSON PATH 🔍	OUTPUT JSON PATH 🔍
item:Index__c	index
typeObj:Amount__c	amount

Figure 9.13 – An overview of the Output tab of the DataRaptor using multiple extract steps

When previewing the DataRaptor, we see 89ms of time spent on the server:

Response   **Performance Metrics - Browser:** 656ms   **Server:** 89ms   **Apex CPU:** 67ms ℹ

```
{
  "index": 300,
  "amount": 300
}
```

Figure 9.14 – An overview of the performance metrics of the DataRaptor using multiple extract steps

The **Debug Log** window shows that we're using three queries—first, extracting data from the child, then using the output to extract from the parent object, and then from the parent object's parent:

```
2024-01-24T12:53:45.734Z: Query: SELECT
test_subtype__c, index__c, id FROM Test_Item__c
WHERE Index__c = 300 LIMIT 50000
2024-01-24T12:53:45.751Z: Query results found: 1
2024-01-24T12:53:45.752Z: Query time: 18
2024-01-24T12:53:45.755Z: Query: SELECT id,
test_type__c FROM Test_SubType__c WHERE Id =
'a1dAq000004agpdIAA' LIMIT 50000
2024-01-24T12:53:45.762Z: Query results found: 1
2024-01-24T12:53:45.762Z: Query time: 7
2024-01-24T12:53:45.763Z: Query: SELECT amount__c,
id FROM Test_Type__c WHERE Id =
'a1LAq000000VLY1MAO' LIMIT 50000
2024-01-24T12:53:45.769Z: Query results found: 1
2024-01-24T12:53:45.769Z: Query time: 6
2024-01-24T12:53:45.772Z: Time in Server: 84
```

Figure 9.15 – An overview of the debug log of the DataRaptor using multiple extract steps

Now, let's try extracting this information in another way.

Using relationship notation

What if we could accomplish the same task using just one query? We should be able to do that because we can extract the Account information along with Contact records in the following familiar query:

```
SELECT Id, Name, Account.Name FROM Contact
```

Let's create a new DataRaptor and begin by adding just one query on the **Extract** tab—that is, querying our lowest-level child:

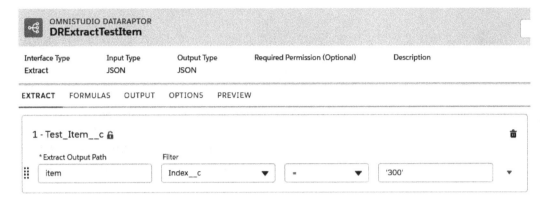

Figure 9.16 – An overview of the Extract tab of the DataRaptor using relationship notation

Then, on the **Output** tab, we could use the same relationship query syntax as in the SOQL query. We will start with our lowest-level `Test_Item__c` object and extract the value from our top-level object, `Test_SubType__r.Test_Type__r.Amount__c` (see *Figure 9.17*):

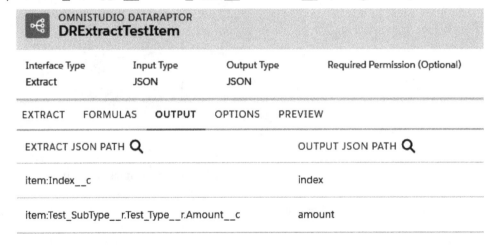

Figure 9.17 – An overview of the Output tab of the DataRaptor using relationship notation

This time, when previewing the DataRaptor, we see a server time of 65ms:

Response   **Performance Metrics - Browser:** 407ms   **Server:** 65ms   **Apex CPU:** 54ms ⓘ

```
{
    "index": 300,
    "amount": 300
}
```

Figure 9.18 – An overview of the performance metrics of the DataRaptor using relationship notation

This also makes complete sense after looking at the **Debug Log** window, as this time, the DataRaptor only uses one query to retrieve our values:

```
2024-01-24T12:54:04.087Z: Query: SELECT
test_subtype__r.test_type__r.amount__c, index__c,
id FROM Test_Item__c WHERE Index__c = 300 LIMIT
50000
2024-01-24T12:54:04.107Z: Query results found: 1
2024-01-24T12:54:04.107Z: Query time: 20
2024-01-24T12:54:04.109Z: Time in Server: 60
```

Figure 9.19 – An overview of the debug log of the DataRaptor using relationship notation

The use of relationship notation allowed our new DataRaptor to extract the same information as our old DataRaptor 37% faster. It has accomplished this with just one query instead of three, which may run even faster in real-life database scenarios.

> **Note**
>
> While many times the use of relationship notation improves performance, this is not always the case. Sometimes, the resulting query may become non-selective. This may happen immediately or over time as data volumes grow—especially when using custom objects. This is why it is always a good idea to test your application with life-like data (or, better yet, a copy of your production data). See *Chapter 8, Non-Selective Queries and Data Skew*, for more information on non-selective queries and query optimization.

And that was it for our quick dive into the use of relationship notation in our Extract DataRaptors. We've seen how to use it to reduce the number of internal queries our DataRaptors use and boost performance,

In the next section, we will look at a seemingly unimportant configuration that may surprise us by offering a sizable performance improvement.

Boosting performance by trimming the response JSON

While adding an extra result field to a query or an extra response node to an Integration Procedure JSON may seem insignificant, let's see how this may affect performance. Let's see whether we should pay attention to this small thing or not. Let's start with DataRaptors and see the exact performance impact that reducing the number of response fields may have.

DataRaptors

Let's compare two DataRaptors that extract the same data from the same object but return a different number of fields. Here's a sample OmniScript with two **DataRaptor Extract Action** elements:

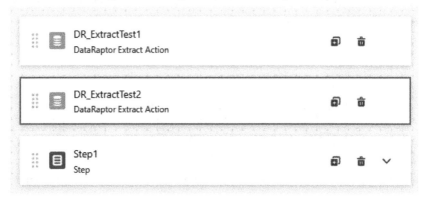

Figure 9.20 – An overview of our test OmniScript with two DataRaptors

Both DataRaptors retrieve a single record from the `Test_Obj__c` object, but the first one retrieves and returns more fields than the second. Both DataRaptors have the same filter criteria and extract the same amount of data but use different records to visually differentiate the results.

Here's how the first DataRaptor's **Extract** tab looks:

Figure 9.21 – An overview of the Extract tab of the test DataRaptor with 10 fields

And here's its **Output** tab:

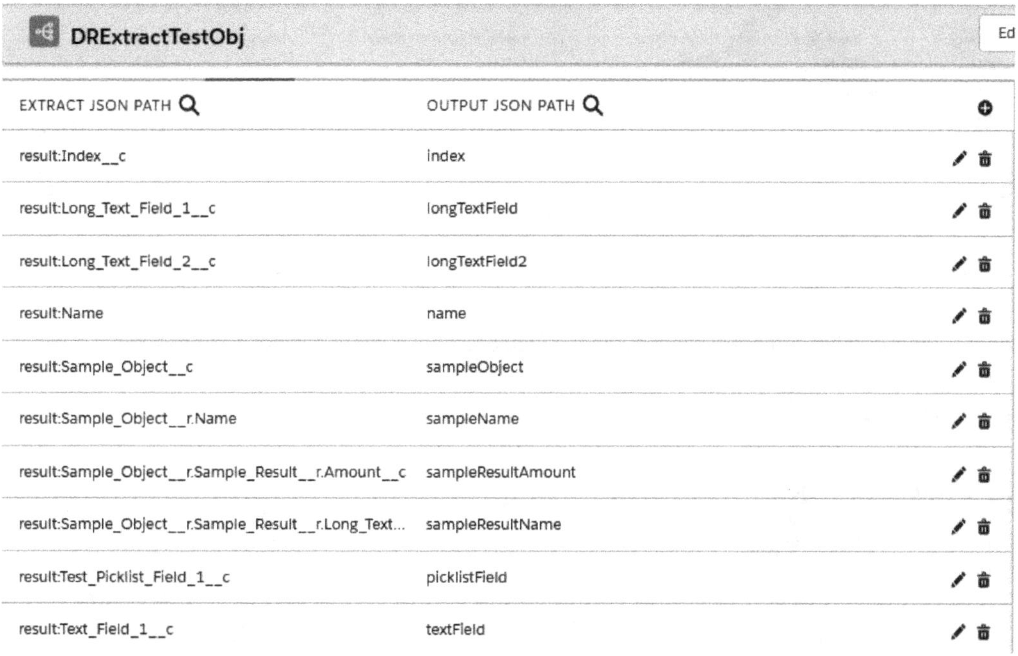

EXTRACT JSON PATH 🔍	OUTPUT JSON PATH 🔍	➕
result:Index__c	index	✏️ 🗑️
result:Long_Text_Field_1__c	longTextField	✏️ 🗑️
result:Long_Text_Field_2__c	longTextField2	✏️ 🗑️
result:Name	name	✏️ 🗑️
result:Sample_Object__c	sampleObject	✏️ 🗑️
result:Sample_Object__r.Name	sampleName	✏️ 🗑️
result:Sample_Object__r.Sample_Result__r.Amount__c	sampleResultAmount	✏️ 🗑️
result:Sample_Object__r.Sample_Result__r.Long_Text...	sampleResultName	✏️ 🗑️
result:Test_Picklist_Field_1__c	picklistField	✏️ 🗑️
result:Text_Field_1__c	textField	✏️ 🗑️

DRExtractTestObj   Ed

Figure 9.22 – An overview of the Output tab of the test DataRaptor with 10 fields

When previewing the DataRaptor, it produces the following query:

```
2023-08-16T07:54:53.726Z: Query: SELECT
sample_object__c, text_field_1__c,
sample_object__r.sample_result__r.long_text_field__c,
 index__c, name, sample_object__r.name, id,
long_text_field_2__c, test_picklist_field_1__c,
long_text_field_1__c,
sample_object__r.sample_result__r.amount__c FROM
Test_Obj__c WHERE Index__c = 500 LIMIT 50000
```

Figure 9.23 – An overview of the debug log of the test DataRaptor with 10 fields

On the other hand, the second DataRaptor only retrieves and returns two fields. Here's what its **Extract** tab looks like:

Figure 9.24 – An overview of the Extract tab of the test DataRaptor with two fields

And here's the **Output** tab:

OMNISTUDIO DATARAPTOR
DRExtractTestObject1

Interface Type	Input Type	Output Type	Required Permission (Optional)	Description
Extract	JSON	JSON		

EXTRACT   FORMULAS   **OUTPUT**   OPTIONS   PREVIEW

EXTRACT JSON PATH Q	OUTPUT JSON PATH Q	
result:Index__c	index	✏ 🗑
result:Sample_Object__r.Sample_Result__r.Amount__c	sampleResultAmount	✏ 🗑

Figure 9.25 – An overview of the Output tab of the test DataRaptor with two fields

When previewing the second DataRaptor, it produces a much simpler query, as seen in the following screenshot:

```
2023-08-16T06:56:35.545Z: Query: SELECT index__c, id,
 sample_object__r.sample_result__r.amount__c FROM
 Test_Obj__c WHERE Index__c = 300 LIMIT 50000
```

Figure 9.26 – An overview of the debug log of the test DataRaptor with two fields

Now, let's run our OmniScript with time tracking turned on and see how long each of the two DataRaptors takes to extract the data. In our test, the first DataRaptor took 860ms while the second one was almost 3 times faster, taking a mere 361ms. You can also see that the amount of data returned from the first and the second DataRaptor is different (see *Figure 9.27*):

```
▼ vlcTimeTracking:   Object
    OmniScriptSessionToken: "abb03f1b-6cf2-4ab5-bc63-0fa4465166a6"
    DR_ExtractTest1: 860
    DR_ExtractTest2: 361
▼ sampleObj:   Object
    textField: "Test 500"
    sampleObject: "a1EAq000000SphHMAS"
    longTextField2: "Lorem ipsum dolor sit amet, consectetur adipiscing elit,
    picklistField: "Value 1"
    index: 500
    name: "Test 500"
    sampleResultAmount: 1000.5
    sampleResultName: "Lorem ipsum dolor sit amet, consectetur adipiscing elit
    longTextField: "Lorem ipsum dolor sit amet, consectetur adipiscing elit, s
    sampleName: "Sample 10"
▼ sampleObj1:   Object
    index: 300
    sampleResultAmount: 1000.5
```

Figure 9.27 – An overview of the time-tracking output of the test OmniScript

This may seem counterintuitive as we might expect most of the time would be spent on database operations. However, the numbers don't lie, and removing unnecessary fields from your DataRaptors output does have a tangible impact on performance. So, it's always best to only return the fields you really need.

> **Note on updating DataRaptors**
>
> Please remember that, unlike Integration Procedures and OmniScripts, DataRaptors, in most OmniStudio installations, do not have internal version support, so there's no easy out-of-the-box way to undo changes. It may also be difficult to see the changes made to a DataRaptor at a glance.
>
> Source control systems come to the rescue, making it easy to visually compare serialized DataRaptor JSON files (see *Chapter 5, Tracking Code Changes and Deployment,* for more information), so remember to commit your OmniStudio components to source control.
>
> A DataRaptor may be used by multiple OmniScripts, Integration Procedures, and FlexCards. So, modifying them in one place can easily break other components where this DataRaptor may be used. When all your OmniStudio components are checked into a source control system, you can search for references to the DataRaptor you are about to modify and assess the impact before making the changes. If not sure, consider cloning a DataRaptor and making your changes to the cloned copy so that existing components' functionality will not be affected.

In the next section, let's see how much of an impact removing unneeded JSON nodes would have on an Integration Procedure.

Integration Procedures

Very often, developers choose to return all JSON nodes produced by all the steps in the Integration Procedure. They do it just in case a data element might be needed and so that they don't have to decide which part of the data to return. Besides, this doesn't cause any additional external service or database calls, so they leave the **Return Full Data JSON** box checked on their Integration Procedure's Response Action (see *Figure 9.28*):

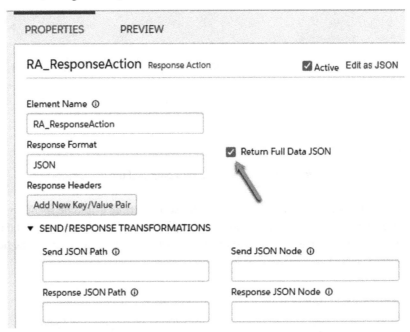

Figure 9.28 – An overview of the Return Full Data JSON checkbox in an Integration Procedure

Let's test and see how much of an impact leaving this box checked may have on performance.

Here's a simple OmniScript with one Integration Procedure Action that calls our sample Integration Procedure:

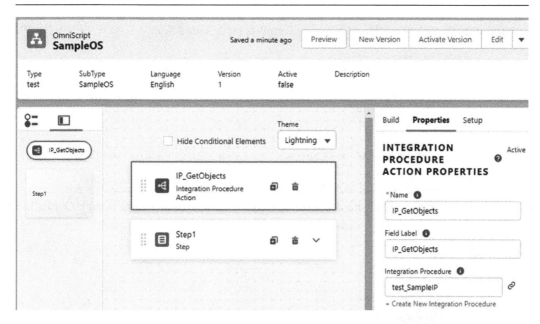

Figure 9.29 – An overview of our sample OmniScript for testing Integration Procedure

The sample Integration Procedure we're calling contains three DataRaptors. The first two—DR_ExtractTestObjects and DR_ExtractSampleObjects—return 500 records each from our test custom object. And the DR_extractAccount DataRaptor only returns one Account record with one related Contact.

Let's leave the **Return Full Data JSON** box checked on the Response Action and run our OmniScript with time tracking turned on (see *Figure 9.30*):

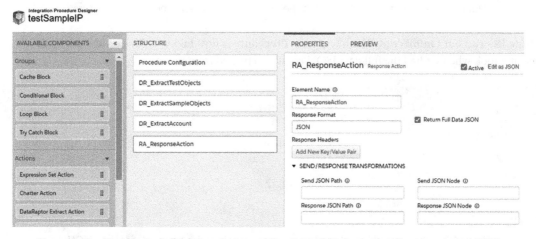

Figure 9.30 – An overview of our sample Integration Procedure for testing the trimming of JSON

Our Integration Procedure is taking 1,576ms to complete (see *Figure 9.31*):

```
▼ vlcTimeTracking:  Object
    OmniScriptSessionToken: "2b19ab21-c58c-482a-8c0b-138eb1fe5654"
    IP_GetObjects: 1576
▼ result:  Object
    RA_ResponseActionStatus: true
```

Figure 9.31 – An overview of the Integration Procedure timing returning full data JSON

Now, let's uncheck the **Return Full Data JSON** checkbox and have our Integration Procedure only return the subset of data we really need. We can specify the node to return in the **Send JSON Path** field (see *Figure 9.32*):

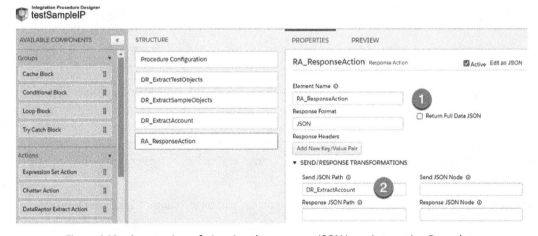

Figure 9.32 – An overview of trimming the response JSON in an Integration Procedure

Now, let's run our OmniScript. The Integration Procedure is now taking 768ms or less than half of what it took when we had the full data JSON content returned from it:

```
▼ vlcTimeTracking:  Object
    OmniScriptSessionToken: "f07eabe1-88d8-4bae-ab97-2336fabe2747"
    IP Get Objects: 768
▼ result:  Object
  ▼ contact:  Object
      email: "johnsmith@test.com"
      description: "Lorem ipsum dolor sit amet, consectetur adipiscing elit
      name: "John Smith"
```

Figure 9.33 – An overview of Integration Procedure timing with trimmed response JSON

Why did trimming the response JSON have this kind of effect on performance? Why does it not spare any database or API calls and make our DataRaptors run any faster? It's hard to tell, and the reason here is far less important than the performance metrics we just received. And they show that this quick configuration change is well worth making virtually every time.

Now, this is the end of our review of how excluding unnecessary fields from DataRaptors may produce tangible performance improvements easily and how trimming the response JSON may produce even greater time saving to our runtime bottom line.

In the next section, let's turn the tables and look at the best practice that too many developers, managers, and architects are often too eager to use—sometimes without reaping the benefits they expect.

How fast the Turbo Extract DataRaptor really is

In this section, let's compare the Turbo Extract DataRaptor with the regular Extract type DataRaptor. **Turbo Extract** places some limitations on functionality in exchange for offering better performance. Let's put it to the test to see how much of a performance improvement we can expect and when it's best to use it in our applications.

Let's use the same sample object we used earlier in this chapter. It has 4 custom fields and 1,000 test records. Let's create a regular **Extract**-type DataRaptor and a **Turbo Extract**-type DataRaptor and use them to retrieve the same set of data. We will search on indexed and non-indexed fields to rule out the query performance factors.

Here's the regular **Extract** DataRaptor, filtering on an indexed Id field:

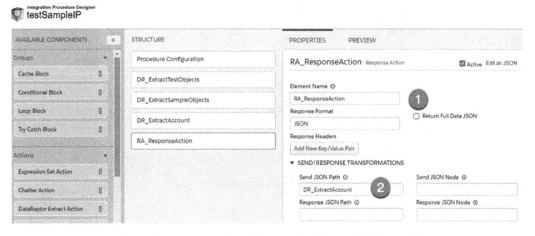

Figure 9.34 – An overview of Extract DataRaptor filtering on Id

And here's the **Output** tab showing the four fields we're going to select:

EXTRACT	FORMULAS	**OUTPUT**	OPTIONS	PREVIEW

EXTRACT JSON PATH 🔍	OUTPUT JSON PATH 🔍	➕
result:Index__c	index	✏️ 🗑️
result:Long_Text_Field_1__c	longTextField	✏️ 🗑️
result:Test_Picklist_Field_1__c	picklistField	✏️ 🗑️
result:Text_Field_1__c	field1	✏️ 🗑️

Figure 9.35 – An overview of the Output tab of the Extract DataRaptor

Now, here's the matching **Turbo Extract** DataRaptor selecting the same object, filtering on the same field with the same criteria:

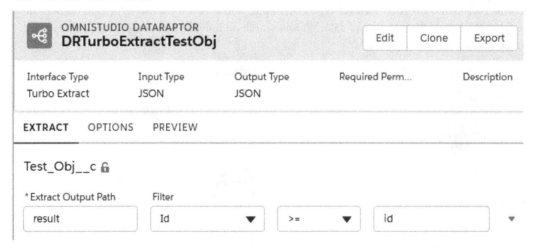

Figure 9.36 – An overview of the Turbo Extract DataRaptor filtering on Id

We're selecting the same four fields as output:

Figure 9.37 – An overview of the output fields of the Turbo Extract DataRaptor

When running both DataRaptors side by side in the **Preview** mode, the regular **Extract** DataRaptor shows a server time of 384ms. The **Turbo Extract** DataRaptor shows a server time of 300ms, performing 28% faster than our regular DataRaptor in this test.

Now, let's do one more extract, this time on a non-indexed *number* field to rule out the impact that query performance may be having on our test. Let's change the field we use in the **Filter** expression in both our DataRaptors (see *Figure 9.38*):

Figure 9.38 – An overview of the updated filter criteria in DataRaptor

This time, the regular **Extract** DataRaptor shows a server time of 374ms and the **Turbo Extract** DataRaptor shows a server time of 296ms, performing 26% faster than our regular DataRaptor in this test.

> **Note**
>
> A search on an indexed field is generally faster than one on a non-indexed field. However, in our case, the query on a non-indexed field returned faster. This could be because the `Index__c` field type is a *number* as opposed to the Salesforce `Id` field, which contains an ID string. Alternatively, it could be because of how the platform was able to apply its internal optimizations in this specific query. Whatever the case might be, this shows how important the data and specific testing scenarios may be for measuring the performance of an OmniStudio app.

As you can see, while the performance improvement offered by the Turbo Extract DataRaptor is tangible, it is not huge and may not be sufficient to justify changes in the architecture. For instance, if you need to extract from two objects or use a formula, the traditional DataRaptor may be a better alternative. But when you need to quickly pull a few fields from a single object, using a Turbo Extract DataRaptor may be a better option for you in that specific case.

> **Note**
>
> We have performed more testing to compare the Turbo Extract and regular Extract DataRaptors. You can go to this book's companion site at `https://maximumvlocity.com/` to see the details as well as other best practice reviews and OmniStudio tips.

And that is the end of our side-by-side comparison of Turbo Extract and regular Extract DataRaptors. We saw a number of performance improvements offered by the Turbo Extract version. That should give us a solid foundation to base our decisions on whether to use them in each specific scenario. This also brings us to the end of our review of the best practices for improving the performance of the Service Layer of OmniStudio applications.

Summary

Well, that's a wrap. I hope you had fun with our new superpower—the ability to use OmniStudio performance metrics to see the exact impact that a best practice may have in the specific case of your application. This unlocks an entirely new level of understanding and makes optimizing your Salesforce Industries solutions more effective and rewarding.

In the chapter, we also looked at some valuable best practices that could make our Service Layer OmniStudio components faster. We looked at scenarios when running our DataRaptors and Remote Actions inside Integration Procedures may bring tangible benefits. Next, we explored how to speed up our Extract DataRaptors by using relationship notation and saw the unexpectedly large impact that trimming the response JSON can have on our Integration Procedure and DataRaptor performance. Finally, we turned the tables and looked at scenarios when using Turbo Extract DataRaptors may not bring the kind of benefits one may expect from them.

These best practices should improve the performance of your applications. More importantly, though, while testing them and measuring the performance improvements, we learned valuable skills. I hope you will continue to put these best practices to the test in your quest for the ultimate OmniStudio application performance. Remember to always be testing at every step. Set up your test scenarios, test, and make decisions based on numbers and not expectations.

In the next chapter, we will look at best practices for better performance of the OmniStudio Presentation Layer and measure the performance improvement that each of these practices may bring.

10

Improving the Performance of the Presentation Layer

In this chapter, we will be looking at the ways to spot and improve substandard performance in the OmniStudio Presentation Layer, regarding OmniScripts and FlexCards. While investigating this, let's explore the impact that some of the recommended Presentation Layer best practices may have on our applications.

You will learn the following topics in this chapter:

- What kind of impact do formulas in OmniScripts have on their performance and how should you measure this impact?
- Should you be avoiding the use of conditional views in your OmniScripts because of performance considerations?
- What is the performance impact of the merge fields in OmniScripts?
- How should you measure the performance of the FlexCards and UI-rich OmniScripts?
- What can you do when your client-side document generation is slow?

Let's begin by reviewing the impact that some of the recommended OmniScript best practices may have on OmniScript performance and how we can go about measuring it.

Technical requirements

To follow along with this chapter, you will need access to an OmniStudio installation. If you don't have one handy, you can always request your free trial development environment from the Salesforce Developers site, which is (at the time of this writing) available at `https://developer.salesforce.com/free-trials`. Once on the site, head over to the **Industry-Based Trials** section and get yourself a trial org for the industry of your choice.

Performance impact of OmniScript best practices

Just as we did in previous chapters, let's review some of the OmniScript best practices and measure their performance impact. If you look at the *Performance Factors* section of the *OmniScript Best Practices* page (`https://help.salesforce.com/s/articleView?id=sf.os_omniscript_best_practices.htm`), among the first recommendations is the suggestion to reduce formulas and merge fields and conditional views.

> **Note**
>
> Salesforce documentation also mentions that *PDFs larger than 250KB generate slowly. PDFs larger than 1MB can take several minutes to generate and sometimes time out.* For more information on other options for generating documents with OmniStudio, see the *Document generation options* section later in this chapter.

So, let's begin by looking at what kind of performance degradation we may expect by adding a lot of formulas to OmniScript. Let's test the performance impact and applicability of the **Reduce Formulas** OmniScript best practice.

Performance impact of formulas on OmniScripts

For this test, I created a simple OmniScript with two empty steps. I've used a simple formula that concatenates two substrings of a hardcoded word, resulting in the same word. Then, I placed my simple formula into the first step of a simple two-step OmniScript:

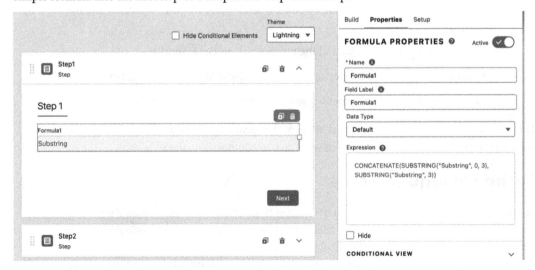

Figure 10.1 – An overview of the test formula in an OmniScript

> **Note**
>
> The formula we're looking at in this test is very simple. More complex formulas will take more time to execute, so you may want to follow the steps presented in this section to measure the performance impact that your formulas may be having on your application.

The documentation suggests that we can test an OmniScript's performance by enabling time tracking (see *Chapter 3, Evaluating the Performance of an OmniStudio Implementation*, for more information on how to enable time tracking in an OmniScript). Let's use OmniScript time tracking and see the performance impact of our formula.

> **OmniScript Time Tracking or the OmniStudio Tracking Service?**
>
> The **OmniStudio Tracking Service** is also an option for measuring the performance of OmniScript components. That is in addition to measuring the performance of other OmniStudio components that it can track. The time values captured by it would be the same as the values captured by the **OmniScript time tracking** feature.
>
> The difference is that OmniScript time tracking places the time values for all of the OmniScript steps neatly into the **Data JSON** on the OmniScript **Preview** UI, while the OmniStudio Tracking Service creates VlocityTrackingEntry__c records for each of the OmniScript steps.
>
> The OmniStudio Tracking Service is, therefore, a better fit for monitoring and error logging applications, while the OmniScript time tracking feature is a better fit for ad-hoc testing, such as the one we're conducting here (see *Chapter 3, Evaluating the Performance of an OmniStudio Implementation*, for more information on the OmniStudio Tracking Service).

After clicking on the **Preview** button in the OmniScript Designer interface, I had to step away from the desk for a moment. Then, I returned and clicked on the **Next** button. When I glanced at the vlcTimeTracking node, it was showing that our empty OmniScript step with just one simple formula took close to 60,000ms (ms, of course, stands for milliseconds) to load (see *Figure 10.2*):

Figure 10.2 – An overview of the initial OmniScript time tracking values

As we've just seen, the OmniScript time tracking (and the OmniStudio Tracking Service) measure the total time a user has spent on the step. So, in addition to the time the OmniScript took to run my formula, the **Step1** number also included the time the system was waiting for me to click on the **Next** button. How do we eliminate the idle time from the step timing?

Eliminating idle time from measured OmniScript step timings

To eliminate the idle time from our numbers, I've created a simple custom **Lightning Web Component** (**LWC**) that advances the OmniScript to the next step the moment it is rendered. The component extends `OmniscriptBaseMixin`—a standard component that we need to extend to create custom LWCs for use in OmniScripts. It includes methods to update data JSON, navigate between steps, and more (see the *OmniScriptBaseMixin* component documentation page for more information: `https://help.salesforce.com/s/articleView?id=sf.os_extend_the_omniscriptbasemixin_component_17717.htm`)

My simple custom LWC advances the OmniScript to the next step simply by calling the `omniNextStep()` method from its `renderedCallback()` function. Here's the full source of the component JavaScript controller:

```
import { LightningElement, api } from 'lwc';
import { OmniscriptBaseMixin } from
    "omnistudio/omniscriptBaseMixin";
export default class SampleElemCmp
    extends OmniscriptBaseMixin(LightningElement) {

    renderedCallback(){
        this.omniNextStep();
```

```
        }
    }
}
```

Then, I added my LWC at the end of **Step 1** and activated the OmniScript:

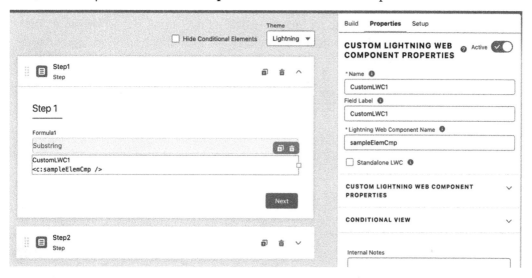

Figure 10.3 – An overview of an LWC for auto-advancing to the next step added to the OmniScript

> **Note**
>
> Just as we saw in *Chapter 2*, *A Sample Application*, when an OmniScript contains custom LWCs, we need to activate it before we can test the OmniScript with the **Preview** tool.

Now, as soon as I click the **Preview** button, the OmniScript immediately moves to **Step 2** and the **Data JSON** shows that **Step 1** of our OmniScript took 33ms (see *Figure 10.4*):

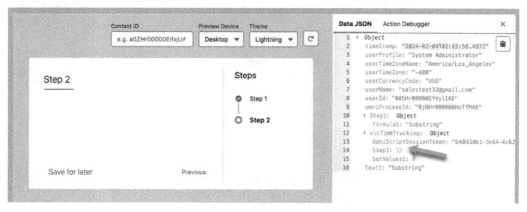

Figure 10.4 – Time tracking value for the single formula test

We're now able to skip the idle time and capture the time it took for the OmniScript to process our formula. Let's see what happens with the time as we add formulas.

Testing with multiple formulas

Now, let's clone our formula 10 times to see how this will affect the OmniScript performance. After cloning our formula 10 times, **Step 1** contains 10 formulas, and we notice that it takes 336ms to run in the **Preview** mode (see *Figure 10.5*):

```
▾ Step1:   Object
    Formula1: "Substring"
    Formula2: "Substring"
    Formula3: "Substring"
    Formula4: "Substring"
    Formula5: "Substring"
    Formula6: "Substring"
    Formula7: "Substring"
    Formula8: "Substring"
    Formula9: "Substring"
    Formula10: "Substring"
▾ vlcTimeTracking:   Object
    OmniScriptSessionToken: "dcf4c20f-5642-40e5-9c38-c96489c0b861"
    Step1: 336
```

Figure 10.5 – An overview of the screen showing the time tracking value for the 10-formula test

Predictably, 20 copies of our formula took 641ms (see *Figure 10.6*):

```
▾ Step1:   Object
    Formula1: "Substring"
    Formula2: "Substring"
    Formula3: "Substring"
    Formula4: "Substring"
    Formula5: "Substring"
    Formula6: "Substring"
    Formula7: "Substring"
    Formula8: "Substring"
    Formula9: "Substring"
    Formula10: "Substring"
    Formula11: "Substring"
    Formula12: "Substring"
    Formula13: "Substring"
    Formula14: "Substring"
    Formula15: "Substring"
    Formula16: "Substring"
    Formula17: "Substring"
    Formula18: "Substring"
    Formula19: "Substring"
    Formula20: "Substring"
▾ vlcTimeTracking:   Object
    OmniScriptSessionToken: "13c9060f-a347
    Step1: 641
```

Figure 10.6 – An overview of the screen showing the time tracking value for the 20-formula test

Now, this concludes our first OmniScript best practice performance evaluation, showing the impact of reducing the number of formulas. We've seen this best practice hold true, but we've also seen how fast the OmniScript formulas can be.

So, while using a lot of formulas will decrease the performance of an OmniScript, the amount of time taken by the formulas is also a very important number to consider. In our test, the simple OmniScript step with a lot of formulas still took less than a second to render. So, if those formulas were implementing the actual business logic, leaving them in place would be perfectly fine from the performance point of view.

We've also found a way to get the OmniScript time tracking feature (and the OmniStudio Tracking Service) to produce accurate performance numbers. This trick may become handy when you need to measure the impact of formulas in your specific OmniScript.

> **Note**
>
> Having a simple LWC advance the OmniScript to the next step only produces accurate step timing for internal OmniScript components, such as the formulas, conditional views, and merge fields described in this section. It will not work for the UI components that load asynchronously. See the *Measuring performance in the Presentation Layer* section later in this chapter for a discussion on the options for measuring the performance of interactive OmniScript components.

Now, let's continue to the next section, where we will be looking at the next OmniScript best practice—reducing conditional views—and the performance benefits it may offer.

Performance impact of conditional views in OmniScripts

Let's test the effect of **reducing conditional views** on OmniScript performance. For this test, I put together a simple OmniScript with three steps. The first step contains one text box. When the user enters a value into the box and advances to the next step, that value is used to control the visibility of the controls in the following step.

The second step contains 20 text boxes with conditional views (see *Figure 10.7*). It also contains the `SampleElemCmp` LWC we discussed in the previous section so that we can get our OmniScript to immediately advance to **Step 3**. In this way, we can get the time tracking feature to measure the loading time of our **Step 2**.

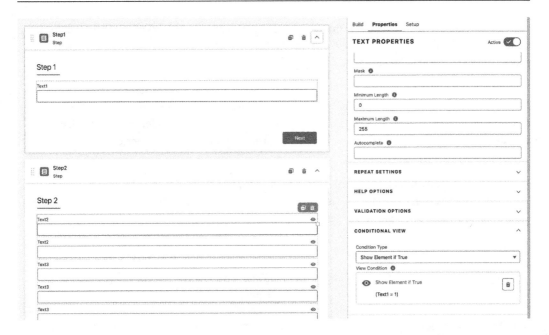

Figure 10.7 – An overview of a sample OmniScript for testing the performance impact of conditional views

After activating the OmniScript version and launching the **Preview** mode, I entered 1 in the text box in **Step 1** and clicked **Next**. In this test, our `vlcTimeTracking` node shows that our **Step 2** containing 20 conditional views (each applied to its own single text box) took 92ms to render (see *Figure 10.8*):

Figure 10.8 – An overview of the time tracking values for 20 conditional views

Now, let's go ahead and remove the conditional views from all the text boxes and see what kind of performance impact this may have (see *Figure 10.9*):

Figure 10.9 – An overview of step 2 of the OmniScript without the conditional views

After removing all the conditional views from all the text boxes, activating the OmniScript and advancing past the first step, I noticed that the loading time of **Step 2** is 63ms (see *Figure 10.10*):

Figure 10.10 – An overview of the time tracking values for 20 text boxes without conditional views

That concludes our review of another OmniScript best practice: reducing conditional views. While the time did drop by 35%, the mere 29ms we saved by removing conditional views is such a tiny amount of time that users are unlikely to notice the difference.

Now, while the use of **conditional view** by itself does not have a significant impact on OmniScript performance, any heavy and complex components added to the step that are only shown in rare circumstances may cause it to load slowly.

Finally, let's look at one more OmniScript best practice: reducing merge fields. Let's check out how the use of merge fields in OmniScripts affects the performance of our apps.

Performance impact of merge fields in OmniScripts

Earlier in this chapter, while looking at the *Performance impact of formulas on OmniScripts* section, we created 20 simple formula fields to test the impact they may have on our OmniScript performance. Let's update these formulas to use merge fields and see how this will affect the performance of our OmniScript.

I've added the **Set Values** action to our OmniScript to create a variable called Text1 so that it can be used in our formulas (see *Figure 10.11*):

Figure 10.11 – An overview of setting values to create a variable

Then, I replaced the hardcoded word Substring with a merge field in all our formulas (see *Figure 10.12*):

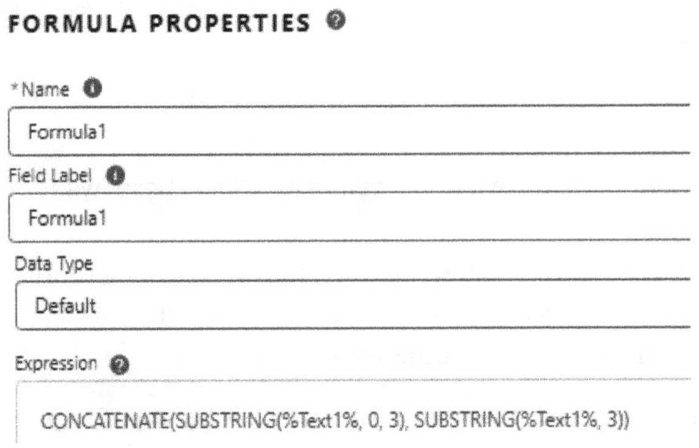

FORMULA PROPERTIES

*Name ❶

    Formula1

Field Label ❶

    Formula1

Data Type

    Default

Expression ❷

    CONCATENATE(SUBSTRING(%Text1%, 0, 3), SUBSTRING(%Text1%, 3))

Figure 10.12 – An overview of adding the merge field to a formula

When running our updated OmniScript with a merge field in all its 20 formulas in the **Preview** mode, it takes virtually the same time, 675ms instead of 641ms, or just about a 5% decrease:

```
▼ vlcTimeTracking:  Object
    OmniScriptSessionToken: "5fede0c4-3
    SetValues2: 0
    Step1: 675
```

Figure 10.13 – An overview of the time tracking value with the merge field applied

That concludes our review of the OmniScript best practice of reducing merge fields. It looks like using merge fields instead of hardcoded text in our formulas did not significantly affect their performance. That was good to know, as now, instead of simply trying to avoid using the merge fields, you can consider the amount of improvement that reducing them may bring to your situation.

If you found these performance insights useful, you may also like the other FlexCard and OmniScript best practice reviews on this book's companion site at `https://maximumvlocity.com/`.

That's the end of our review of the impact that some of the recommended best practices may have on the performance of OmniScripts in our OmniStudio apps. We looked at reducing the number of formulas, conditional views, and merge fields in our OmniScripts. We saw the effect that this recommendation had on our run times. These numbers are valuable as they will help you decide whether you should be concerned about performance when using formulas, conditional views, and merge fields in OmniScripts in your OmniStudio applications.

In this section, we also found out how to use time tracking in OmniScripts to obtain accurate step-timing measurements. In the next section, we will explore the limitations of this approach and how to address those limitations and measure the performance of our OmniScripts and FlexCards.

Measuring the performance of the Presentation Layer

In the previous section, we found out that OmniScript time tracking simply records the time a user spends on the step. So, for UI steps, we used a simple LWC to immediately advance the user to the next step so that the step loading time can be recorded.

This approach worked well for the internal OmniScript components we were testing in the previous section (*Performance impact of the OmniScript best practices*). Now, what if we need to measure the performance of a step with UI controls that also take time to load? Let's look at an example.

Let's say we have a FlexCard on an OmniScript step and would like to measure how long it is taking to load. Let's use the sample **OpportunitiesCard** we used in *Chapter 2, A Sample Application*. This card displays the list of Opportunities in a specified Account:

Figure 10.14 – An overview of a sample FlexCard displaying the list of Opportunities

We can then add our **SampleElemCmp** LWC, which will immediately advance to the following step so that the time the step took to load can be recorded:

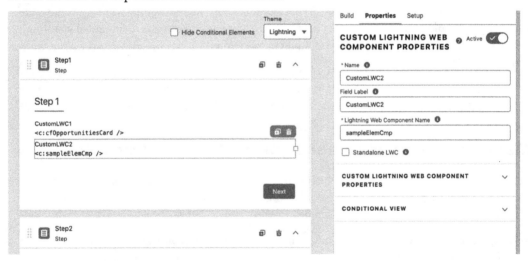

Figure 10.15 – An overview of a sample OmniScript displaying FlexCard

However, after activating and running our OmniScript in the **Preview** mode, the time tracking node shows a step time of only 48ms (see *Figure 10.16*):

Figure 10.16 – An overview of OmniScript time tracking showing an incorrect loading time for the FlexCard

This doesn't sound right because when we run this in its own **Preview** mode, the FlexCard takes about a second to load. Looks like the redirect in our LWC is firing before the FlexCard has a chance to complete loading. So how do we measure the load time of our FlexCard? The following sections present some options.

Measuring load times with LWC Debug Mode

When enabled, LWC Debug Mode tracks the **experienced page time** (EPT). **EPT** is shown in a bubble on the top right of the screen (see *Figure 10.17*):

Figure 10.17 – An overview of a page with LWC Debug Mode enabled

What does it stand for? The **EPT** measures how long the page takes to load before a user can meaningfully interact with it. Unlike Salesforce Classic, LWCs (and the OmniScripts and FlexCards that are also rendered as LWCs) can involve multiple asynchronous calls while loading, retrieving data, and loading child components. The load time is also affected by browser and network performance. This is why the **EPT** measurement provided by the LWC framework is very useful.

To get the **EPT** value displayed, we will need to enable the LWC **Debug Mode**. Begin by typing debug in the **Quick Find** box on the top left of the Salesforce **Setup** screen. You can then enable the **Debug Mode** for one or more users (see Figure *10.18*):

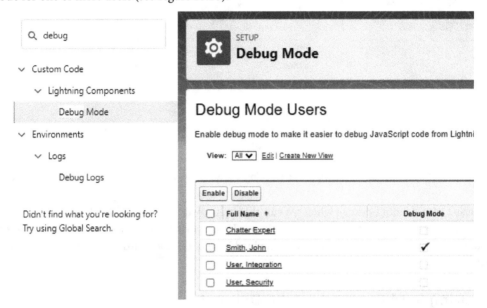

Figure 10.18 – An overview of enabling LWC Debug Mode

Note

Once the LWC **Debug Mode** is enabled, you will also be able to see the full readable source code of your LWCs in the browser's **DevTools**. See the *Debug Using Chrome DevTools* page (`https://developer.salesforce.com/docs/platform/lwc/guide/debug-dev-tools.html`) for more information.

Now, while the LWC **Debug Mode** enables the **EPT**, watching it in the OmniScript or FlexCard **Preview** mode is not very useful, as this will measure the loading time of the **Preview** tool and not just our component.

To measure the **EPT** of an OmniScript, select **How To Launch** from the dropdown menu on the top right of your OmniScript Designer interface (see *Figure 10.19*):

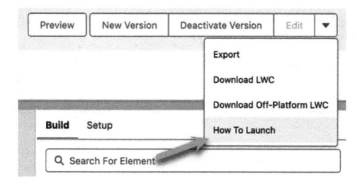

Figure 10.19 – An overview of how to launch an OmniScript shortcut

Then, copy and paste the **Lightning** or the **Newport** link into your browser, as shown in *Figure 10.20*:

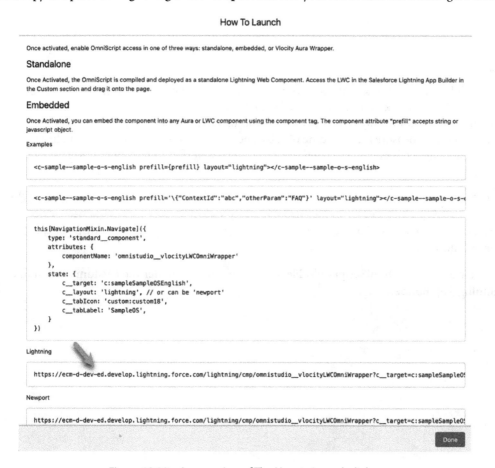

Figure 10.20 – An overview of The How to Launch dialog

And there you go! We now have the OmniScript shown in a separate tab with the **EPT** measurement showing the time it took to load (see *Figure 10.21*):

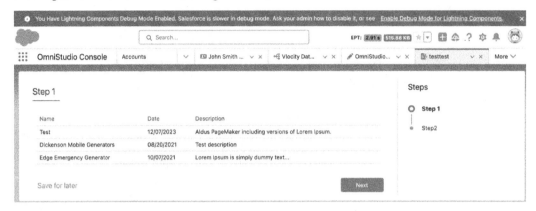

Figure 10.21 – An overview of an OmniScript running in its own tab

> **Note**
>
> The EPT value is approximate, and you will also notice that the first time you load your OmniScript, it will take longer for it to load than the second time after you refresh your browser. Additionally, you will only be able to measure the load time of the first step of an OmniScript. If you need to measure the load time of subsequent steps, consider using Selenium browser automation (see *Chapter 4, An Introduction to Load Testing*, for more information).

You can also measure the EPT of your OmniScripts and FlexCards by placing them in a Lightning Page. See *Create an App Home Page with the Lightning App Builder* (https://help.salesforce. com/s/articleView?id=sf.lightning_app_builder_create_app_page.htm) for more information.

Once activated, your OmniScripts and FlexCards are available under the **Custom** section in the **Lightning App Builder**:

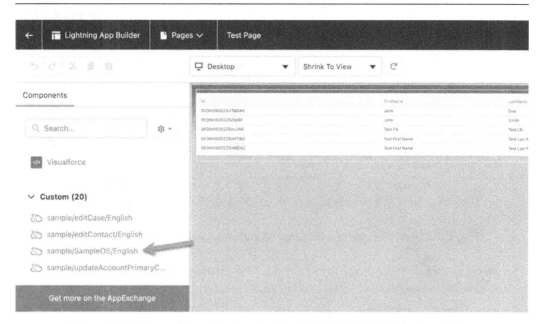

Figure 10.22 – An overview of finding OmniScript LWC in the Lightning App Builder

We're now able to measure the load times of our FlexCards and one-step OmniScripts with the EPT tool using LWC Debug Mode. But what if we need to measure the load time of the second or the third step in an OmniScript? This is what we will discuss in the next section.

Measuring performance with Selenium

OmniScripts and FlexCards run asynchronously on the client side. So, to measure the load time of a step in the middle of an OmniScript or to time an operation that happens after the user clicks on a button, Selenium comes in very handy.

The Java code snippet shown in *Figure 10.24* measures the time from the moment that the Lightning App page title (1) is loaded to the moment when the last record on the FlexCard (2) is loaded (see *Figure 10.23*):

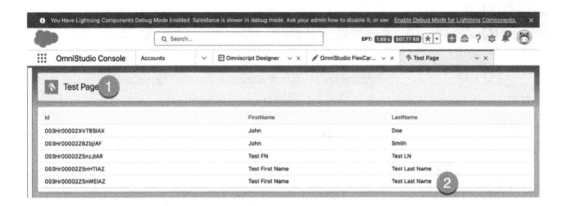

Figure 10.23 – An overview of a FlexCard LWC running in a custom Lightning App

See *Chapter 4*, *An Introduction to Load Testing*, for more information on how to download and set up Selenium, simulate user actions, and measure the execution time:

```
long start = System.currentTimeMillis();
driver.get("https://ecm-d-dev-ed.develop.lightning.force.com/lightning/n/Test_Page");
Wait<WebDriver> wait1 = new FluentWait<>(driver)
        .withTimeout(Duration.ofSeconds(5))
        .pollingEvery(Duration.ofMillis(250))
        .ignoring(NoSuchElementException.class);
wait1.until(ExpectedConditions.presenceOfElementLocated(By.xpath("/html/body/div[4]/div[1]/section/div[1]/div
long start1 = System.currentTimeMillis();
WebElement cellElem = wait1.until(ExpectedConditions.presenceOfElementLocated(By.xpath("/html/body/div[4]/div
long finish = System.currentTimeMillis();
long loadingTime = finish - start;
System.out.println("Total Time: " + (finish - start));
System.out.println("Card loading: " + (finish - start1));
```

Figure 10.24 – An overview of a Java code used with Selenium automation

With just a few more lines of code, you can simulate and measure the performance of complex use cases, such as the modal dialogs, typeahead blocks, and everything else your users can do with your app.

Finally, the following section is a quick reminder of how we can use the LWC lifecycle events to measure the performance of our custom LWCs.

Consider LWC lifecycle events

If you are developing a custom LWC for use in your OmniScript, FlexCard, or just anywhere in Salesforce, you can simply print and compare the values produced by the getTime() method of Date instances at various significant time points in your LWC lifecycle.

For instance, we can implement the constructor() method, and it will be called when our component instance is created. We can also implement the renderedCallback() method that will be called after a component has finished rendering.

The following is a simple LWC with a long-running calculation added into the `connectedCallback()` method to simulate increased loading time. I'm calculating the time between the beginning and the end of the component's loading and then printing it to the **Console**:

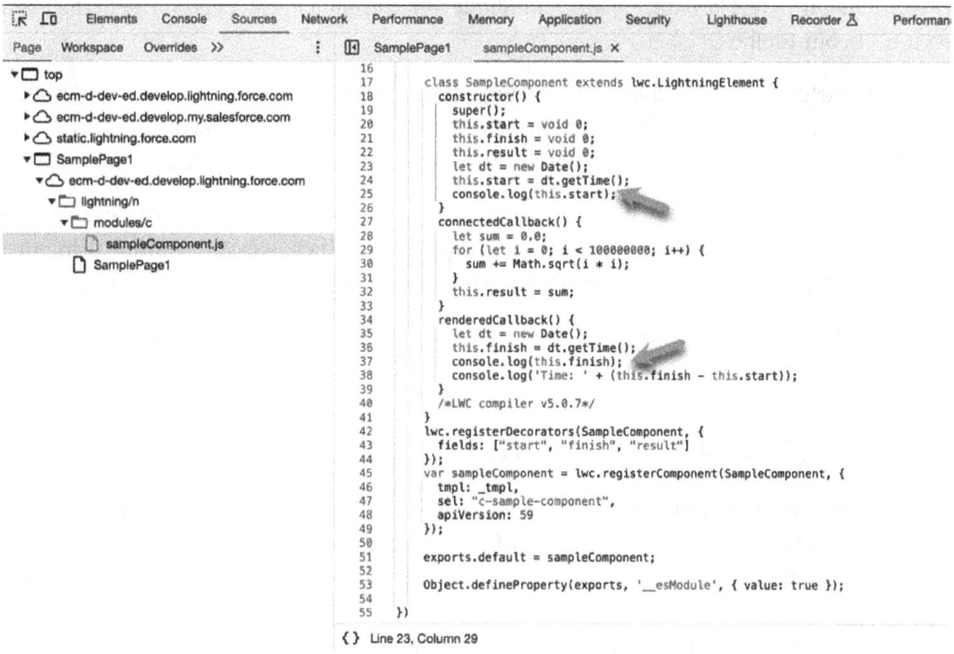

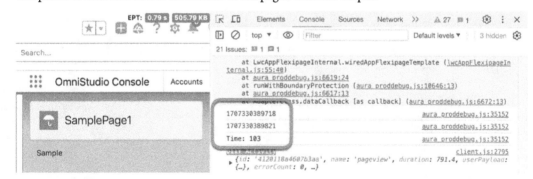

Figure 10.25 – An overview of a sample LWC with manual time tracking

The printout is then found in the middle of the page's **Console** output:

Figure 10.26 – An overview of an LWC manual time tracking printout on the Console

Adding these simple manual time checks to your LWCs can be easier than setting up Selenium and more flexible and accurate than using the **EPT** number provided by the LWC **Debug Mode**.

With that, we have come to the end of this section. We have learned about three additional practical ways of measuring the performance of our OmniScripts, FlexCards, and their components. Knowing these in addition to the execution times and the OmniStudio Tracking Service that we learned about in *Chapter 3, Evaluating the Performance of an OmniStudio Implementation*, places powerful performance tracking tools in our toolbox.

We looked at the helpful and easy-to-use LWC **Debug Mode**, circled back on the powerful and versatile browser automation we can obtain by using the Selenium WebDriver, and looked at the easy-to-use but powerful coding technique of using lifecycle events to track the performance of custom LWCs.

Having these tools under our belt will make it easier for us to narrow down performance issues in our OmniScripts and FlexCards to a specific step or component. Then, we can continue using these tools to compare the measurements and track the performance improvements we're able to achieve.

Now let's look at one more potential area of slow performance in the OmniStudio Presentation Layer—the client-side document generation.

Document generation options

If your application needs to produce printable documents, OmniStudio has you covered. You can create PDF, Word, and PowerPoint documents in your OmniScripts based on the pre-defined templates. While different options are available, many implementations use **DataRaptor Transform** to map the values in the OmniScript JSON to the fields in the document template. The common practice is then to insert the document generation LWC into your OmniScript step. The LWC will then generate and attach Word and PDF versions of the document to the Salesforce Object of your choice:

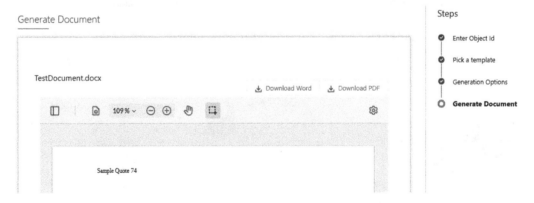

Figure 10.27 – An overview of the client-side document generation LWC on a sample OmniScript step

> **Note**
>
> For more information on OmniStudio document generation, refer to its documentation page at `https://help.salesforce.com/s/articleView?id=ind.doc_gen_foundation_document_generation_overview_389381.htm`.

While this setup fits perfectly to most document generation scenarios, in some cases, the applications experience a slowdown when attempting to generate larger documents or create multiple documents in the same OmniScript step. If this is the case for your application, consider switching to server-side document generation. The documents will then get generated in the background, so your users will be able to continue using the application instead of waiting for the generated documents to load.

Server-side document generation uses the same Word or PowerPoint document templates and attaches generated documents to a Salesforce Object of your choice. It can also generate large batches of documents.

Once the server-side document generation is enabled (refer to `https://help.salesforce.com/s/articleView?id=ind.doc_gen_enable_server_side_docgen_setting_omnistudio_pkg.htm` for more information), you will need to insert record(s) into the `DocumentGenerationProcess` object. The OmniStudio internal job will then pick them up, generate your documents on the server, and attach them to the records you specify.

This can be done in a DataRaptor, Integration Procedure, or an Apex class. The following is a sample Apex class that inserts a server-side document generation request record:

```
public class DocGenServerSideSample
    public void genDoc(){
        String requestText = '{\"templateContentVersionId\":\"068Aq000001bcP7IAI\",\"title\":\"NewDocDemo\",\"keepIntermediate\":true}';
        String type = 'GenerateAndConvert';
        String tokenData = '{\"testtag\":\"SAMPLE\"}';
        DocumentGenerationProcess request = new DocumentGenerationProcess();
        request.Type = type;
        request.RequestText = requestText;
        request.ReferenceObject = '0Q0Aq00000089vLKAQ';
        request.TokenData = tokenData;
        insert request;
    }
```

Figure 10.28 – An overview of a sample code for creating a server-side document generation request

The parameters are as follows:

- `requestText` is the JSON object specifying `templateContentVersionId`, which is the content version ID of the document template, the `title` for the generated document, and the `keepIntermediate` flag that controls whether the system should also attach the generated intermediate Word document along with the final PDF document.

- The `type` parameter should always be `GenerateAndConvert` so that the system generates a Word document and creates a PDF document.

- `tokenData` is the JSON object containing values to be filled into the document template.

- `ReferenceObject` is the object to which the generated document is going to be attached.

Once the record is inserted, you will be able to monitor the progress by querying the `DocumentGenerationProcess` object. As the OmniStudio internal job processes the request, it updates the **ResponseText, TokenData,** and **Status** fields:

Figure 10.29 – An overview of a query showing the status of the server-side document generation jobs

Once the status changes to **Success**, the generated file is attached to the object specified in the `ReferenceObject` parameter:

Figure 10.30 – A sample generated document

And that is the end of our quick review of server-side document generation. You have seen what it takes to implement it and now have an alternative solution that you can use when your client-side document generation is not meeting your performance or user experience expectations.

You now also have a tool for generating large batches of documents (for more information, see the *Document Generation Batch Process* section of OmniStudio documentation available at `https://help.salesforce.com/s/articleView?id=ind.doc_gen_Document_Generation_Batch_Process.htm`) This also brings us to the end of this chapter.

Summary

Well, this is the end of our brief tour of the best practices for improving the performance of the OmniStudio Presentation Layer. We tackled challenges using the OmniScript time tracking feature for measuring the performance of steps with UI components and learned several ways to overcome them.

Then, we measured the impact that OmniScript formulas may have on its performance. We followed that up by reviewing the impact of conditional views and merge fields on the performance of OmniScript apps, which, in our tests, were insignificant. Armed with this knowledge, we can now focus our efforts and develop better performing and more usable OmniScripts.

We continued to explore other ways to measure the performance of OmniScripts and FlexCards and learned how to use the handy LWC Debug Mode and LWC lifecycle events and took another look at the powerful Selenium browser for automation. I'm sure these will come in handy for troubleshooting and tuning the performance of your OmniStudio Presentation Layer components.

Finally, we looked at client-side document generation. While the out-of-the-box document generation LWC can produce large documents quickly, we now have another option we can use when it does not fit our goals. We're now equipped with the OmniStudio server-side document generation that can produce hundreds of documents in the background without making our users wait.

In the next chapter, we will look at DataRaptor formula performance considerations and explore different implementation options to better use the power of formulas in our OmniStudio applications.

DataRaptor Formula Performance Considerations

DataRaptor and Integration Procedure formulas can be very handy for data manipulation, but they too can become a cause for sub-optimal performance. In this chapter, we will look at out-of-the-box and custom Apex-based formula performance considerations and different implementation options available to improve the performance of our OmniStudio apps. We will also look at a few best practices and put them to the test so that we can see the exact impact they may have on our OmniStudio apps, as well as learn how to measure the performance impact of other best practices that we're thinking about applying. In this chapter, we will cover the following topics:

- Getting a feel of DataRaptor and Integration Procedure formula performance

- Looking at the powerful QUERY function and seeing if using it comes with a performance penalty

- Seeing the effect that filtering the input JSON may have on custom Apex formula functions

This should be another fun read, filled with examples and actionable numbers. Let's begin by seeing how fast DataRaptor formulas are.

Technical requirements

To follow along with this chapter, you will need access to an OmniStudio installation. If you don't have one handy, you can always request your free trial development environment from the Salesforce Developers site, which is (at the time of this writing) available at https://developer.salesforce.com/free-trials. Once on the site, head over to **Industry-Based Trials** and get yourself a trial org for the industry of your choice.

How fast are DataRaptor formulas?

DataRaptors and Integration Procedures share the same set of formulas. Let's begin by getting a feel for how fast these formulas really are by comparing them with Salesforce formulas. Often, we have an option to use either of the two. So, instead of just making it a matter of preference, let's look at the performance of both DataRaptor and Salesforce formulas so that we can make a decision based on that.

> **DataRaptor formula reference**
>
> Some of the functions, such as the `SORTBY` one that sorts a list of JSON objects, are only available in DataRaptor Transforms.
>
> For more information on formulas and functions available, refer to the OmniStudio documentation for your edition of OmniStudio. While DataRaptor formulas in *OmniStudio Standard* and *OmniStudio for Vlocity* are largely the same, it is best to refer to the documentation for your edition of OmniStudio.
>
> Here's the DataRaptor formula and function reference for OmniStudio Standard: `https://help.salesforce.com/s/articleView?id=sf.os_function_reference_56716.htm`
>
> You can tell that you are running OmniStudio Standard if your **Omni Interaction Configuration** page in Salesforce **Setup** has the `TheFirstInstalledOmniPackage` entry.

I've created a sample DataRaptor that extracts one row from the **Account** object:

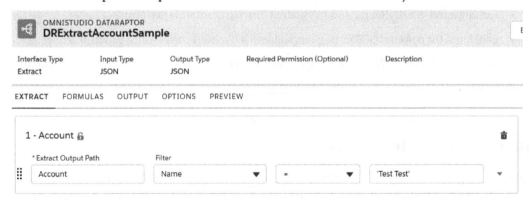

Figure 11.1 – An overview of sample DataRaptor for testing formula performance

I'm now going to add a formula that concatenates all the components of the `address` field with non-blank values: `BillingStreet`, `BillingCity`, `BillingState`, `BillingCountry`, and `BillingPostalCode`. *Figure 11.2* shows our formula on the DataRaptor **Formulas** tab:

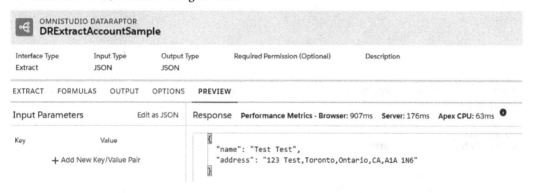

Figure 11.2 – An overview of the Formulas tab of our sample DataRaptor

The **Preview** tab confirms that the formula is working, correctly concatenating the components of the address field, as shown in *Figure 11.3*:

Figure 11.3 – An overview of previewing the sample DataRaptor with the address formula

Now, let's go ahead and add the same logic to a custom formula field to the **Account** object itself:

Account Custom Field
Address Formula
Back to Account Fields

Custom Field Definition Detail	Edit	Set Field-Level Security	View Field Accessibility	Where is this used?

Field Information

Field Label	Address Formula		Object Name	Account
Field Name	Address_Formula			
API Name	Address_Formula__c			

Figure 11.4 – An overview of the Address Formula custom field added to the Account object

Our formula now concatenates the non-blank components of the `address` field:

Figure 11.5 – An overview of the custom field formula content

Now, let's create a second DataRaptor, this time, using the new field instead of a DataRaptor formula. Let's begin by adding the **Account** object with the same filter criteria to the **Extract** tab:

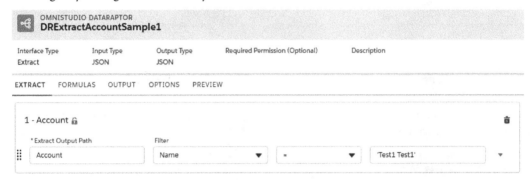

Figure 11.6 – An overview of a sample DataRaptor for testing Salesforce formulas

This time, we will leave the **Formulas** tab blank and simply add our new **Address Formula** field to the **Output** tab:

Figure 11.7 – An overview of the Output tab of the sample DataRaptor

The second DataRaptor yields the same result in the **Preview** mode: name and the concatenated address fields. See *Figure 11.8*:

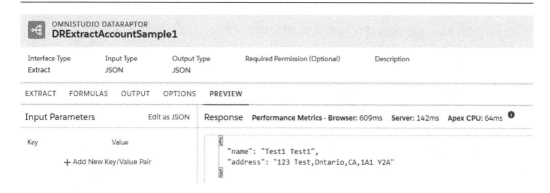

Figure 11.8 – An overview of previewing the second DataRaptor

Now, let's add both DataRaptors to a sample OmniScript so that each step runs one of our DataRaptors. We can then measure and compare the performance of both steps. Here's our sample OmniScript with the two DataRaptors for us to compare:

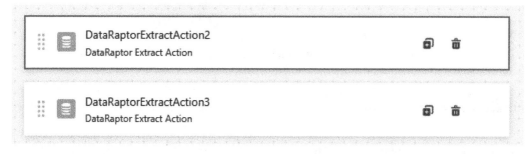

Figure 11.9 – An overview of a sample OmniScript for comparing the DataRaptors

And here's how the step timing looks (remember—the step timings are measured in milliseconds or ms. The first DataRaptor, which was combining the address components, took 420ms. Then, the second DataRaptor, which was consuming the output of a Salesforce formula field, took 261ms to complete, running about 40% faster:

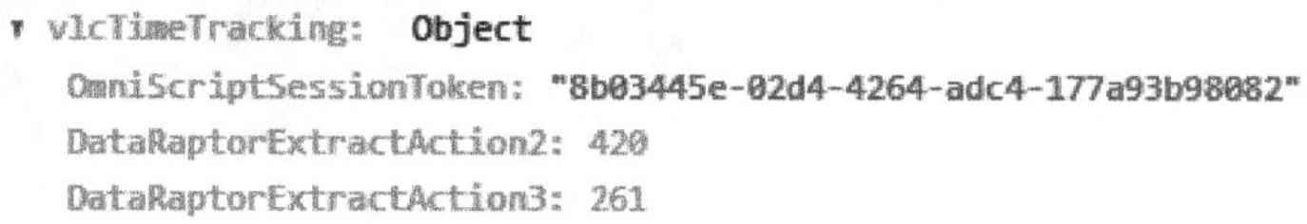

```
▼ vlcTimeTracking:  Object
    OmniScriptSessionToken: "8b03445e-02d4-4264-adc4-177a93b98082"
    DataRaptorExtractAction2: 420
    DataRaptorExtractAction3: 261
```

Figure 11.10 – An overview of the OmniScript time-tracking output

Please note that the formula we tested was fairly simple. With complex formulas, especially when many formulas are implemented in the DataRaptor, the difference would likely be more profound.

Now, this concludes our quick exploration of the efficiency of DataRaptor formulas. We compared their performance to Salesforce formula fields and saw that the former were about 40% slower in our test.

Should we avoid using formulas in DataRaptors? Definitely not. There are formulas that are not available on the Salesforce object side, and the local JSON manipulation is much easier to do on the DataRaptor side.

While DataRaptor formulas are extremely useful and versatile, this power comes with responsibility. They do come with a performance penalty, especially when we are using many formulas in the same component, so we need to consider that.

In the next section, we will look at the powerful QUERY function and compare its performance with that of a standalone DataRaptor, revealing numbers that would've been difficult to guess!

The QUERY function or another Extract?

The QUERY function in DataRaptors in Integration Procedures allows us to run a SOQL query and returns a list of values in its response JSON node. It is just as if we were to run a separate Extract DataRaptor right inside a formula. While this function is very powerful, it's also easy to abuse by calling it multiple times to retrieve more than one field, using it in Transform-type DataRaptors, and so on.

> **Note**
>
> The QUERY function only selects a single field, so if we need to extract multiple fields with it, we will need to create multiple formulas.
>
> Try to avoid using the QUERY function in *DataRaptor Transforms*. This introduces new data; thus, input and output will no longer match, making the DataRaptor difficult to debug.

Let's put the QUERY function to the test to see how it affects the performance of our OmniStudio apps. The following DataRaptor extracts data from the **Contact** object and then uses three QUERY formulas to extract three **Opportunity** object fields. Here's the **Extract** tab of our test DataRaptor:

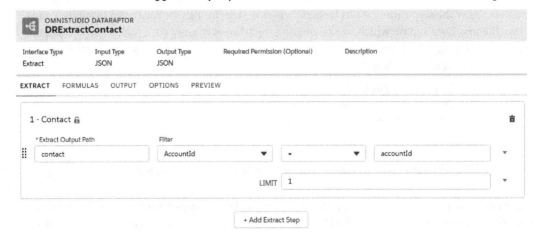

Figure 11.11 – An overview of our sample DataRaptor for testing the QUERY function

And here's the **Formulas** tab where we extract the values from the **Opportunity** object using the same `accountId` value:

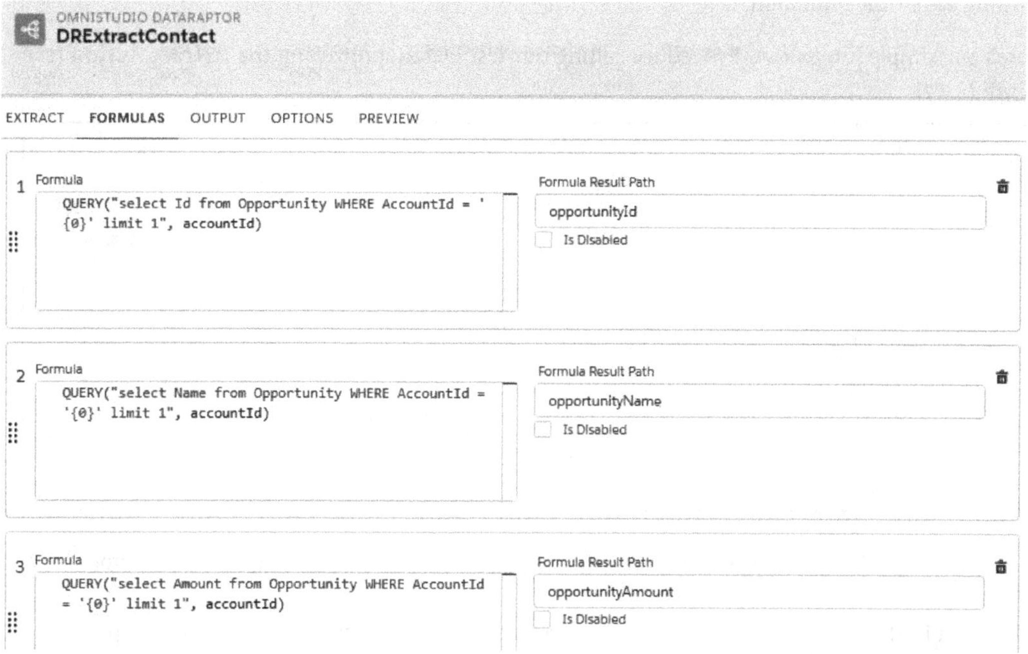

OMNISTUDIO DATARAPTOR
DRExtractContact

EXTRACT   **FORMULAS**   OUTPUT   OPTIONS   PREVIEW

1 Formula
```
QUERY("select Id from Opportunity WHERE AccountId = '
{0}' limit 1", accountId)
```
Formula Result Path
opportunityId
☐ Is Disabled

2 Formula
```
QUERY("select Name from Opportunity WHERE AccountId =
'{0}' limit 1", accountId)
```
Formula Result Path
opportunityName
☐ Is Disabled

3 Formula
```
QUERY("select Amount from Opportunity WHERE AccountId
= '{0}' limit 1", accountId)
```
Formula Result Path
opportunityAmount
☐ Is Disabled

Figure 11.12 – An overview of the Formulas tab of the sample DataRaptor

And here's the **Output** tab showing the Contact fields we extracted, as well as the new JSON nodes created by our formulas:

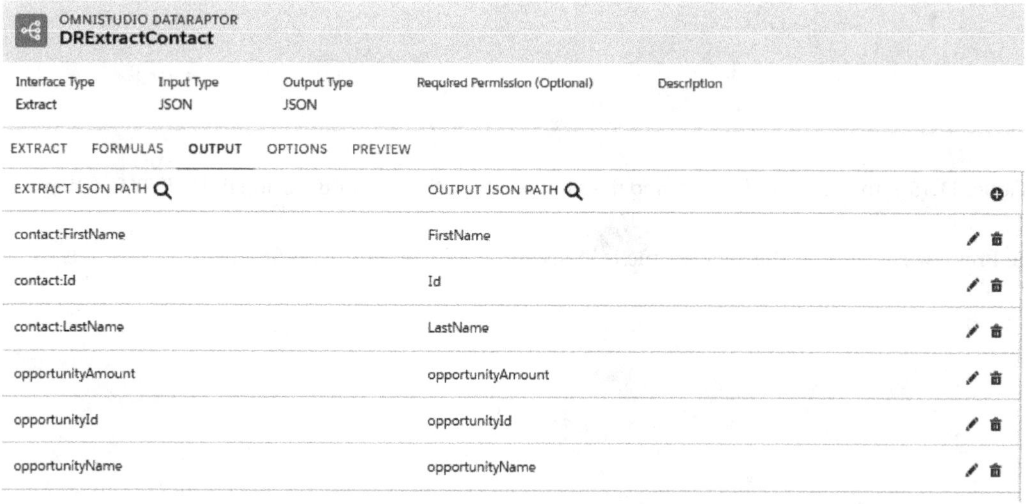

OMNISTUDIO DATARAPTOR
DRExtractContact

Interface Type	Input Type	Output Type	Required Permission (Optional)	Description
Extract	JSON	JSON		

EXTRACT   FORMULAS   **OUTPUT**   OPTIONS   PREVIEW

EXTRACT JSON PATH 🔍	OUTPUT JSON PATH 🔍	➕
contact:FirstName	FirstName	✏️ 🗑️
contact:Id	Id	✏️ 🗑️
contact:LastName	LastName	✏️ 🗑️
opportunityAmount	opportunityAmount	✏️ 🗑️
opportunityId	opportunityId	✏️ 🗑️
opportunityName	opportunityName	✏️ 🗑️

Figure 11.13 – An overview of the Output tab of the sample DataRaptor

Let's place our DataRaptor into an Integration Procedure. This way, we can later compare it with another Integration Procedure running two DataRaptors that will replace our single DataRaptor running the QUERY function.

Here's our simple Integration Procedure calling our test DataRaptor using the **Extract Action** (see *Figure 11.14*):

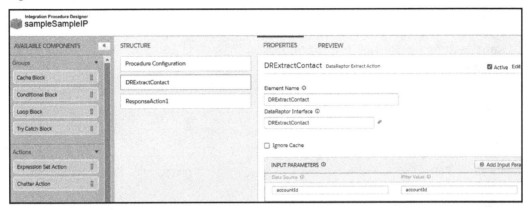

Figure 11.14 – An overview of our sample Integration Procedure for running the DataRaptor

When run in the **Preview** mode, this produces the result we expect: the Contact and Opportunity fields. See *Figure 11.15*.

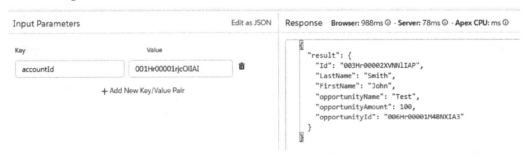

Figure 11.15 – An overview of previewing the sample Integration Procedure using the QUERY function

The **Preview** pane shows the **Server** time is 78ms and the **Browser** time is 988ms.

Now, let's replace our QUERY function with a second DataRaptor. The first DataRaptor would virtually stay the same. The following screenshot shows its **Extract** tab:

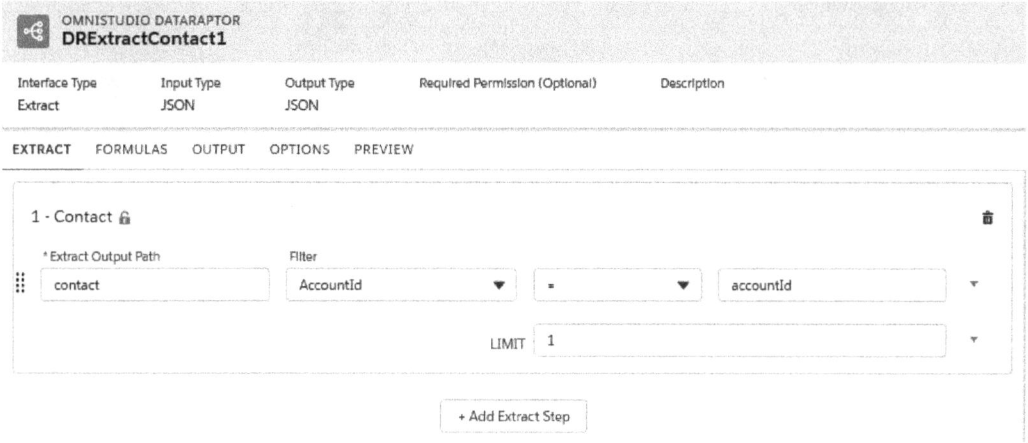

Figure 11.16 – An overview of a test DataRaptor not using the QUERY function

There are no formulas this time, and the **Output** tab only shows the **Contact** object fields; we're no longer extracting the Opportunity fields here:

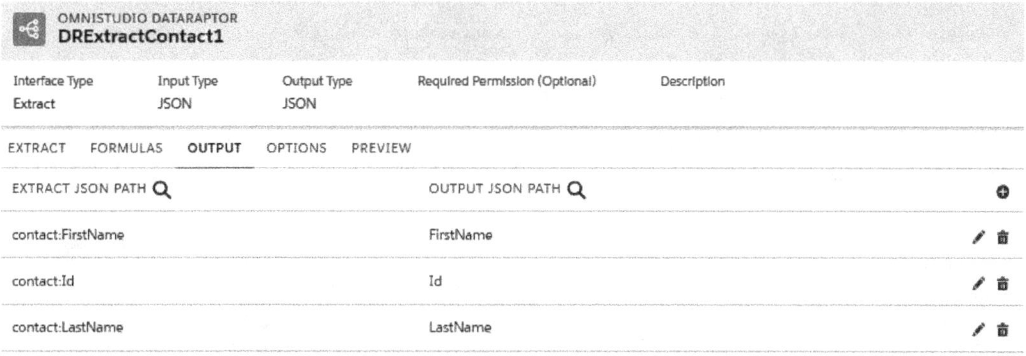

Figure 11.17 – An overview of the Output tab of the test DataRaptor not using the QUERY function

Now, here's our second DataRaptor extracting from the **Opportunity** object:

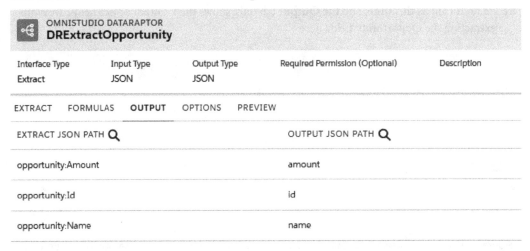

Figure 11.18 – An overview of the Extract tab of the test DataRaptor replacing the QUERY function

This DataRaptor has no formulas either; only the three **Opportunity** object fields we used to extract with the QUERY function are added to the **Output** tab:

OMNISTUDIO DATARAPTOR **DRExtractOpportunity**				
Interface Type Extract	Input Type JSON	Output Type JSON	Required Permission (Optional)	Description

EXTRACT   FORMULAS   **OUTPUT**   OPTIONS   PREVIEW

EXTRACT JSON PATH 🔍	OUTPUT JSON PATH 🔍
opportunity:Amount	amount
opportunity:Id	id
opportunity:Name	name

Figure 11.19 – An overview of the Output tab of the test DataRaptor replacing the QUERY function

And here's our simple Integration Procedure that hosts our two new DataRaptors:

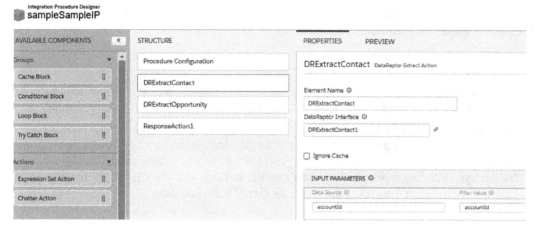

Figure 11.20 – An overview of a test Integration Procedure not using the QUERY function

When run in the **Preview** mode, it shows a **Server** time of 67ms and a **Browser** time of 622ms:

Figure 11.21 – An overview of a test Integration Procedure
without the QUERY function in the Preview mode

The time difference is 37% when measured by the browser and only 12% when measured by the server-side Apex runtime. Now, the DataRaptor running the QUERY function ended up firing four queries instead of two as we had to call the function once for every field we retrieved from the **Opportunity** object. Considering that we had to use two more queries, the function performed surprisingly well!

That concludes the tests for measuring the quick performance of the DataRaptor and Integration Procedure QUERY function. We've seen that the function performed well in our tests and did not result in much of a slowdown in our Integration Procedure. This fact may help you decide when to use the QUERY function to run your SOQL statement and when to use a standalone DataRaptor. Now, knowing that the performance may not be much of a concern, you will be able to pay more attention to clarity and readability. In the next section, we will look at the performance nuances of using custom Apex functions in our Integration Procedure and DataRaptor formulas.

Limiting custom function payload size

We can use custom functions in our DataRaptor and Integration Procedure formulas that will call Apex code implementing our custom function logic.

> **OmniStudio Standard or OmniStudio for Vlocity?**
>
> Custom functions features are different between OmniStudio Standard and OmniStudio for Vlocity. See earlier in this chapter on how to tell which OmniStudio edition you are running.
>
> While the OmniStudio for Vlocity edition allows you to use custom metadata types to define custom functions (`https://help.salesforce.com/s/articleView?id=sf.os_define_the_metadata_for_the_custom_function.htm`), with OmniStudio Standard, you will need to pass the Apex class, method, and input data directly into the function. Examples in this section are using the syntax for OmniStudio Standard.

This best practice goes along the same lines as the ones we saw in *Chapter 9, Improving the Performance of the Service Layer*, where we looked at trimming the response JSON. We looked at the JSON produced by Integration Procedures and at reducing the number of fields returned by DataRaptors. This best practice deals with the size of the input we send to custom Apex functions. Let's see what kind of effect the size of the `input` JSON has on the custom function performance.

The following Apex code implements a simple custom formula function that returns the sum of the `index` values we send (see *Figure 11.22*):

```
1   global class CustomFuncImpl implements Callable
2 ▾ {
3       global Object call(String methodName, Map<String, Object> args)
4 ▾     {
5 |         Map<String, Object> inputMap = (Map<String, Object>)args.get('input');
6           Map<String, Object> outputMap = (Map<String, Object>)args.get('output');
7           Map<String, Object> optionsMap = (Map<String, Object>)args.get('options');
8
9           return invokeMethod(methodName, inputMap, outputMap, optionsMap);
10      }
11      global Object invokeMethod(String methodName, Map<String, Object> inputs, Map<String, Object> output, Map<String, Object> options)
12 ▾    {
13          if (methodName == 'sum')
14 ▾         {
15              List<Object> arguments = (List<Object>)inputs.get('arguments');
16              output.put('result', sum(arguments));
17          }
18
19          return true;
20      }
21      Double sum(List<Object> arguments)
22 ▾    {
23          Double result = 0;
24          for(Object elem : arguments)
25 ▾         {
26              if (elem != null)
27 ▾             {
28                  Map<String, Object> m = (Map<String, Object>)elem;
29                  result += (Double)m.get('index');
30              }
31          }
32          return result;
33      }
34 }
```

Figure 11.22 – An overview of a simple custom DataRaptor formula function

And here's how we invoke the function in a DataRaptor. This formula sends the full `input` JSON to our custom function:

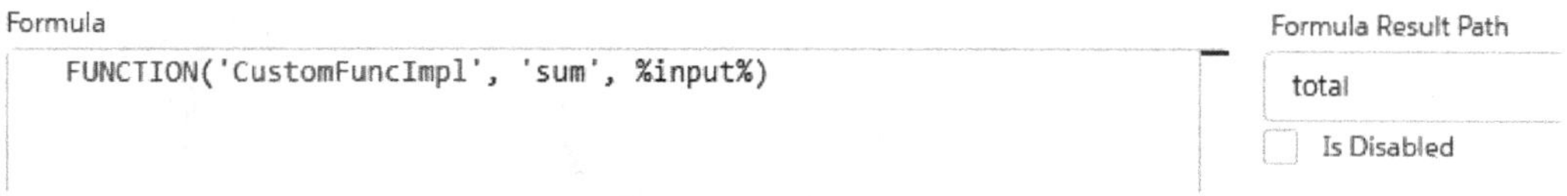

Formula
```
FUNCTION('CustomFuncImpl', 'sum', %input%)
```

Formula Result Path

total

☐ Is Disabled

Figure 11.23 – An overview of a sample formula using our function

When running our DataRaptor in the **Preview** tab, we see that the `input` JSON contains our `index` elements in addition to a lot of different other values:

Input

```
{
    "input": [
        {
            "textField": "Test 501",
            "picklistField": "Value 1",
            "index": 501,
            "name": "Test 501",
            "formulaOutput": "test",
            "longTextField": "Lorem ipsum dolor sit amet,
consectetur adipiscing elit, sed do eiusmod tempor
incididunt ut labore et dolore magna aliqua. Ut
enim ad minim veniam, quis nostrud exercitation
ullamco laboris nisi ut aliquip ex ea commodo
consequat. Duis aute irure dolor in reprehenderit
in voluptate velit esse cillum dolore eu fugiat
nulla pariatur. Excepteur sint occaecat cupidatat
non proident, sunt in culpa qui officia deserunt
mollit anim id est laborum."
        },
        {
            "textField": "Test 502",
            "picklistField": "Value 1",
            "index": 502,
```

Figure 11.24 – An overview of a test JSON sent to the custom function

The preview of our DataRaptor shows a **Server** time of 269ms and a **Browser** time of 1,042ms (see *Figure 11.25*):

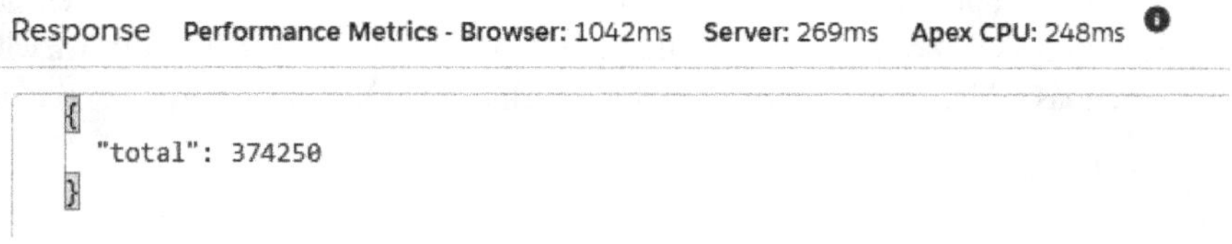

Response   **Performance Metrics - Browser:** 1042ms   **Server:** 269ms   **Apex CPU:** 248ms ⓘ

```
{
    "total": 374250
}
```

Figure 11.25 – An overview of a DataRaptor preview with full JSON sent to a custom function

Now, what if we only send our function the values it needs? If we filter the JSON prior to invoking our custom function, what kind of impact will it have on performance? Let's change the DataRaptor and find out. Let's add another formula this time to extract the index nodes out of the child nodes of the input JSON. We would then feed this filtered JSON to our custom function (see *Figure 11.26*):

1	Formula		Formula Result Path
	`LIST(input:index)`	—	indexes
			☐ Is Disabled

2	Formula		Formula Result Path
	`FUNCTION('CustomFuncImpl', 'sum', indexes)`	—	total
			☐ Is Disabled

Figure 11.26 – An overview of the updated Formulas tab implementing the filtering

Let's preview the updated DataRaptor now. Just as before, our custom function has returned the same value, but for this item, the **Server** time is 55ms, showing about 80% improvement over our previous run, and the **Browser** time is 681ms, which is about 35% better:

Response   Performance Metrics - Browser: 681ms   Server: 55ms   Apex CPU: 101ms

```
{
    "total": 374250
}
```

Figure 11.27 – An overview of a DataRaptor preview with filtered input JSON sent to a custom function

Wow! We have achieved a significant improvement in our runtime simply by adding one function call to our DataRaptor! Just like we saw in the examples in *Chapter 9*, *Improving the Performance of the Service Layer*, JSON operations in OmniStudio have proven to be computationally expensive, while adding the filtering logic is quick and easy and has proven to bring sizable benefits.

That is it for our quick tour of custom Apex DataRaptor and Integration Procedure formula functions. We now have the numbers that direct us to pay attention to the content of the data JSON we will send to our custom functions so that they perform at their best. This also brings us to the end of the chapter.

Summary

Well, we have come to the end of our quick review of important DataRaptor and Integration Procedure formula performance considerations. We got a feel of the formula performance, looked at the powerful QUERY function, and compared its performance with that of a standalone DataRaptor. We've also seen the impressive effect that filtering the input data may have on custom Apex formula functions. Armed with these insights, we can make better use of DataRaptor and Integration Procedure formulas.

And even more importantly, we looked at a few more practical examples of how to measure the performance impact of best practices. This will help us make more informed decisions about the fit of specific best practices in our specific OmniStudio application scenarios.

In the following chapter, we will look at some dangerous OmniStudio performance and scalability anti-patterns and ways for us to avoid them.

12
OmniStudio Performance Anti-Patterns

Vlocity, now renamed as OmniStudio, has been experiencing unprecedented growth since the day it was founded in 2014. The number of industries served has also significantly increased over time. In keeping pace with this, the platform functionality has grown to support the expanding ecosystem. However, as the platform grew, so did the complexity of the projects.

Along with the growing complexity, a few common mistakes have emerged over time, which seemed like a good idea or the right way of doing things at that time. Those common mistakes are the OmniStudio anti-patterns, and they cause performance, reliability, and scalability issues in many applications.

What's a **design pattern**? Wikipedia defines it as *a reusable solution to a commonly occurring problem within a given context* (`https://en.wikipedia.org/wiki/Software_design_pattern`). Most developers and architects are familiar with design patterns such as **fire and forget**, **publish/subscribe**, and **singleton**. Just like design patterns, an **anti-pattern** is a commonly occurring solution to a common problem. However, unlike its desirable counterpart, anti-patterns occur in unsuccessful apps and lead to negative consequences.

In previous chapters, we looked at the best practices that lead to improved performance in OmniStudio solutions. In this chapter, we will look at the common OmniStudio anti-patterns that cause performance and scalability issues and the ways to avoid them in our apps.

In this chapter, we will review the following:

- A family of **Loop Block** anti-patterns that often produce sporadic governor limit errors
- Poor error-handling issues that may cause data corruption and performance impact
- DataRaptor Extract anti-patterns that may cause unexpected and significant performance degradation and governor limit errors

Let's begin with Loop Block anti-patterns—the OmniStudio version of the famous **SOQL in a loop** Apex code malady.

Technical requirements

To follow along with this chapter, you will need access to an OmniStudio installation. If you don't have one handy, you can always request your free trial development environment from the Salesforce Developers site, which is (at the time of this writing) available at `https://developer.salesforce.com/free-trials`. Once on the site, head over to the **Industry-Based Trials** and get yourself a trial org for the industry of your choice.

DML, API, and Remote Action calls from Loop Block

While virtually any Salesforce developer knows not to use database or external service calls in Apex loops, I have personally witnessed a surprisingly large number of OmniStudio applications where developers were applying similar logic without realizing the consequences.

Those apps have DataRaptors, HTTP, and remote actions sitting inside the **Loop Block** of the Integration Procedures. Perhaps, the declarative nature of Integration Procedures makes the developers feel that the rules of the Salesforce platform somehow do not apply. However, when SOQL queries and HTTP calls are run either from the inside of an Apex loop or from inside a **Loop Block** in an Integration Procedure, they impact performance and risk hitting governor limits the same way.

Let's look at an example. The Integration Procedure shown in the following image extracts `Quote` objects on its first step. Then, for each of the retrieved records, it queries and updates the corresponding quote line items (see *Figure 12.1*):

INTEGRATION PROCEDURE DESIGNER
sampleIPProcessQLI

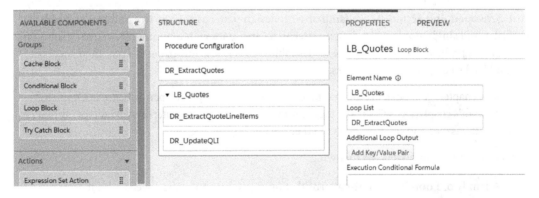

Figure 12.1 – An overview of an Integration Procedure with DataRaptors for Loop Block

Some of its DataRaptor calls, **DR_ExtractQuoteLineItems** and **DR_UpdateQLI**, are made from within the **Loop Block** and may easily hit governor limits as the number of **Quotes** fed to the **Loop Block** grows. For example, here's **Debug Log**, showing our **Loop Block** hitting the `Too many DML statements` limit, causing the Integration Procedure to fail:

```
Errors/Debug Output                                              →

∨ Debug Log

                              Debug Response Full            ▼

        },
        {
          "quoteId": "0Q0Aq00000089xKKAQ",
          "name": "Sample Quote 197"
        },
        {
          "quoteId": "0Q0Aq00000089xLKAQ",
          "name": "Sample Quote 198"
        },
        {
          "quoteId": "0Q0Aq00000089xMKAQ",
          "name": "Sample Quote 199"
        }
      ]
    },
    "DR_UpdateQLI": {
      "error":
"common.apex.runtime.impl.LimitException:
omnistudio:Too many DML statements: 151",
        "success": false
    },
    "elapsedTimeActual": 15883,
    "originalInput": {}
}
```

Figure 12.2 – An overview of the error produced by a failed DataRaptor in Loop Block

A similar situation is shown in the next image:

Figure 12.3 – An overview of an Integration Procedure with a Remote Action in Loop Block

The `RA_ProcessQuote` **Remote Action** is called from within **Loop Block**. If **Remote Action** runs SOQL queries or makes HTTP calls, this **Loop Block**, too, can hit governor limits, causing the Integration Procedure to fail. The following screenshot shows an example of how that exception may look:

Errors/Debug Output   →

> Debug Log

∨ Errors

```
[
  "Too many SOQL queries: 101",
  {
    "statusCode": 400,
    "type": "exception",
    "tid": 50,
    "ref": false,
    "action":
"omnistudio.OmniScriptDesignerController",
```

Figure 12.4 – An overview of the error produced by a failed Remote Action in Loop Block

Even if the **Remote Action** does not make database or HTTP calls but runs some heavy processing logic, this, too, may cause **Loop Block** to hit governor limits, and here's how that error may look:

Figure 12.5 – An overview of the timeout error produced by a Remote Action

I hope I was able to show you how making DML, API, and **Remote Action** calls from within **Loop Block** can be dangerous and put your app at risk as your data volume grows.

How do you make your apps more resilient and future-proof?

Better solutions

There are two basic ways to make your apps more robust: reconfigure your logic to run without Loop Block or make your Loop Block more fail-proof. Consider applying one of the following options:

- If you have control over the Remote Action you are calling from your Loop Block, consider making it more bulky so that it accepts a JSON object array rather than a single object.

- If you are using a service from the Industry Service Catalog, see if a bulkier version of the service is available so that you can call the service once for your entire list of JSON objects instead of calling it multiple times for each of them.

- When using an HTTP Action, see if a bulkier version of an endpoint is available:

- Pass a JSON array to DataRaptor Load or Extract so that it is called once instead of multiple times in the loop

- Finally, if you have to keep your logic running in a Loop Block, then apply **Chainable** or a **Queueable Chainable** configuration to your Integration Procedure, as described in *Chapter 6, Options for Async Execution.*

And that is the end of our review of the Loop Block family of anti-patterns. We've seen why we need to try to avoid placing database and action calls inside the loops. Staying clear of these anti-patterns or exercising extreme care while applying these would help our OmniStudio apps become more reliable, and we will be better prepared to handle the ever-increasing data volumes.

In the next section, we will continue to review the OmniStudio anti-patterns and look at the kind of issues that can result from poor error handling in Integration Procedures.

Integration Procedure running after an error

This dangerous Integration Procedure anti-pattern relates to the lack of error handling. Let's see what may happen when we neglect to check on the outcome of a step that is not guaranteed to always be completed successfully.

The following Integration Procedure has three steps: the first step creates a **Quote**, and the second and third steps process this **Quote** and its line items (see *Figure 12.6*):

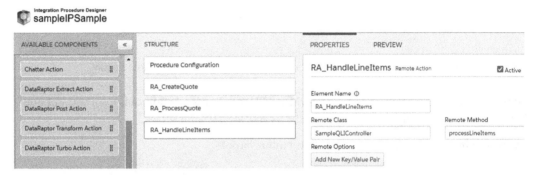

Figure 12.6 – An overview of a sample Integration Procedure for creating Quotes

If we don't check whether the **Quote** was successfully created, steps two and three will still be invoked after step one. They will continue processing, possibly making updates, as if their data comes from a correctly created **Quote**. This may result in additional errors, produce invalid entries, or corrupt the data in our systems.

For example, if the **Quote** in our sample Integration Procedure shown in *Figure 12.6* was not created successfully in the first step, the subsequent steps will also fail. Here's a sample error message that will be produced by the second step:

```
Response    Browser: 774ms ⓘ · Server: 108ms ⓘ · Apex CPU: 123ms ⓘ

{
  "success": false,
  "result": {
    "errorCode": "INVOKE-500",
    "error": "Attempt to de-reference a null object"
  }
}
```

Figure 12.7 – An overview of the error caused by an issue with creating a Quote

Then, our third step will produce multiple errors because more things have gone wrong before we have arrived at it:

```
 -
"RA_HandleLineItems": {
  "errorCode": "INVOKE-500",
  "error": "Attempt to de-reference a null
object"
},
"RA_HandleLineItemsStatus": false,
"RA_ProcessQuote": {
  "errorCode": "INVOKE-500",
  "error": "Attempt to de-reference a null
object"
},
"RA_ProcessQuoteStatus": false,
```

Figure 12.8 – An overview of the error caused by the inability to process the Quote

Now, how can we deal with these issues and make our Integration Procedures more robust?

Better solutions

We can make our Integration Procedures more robust in one of these two ways:

- Add **Failure Condition Formula** to the first step that the following steps depend on. This will ensure that the step will be considered failed when this formula evaluates to TRUE. At this point, you can also consider checking the **Fail On Step Error** box, which will terminate the Integration Procedure if the **Failure Condition Formula** has been evaluated to TRUE.

- Add **Execution Condition Formula** to subsequent steps so that they only run if the operations that they depend on have been successful. If **Execution Condition Formula** is specified, the step will only run when that formula evaluates to TRUE.

The following screenshot shows our first step updated with **Failure Condition Formula**:

Figure 12.9 – An overview of the Integration Procedure updated to handle errors

I have also checked the **Return Only Failure Response** checkbox, which, if checked, causes the step to return only the key-value pairs specified in the **Failure Response** section just below the checkbox.

In our case, if the `result` JSON node does not contain the string value of `success`, the step will fail, and an error message specified in the **Failure Response** section will be returned:

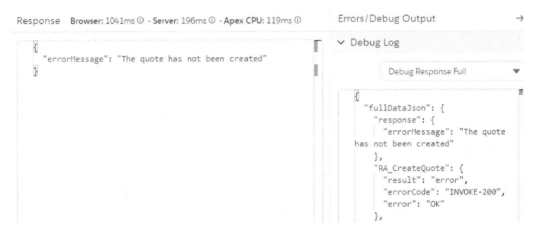

Figure 12.10 – An overview of the message produced by the Integration Procedure Failure Response

The second way to make our Integration Procedure more robust is to add **Execution Condition Formulas** to each of the steps that require certain data or conditions to be successful. Let's assume that the **RA_CreateQuote** step sets the `result` JSON node to `success` when it is successful. We can then specify the **Execution Condition Formula** values for step two as follows:

Figure 12.11 – An overview of Execution Condition Formula added
to step two of the sample Integration Procedure

Similarly, we can specify **Execution Condition Formula** for **RA_HandleLineItems**, which is our third step:

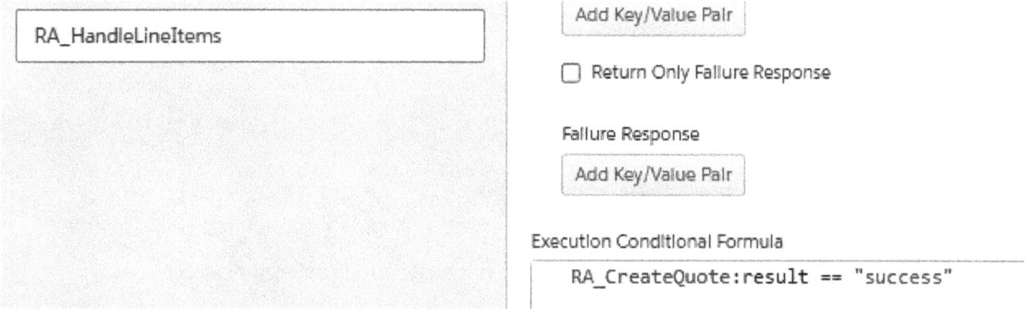

Figure 12.12 – An overview of Execution Condition Formula added
to step three of the sample Integration Procedure

These steps will then be skipped if things in step one do not go according to plan.

That is the end of our review of the *Integration Procedure running after an error*, the typical Integration Procedure error handling anti-pattern. We've seen how this easy-to-fix misconfiguration can cause serious data quality and performance issues. Then, we learned the two simple ways we can correct the situation and proceed toward the more reliable and better-performing OmniStudio apps.

In the next section, we will look at the Extract type DataRaptors anti-patterns that cause poor performance and time-outs in their queries.

Non-selective queries in DataRaptors

The last OmniStudio anti-pattern we will review in this chapter traces back to the non-selective query issues we looked at in *Chapter 8, Non-Selective Queries and Data Skew*. Let's look at a few examples that show DataRaptors with potentially non-selective **Filter** criteria and their alternatives, along with their improved execution times.

Wildcards in Filter criteria

When a wildcard is used in the DataRaptor **Filter** criteria along with the LIKE operator, the resulting SOQL query created by the DataRaptor will most likely become non-selective. This will negatively affect its performance and may also cause a query to time out as your data volume grows. The following is a sample DataRaptor that uses the LIKE operator along with the % wildcards that look for a substring value in the field (see *Figure 12.13*):

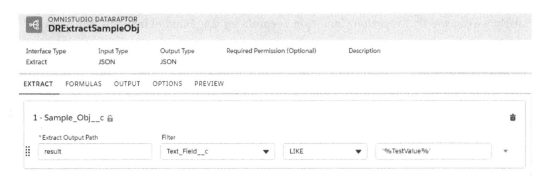

Figure 12.13 – An overview of the LIKE operator used in a DataRaptor Extract

In my test, this DataRaptor takes 2,030ms, i.e., 2,030 milliseconds, to run in the **Preview** mode:

Figure 12.14 – An overview of the Preview mode of a DataRaptor with the LIKE operator

Now, how do we make these DataRaptors more robust and future-proof?

Better solutions

For more robust and future-proof queries, especially on objects with a large number of records, try to avoid the use of LIKE comparisons or partial text comparisons in your DataRaptor **Filter** criteria. If in doubt, grab the query from the DataRaptor's **Debug Log**, and make sure it is selective by running it inside the **Query Plan** tool in your **Developer Console**.

The following DataRaptor Extract returns the same result on the same dataset but uses a different **Filter** criterion:

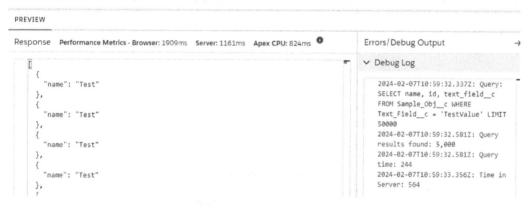

Figure 12.15 – An overview of a DataRaptor without the use of the LIKE operator

Since we're avoiding the LIKE operator this time, the resulting SOQL query has a much better chance of being selective. That allows it to perform significantly faster, taking 1,161ms or nearly half the time than our previous attempt at this **Filter** criteria:

Figure 12.16 – An overview of the Preview mode of the DataRaptor with the use of the LIKE operator

Now, let's look at the next DataRaptor anti-pattern that brings our attention to the use of NULL values in the **Filter** condition.

Use of NULL values

When = or <> **Filter** criteria are used along with the NULL value, especially as the primary or the only criteria in the filter expression, this will very likely make the SOQL query of the DataRaptor non-selective. Moreover, using NULL values in the **Filter** expression has a similar effect in terms of making the query non-selective and often causes it to run very slowly:

> **Note**
>
> If you must use NULL values in a DataRaptor **Filter** criteria, use the `'$Vlocity:NULL'` merge field syntax, as shown in *Figure 12.17*.

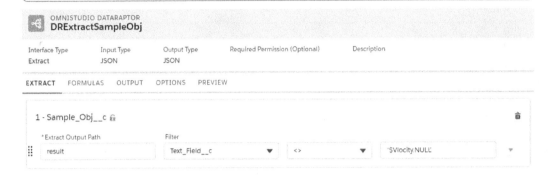

Figure 12.17 – An overview of a DataRaptor with the NULL value comparison

This produces the SOQL query we expect, using the NULL value in its WHERE clause:

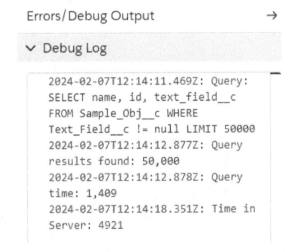

Figure 12.18 – An overview of the SOQL query produced by the DataRaptor with NULL value comparison

In my test, this query took 6,949ms on the same test dataset, or about five times slower than a comparable query filtering on a non-NULL value:

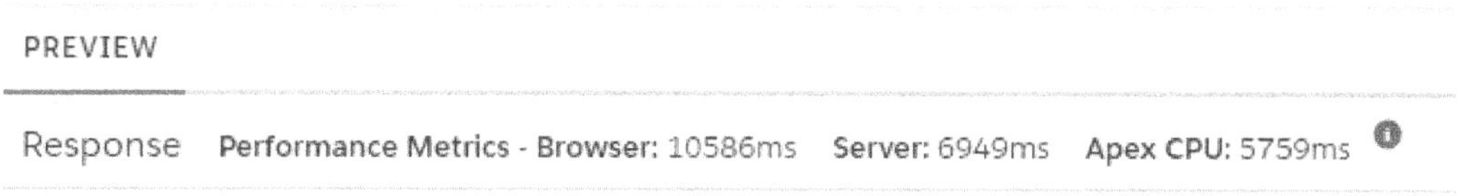

PREVIEW

Response   Performance Metrics - Browser: 10586ms   Server: 6949ms   Apex CPU: 5759ms ⓘ

Figure 12.19 – An overview of the Preview execution times of the DataRaptor with NULL value comparison

o, how do we make this DataRaptor more efficient and future-proof?

Better solutions

There are two things to remember about the use of NULL values in your DataRaptor **Filter** criteria:

- Unless the DataRaptor is extracting from an object with a very small number of records, avoid the use of NULL values in your **Filter** criteria.
- If you have to compare with NULL and there is no way for you to avoid it, add a positive comparison operator, such as =, INCLUDES, < or >, compare it with a non-NULL value first, and then use your NULL comparison as a second **Filter** criteria.

If in doubt, grab the query from the DataRaptor's **Debug Log** and make sure it is selective by running it inside the **Query Plan** tool in your **Developer Console**.

Finally, let's look at a few more DataRaptor **Filter** operators that we need to be careful with.

Use of EXCLUDES and NOT LIKE operators

This anti-pattern states that the use of the negative operators in a DataRaptor **Filter** can produce a lot of matches and make the resulting query non-selective. When filtering by a column that contains multi-select picklist values, be careful with the use of the EXCLUDES keyword. Additionally, be careful with the NOT LIKE operator on other data types.

Let's compare the performance of using the negative vs. positive **Filter** logic on the sample dataset we used in previous examples. Let's create a simple DataRaptor and use the EXCLUDES operator in its **Filter**:

OMNISTUDIO DATARAPTOR
DRExtractSampleObj
Interface Type
Extract
Input Type
JSON
Output Type
JSON
Required Permission (Optional)
Description
EXTRACT
FORMULAS
OUTPUT
OPTIONS
PREVIEW
1 - Sample_Obj__c
* Extract Output Path
result
Filter
Choice__c
EXCLUDES
'Value1'

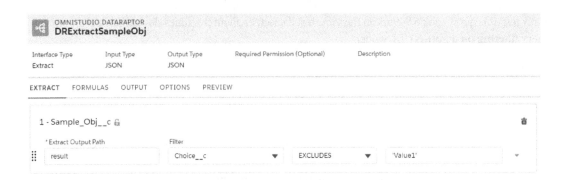

Figure 12.20 – An overview of a DataRaptor using the EXCLUDES operator

Predictably, this results in the `excludes` keyword being used in the `WHERE` clause of the generated query:

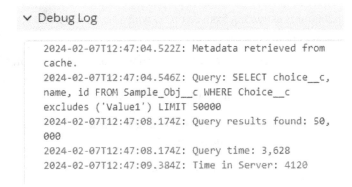

Debug Log
2024-02-07T12:47:04.522Z: Metadata retrieved from cache.
2024-02-07T12:47:04.546Z: Query: SELECT choice__c, name, id FROM Sample_Obj__c WHERE Choice__c excludes ('Value1') LIMIT 50000
2024-02-07T12:47:08.174Z: Query results found: 50,000
2024-02-07T12:47:08.174Z: Query time: 3,628
2024-02-07T12:47:09.384Z: Time in Server: 4120

Figure 12.21 – An overview of the Query produced by the DataRaptor with the EXCLUDES operator

And the DataRaptor takes 4,897ms when it is run in the **Preview** mode:

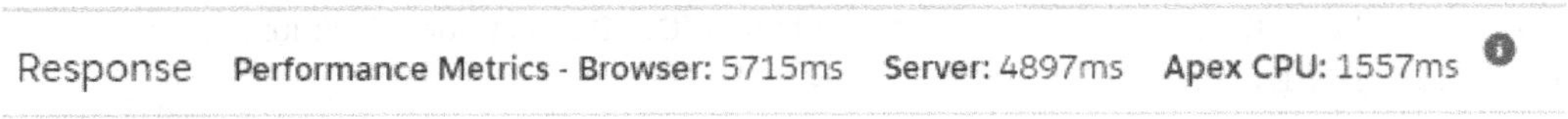

Response
Performance Metrics - Browser: 5715ms
Server: 4897ms
Apex CPU: 1557ms

Figure 12.22 – An overview of the Preview execution times of the DataRaptor with the EXCLUDES operator

Now, how do we make these DataRaptors more robust and future-proof?

Better solutions

There are two ways to make them more robust, efficient, and future-proof:

- Avoid the use of the negative EXCLUDES and NOT LIKE operators. Use the positive INCLUDES operator instead.

- If you absolutely have to use the EXCLUDES operator, use it on the second or the further down items in the list of your DataRaptor **Filter** expressions.

If in doubt, grab the query from the DataRaptor's **Debug Log** and make sure it is selective by running it inside the **Query Plan** tool in your **Developer Console**.

Now, let's change the **Filter** operator to its opposite: the INCLUDES operator. We will then run the DataRaptor on the same data set:

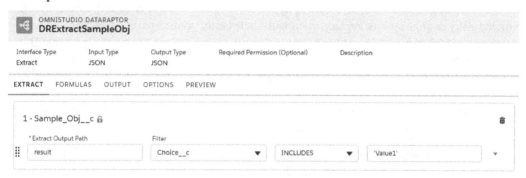

Figure 12.23 – An overview of an updated DataRaptor using the INCLUDES operator

When run in the **Preview** mode, this DataRaptor takes 1,531ms, running over three times faster than the same DataRaptor using the EXCLUDES operator on the same dataset:

Figure 12.24 – An overview of the Preview execution times of DataRaptor without the EXCLUDES operator

That is the end of our review of the dangerous **Filter** operators that often cause the queries produced by our DataRaptor Extracts to become non-selective. Non-selective queries may not only cause our apps to perform slowly but can also crumble under loading, timing out sporadically as our data volumes grow. Learning to use extreme caution with these operators or keep them out of our DataRaptor Extracts will result in better-performing queries and make our apps more reliable. This also brings us to the end of the chapter.

Summary

Well, this is the end of our tour of the OmniStudio performance and scalability anti-patterns and the better solutions we can apply to make our apps more robust on future-proof. We began by defining what an anti-pattern is and then continued to look at the three families of common performance anti-patterns, any of which could produce serious negative effects in our apps.

We began by looking at typical Loop Block configuration errors that often cause sporadic governor limit exceptions in addition to performance degradation. Then, we proceeded to review configurations where the lack of error handling was allowing Integration Procedures to continue running after a failed operation, causing performance and even more serious data corruption issues. Finally, we looked at the risky DataRaptor Extract Filter operators that frequently cause poorly performing and non-selective queries.

With this knowledge under our belt, we are equipped to recognize and stay clear of these commonly occurring risky configurations, replace them with their better counterparts, or apply them with extreme caution. We have also learned to keep our eyes out for other OmniStudio anti-patterns. This also brings us to the end of the book. Thank you for staying with me on this journey! We began with essential insights into the Vlocity OmniStudio platform and Salesforce Industries and continued with code management, performance evaluation, and patterns for improvements in various layers of the platform. We have reviewed the best practices and ways to apply them to ensure the optimal performance of your OmniStudio installations.

While celebrating its tenth anniversary in 2024, the Vlocity OmniStudio platform is still rapidly changing to better fit the increasing and ever-changing demands of Salesforce Industries Solutions. As my clients and I continue to work hard to achieve the maximum OmniStudio performance in our apps, I will continue to publish new tips, tricks, and best practices on this book's companion site, `https://maximumvlocity.com/`. So be sure to visit often, or, better yet, subscribe to our mailing list to get notified when new insights become available. I'm also personally available for a limited number of speaking, training, and consulting engagements.

Here's to the next level of performance with your Vlocity OmniStudio apps!

Yours truly,

Dmitri Khanine

Index

packtpub.com

Subscribe to our online digital library for full access to over 7,000 books and videos, as well as industry leading tools to help you plan your personal development and advance your career. For more information, please visit our website.

Why subscribe?

- Spend less time learning and more time coding with practical eBooks and Videos from over 4,000 industry professionals

- Improve your learning with Skill Plans built especially for you

- Get a free eBook or video every month

- Fully searchable for easy access to vital information

- Copy and paste, print, and bookmark content

Did you know that Packt offers eBook versions of every book published, with PDF and ePub files available? You can upgrade to the eBook version at packtpub.com and as a print book customer, you are entitled to a discount on the eBook copy. Get in touch with us at customercare@packtpub.com for more details.

At www.packtpub.com, you can also read a collection of free technical articles, sign up for a range of free newsletters, and receive exclusive discounts and offers on Packt books and eBooks.

Other Books You May Enjoy

If you enjoyed this book, you may be interested in these other books by Packt:

Salesforce AppExchange Success Blueprint

Jakub Stefaniak

ISBN: 978-1-83508-954-5

- Find out how to become a successful ISV partner on the AppExchange

- Understand how to tackle the challenges of AppExchange development

- Uncover how to avoid common security review pitfalls

- Discover the best practices for configuring an AppExchange listing

- Maximize the revenue potential through pricing and monetization

- Understand how to manage technical debt to maintain product quality

- Build a successful and sustainable ISV partnership with Salesforce

ChatGPT for Accelerating Salesforce Development

Andy Forbes, Philip Safir, Joseph Kubon, Francisco Fálder

ISBN: 978-1-83508-407-6

- Masterfully craft detailed and engaging user stories tailored for Salesforce projects
- Leverage ChatGPT to design cutting-edge features within the Salesforce ecosystem, transforming ideas into functional and intuitive solutions
- Explore the integration of ChatGPT for configuring Salesforce environments
- Write Salesforce flows with ChatGPT, enhancing workflow automation and efficiency
- Develop custom LWCs with ChatGPT's assistance
- Discover effective testing techniques using ChatGPT for optimized performance and reliability

Packt is searching for authors like you

If you're interested in becoming an author for Packt, please visit `authors.packtpub.com` and apply today. We have worked with thousands of developers and tech professionals, just like you, to help them share their insight with the global tech community. You can make a general application, apply for a specific hot topic that we are recruiting an author for, or submit your own idea.

Share Your Thoughts

Now you've finished *Optimizing Salesforce Industries Solutions on the Vlocity OmniStudio Platform*, we'd love to hear your thoughts! Scan the QR code below to go straight to the Amazon review page for this book and share your feedback or leave a review on the site that you purchased it from.

`https://packt.link/r/1835468470`

Your review is important to us and the tech community and will help us make sure we're delivering excellent quality content.

Download a free PDF copy of this book

Thanks for purchasing this book!

Do you like to read on the go but are unable to carry your print books everywhere?

Is your eBook purchase not compatible with the device of your choice?

Don't worry, now with every Packt book you get a DRM-free PDF version of that book at no cost.

Read anywhere, any place, on any device. Search, copy, and paste code from your favorite technical books directly into your application.

The perks don't stop there, you can get exclusive access to discounts, newsletters, and great free content in your inbox daily

Follow these simple steps to get the benefits:

1. Scan the QR code or visit the link below

https://packt.link/free-ebook/9781835468470

2. Submit your proof of purchase
3. That's it! We'll send your free PDF and other benefits to your email directly

www.ingramcontent.com/pod-product-compliance
Lightning Source LLC
Chambersburg PA
CBHW080632060326

40690CB00021B/4904